WOMANING

*A Memoir
by
Meta Commerse*

Story Medicine Worldwide Publications
ASHEVILLE, NORTH CAROLINA

Also by Meta Commerse

Landscapes of Abuse (2001)

The Sixth Commandment, a play (1999)

Rainsongs: Poems of a Woman's Life (2012)

The Mending Time, a novel (2014)

Blues Doula, poems by Meta Commerse (2019)

Diamonds and Pyramids: Story Medicine for Racial Healing (forthcoming)

This project was supported by
the North Carolina Arts Council,
a division of the Department of Natural
and Cultural Resources. www.NCArts.org.

Cover photo from the family collection

Womaning: A Memoir by Meta Commerse
Copyright © 2021 by Meta Commerse

All rights reserved. No part of this book may be reproduced or transmitted in any form by any means, electronic or mechanical, including photocopying, recording, or by any information storage and retrieval system without express, written permission from the publisher.

Story Medicine Worldwide Publications
P.O. Box 1471
Asheville, N.C. 28802-1471
www.storymedicineworldwide.com

Womaning, a Memoir / Meta Commerse. — 1st ed.
ISBN 978-0-578-34828-5

Design, illustration & book services: Carol Majors, PUBLICATIONS UNLTD, Raleigh, NC

for my children:
the catalyst, the rebel, the prodigal,
with my love

PREFACE

Pennsylvania, 1934

Reflecting across bands of time, I imagine her emergence as a conflicted thing. Conflicted, all the way from an unwelcoming womb to the fresh air she finally breathed after the great squeezing and shoving, then to her innocent hope for a more loving home where she could grow. Conflicted, as her arrival placed her into the arms of a grandmother still tasting bile.

Grandmother's bile resulted from their betrayal. "Their" meaning the two people closest to her, her own husband and jealous daughter. "Their" included Life itself because, after all, Grandmother had indeed raised her own children alone, having long suffered their father's, that is, her first husband's, willful abandonment. Together she and her children had, with the help of the Good Lord, managed to survive those hard times none the worse. There had been days during this particular hardship when she noticed something hurtful, almost vengeful in her daughter's eyes, but since Grandmother's heart was as tender as it was blind, she dismissed what she almost saw. And, through it all, she told the Good Lord, that she would endure whatever hardship He had in store. She would faithfully bear it in exchange for her golden crown in Glory. Bear it because this was and had always been a woman's lot. That is, bearing the world's burdens, cleaning up its messes. And Grandmother began the silent practice of smiling in the mirror to be sure that the bitterness did not steal her natural beauty.

* * * * *

Now, in the midst of what people called the "Depression," came this new, cute-as-a-button baby. The little bitty thing would never have made it here had Grandmother not put her foot down and kept them from doing away with her. No. As a pastor's wife, she was pressed to keep the peace, keeping her mouth shut, starting in her own household and then in her community. She kept the peace by taking her daughter over to the white neighborhood and renting a room for her there, where she would stay quietly holed up until time for the birth.

Grandmother also kept the peace by wearing loose clothing and — with the help of a small pillow under her belt — appearing heavier than usual. And, as she went through this trial, figuring it all out, preparing herself and her mind for the birth, there was no one in the world except for her Papa that she could confide in. But Papa was surprisingly quiet about this. Without friends she could trust with this particular secret, her afternoon naps and radio stories became her consolation. Through her soul's secret agony and the comfort of her favorite stories, Grandmother's imagination began to sprout. She began to ponder that there was probably as much unheard in these stories as heard. She began to imagine that the characters in her stories just might in truth be hurting as much as she.

She held out a peculiar hope that keeping this secret would preserve her marriage. It would surely preserve the congregation, her husband's place there and in the community. But, most of all, she hoped it might also protect her daughter's future, that it might assure for her a life not ruined by this nameless, selfish indulgence.

Still, she implored God.

"Why, oh why did You allow *this*?"

"Why must I go through this alone?"

And soon she felt a stir, a wisp of reassurance that she was indeed not going through it alone, but that she would surely need her deepest, most hidden strength to get through.

Now, there had been other secrets, of course. But, as she pondered the whole of it, as she learned to live with the taste of bitter, she saw that this was the way it would have to be. That this way, they could all go on, and no one need be the wiser. She would bring this baby home as her own, and raise her in spite of it all, which is exactly what she did. She raised innocence and hope in spite. Surely, she loved the sweet little thing, but couldn't help what she felt deep down, what this thing had awakened in her. Couldn't help tasting bitter until she looked at her, feeling pulled between her duty as a faithful servant of God and her husband on one side of herself, and her broken heartedness, the aching hole at the center of her life, put there so willingly by her daughter on the other. And as she kept her part of the bargain, the pain of it wound its way into her depths and eventually became unforgettable if not unforgivable. Although she prayed continually over it, the pain melted much too slowly for her to notice. So, she held onto her secret pain, held it like a dog holds its bone, for the rest of her life.

* * * *

This humble child hadn't at all been hard to raise. Quite the contrary, she was precocious and curious, almost in a hurry to learn and to grow up and out of Grandmother's way. It wasn't hard for Grandmother to be very patient with the child. She was almost no trouble at all. Grandmother had by the time she was three taught her to read, had started taking her on slow walks to the neighborhood library, and, to occupy her active mind, taught her the habit of checking out and reading books by the armfuls.

At age five, Baby was reading adult fiction because by then the children's books bored her. On top of everything else, Grandmother was now too distracted with her writing, praying, and healing work to control the titles! Grandmother enrolled Baby in school at age four because of how astonishing she was, how much and how fast she learned. For this reason, right away, the school officials put her in the second grade.

Her childhood slipped by Grandmother in a blurry haze that felt somewhat familiar. A clairvoyant healer, Grandmother recognized the spirit of that something this baby possessed, or shall we say something possessing this baby. Was it that same empty longing she'd thought she'd almost glimpsed in her daughter? That same grown folks,' yearning for something indescribable, that indulgent, Sunday kind of lazy love no girl her age had any business expecting, let alone outright looking for inside her own home?

Grandmother figured that when a child reached the age of 12, that child deserved to know the truth. This rule itself evidenced old, inherited secrets locked away somewhere in the family home. Or in somebody's mind. Of forbidden desire, of legitimacy or the lack of it, secrets many women of her time took with them to their graves. These shameful secrets, this white man's world, this is the world that this child was born into. And just as soon as she could, this little girl got busy doing everything to fit in and belong, to excel and win approval, wherever, however she could.

This atmosphere, family, these circumstances stamped her birth. Baby dropped into the midst, and although it was not of her making, she had to move through and beyond this atmosphere that would color and shape her life. In this place, she would feel a permanent need to live down and disprove the unspoken. Untouched and uninterrupted, this secret lived. It might lay dormant now and again, but although unspoken it reminded her that she was, from the moment of conception, their mistake. From her earliest memories, she had sensed something was wrong, amiss, feeling the conflict, never knowing the truth of it, not even a hint. That is, until her 12th year when Grandmother finally sat her down and carefully told her. The clean bones version. And as Baby listened, she breathed, "ohhhhh," with a huge sigh and cried.

Then a flood of questions and more tears also came chattering in her head.

How in the world could my mother give me away?
Didn't she love me?
*How **could** she?*
Wasn't I good enough for her?

Illinois, 1960s

When the work of raising this child was done, when Baby was finally grown and with children of her own — children, for whom Grandmother had also very much helped in the raising — Grandmother figured enough time had gone by that she started telling this "hard story" more freely within the family.

* * * * *

Grandmother told her story's clean bones version, the one that put the onus of the whole thing in her now former husband's lap and left it there. She told it every chance she got. Told it, and I don't remember if she repelled others within earshot, if they recoiled and hid from her then, or if this made her tell it just to me all those times, but once I turned 12, tell it she did, and I never stopped to consider what the dreaded telling was doing to me.

She told it, as if obliged, as if every telling left her with a little more peace, as if the story's residue worked on her behalf and opened up a little more room in her head. And to the folks who knew her, it looked by now as if the old bitter taste must have slowly neutralized and then turned sweet. As if eventually, Grandmother finally rediscovered life as bittersweet, and that despite or perhaps through the pain, sure enough, good was bound to come.

INTRODUCTION

Carousel
Father lost to this or that
Coveted, innocent;
Mother suffers silently
Barely, rarely home;
Daughter lives love starved, blind;
Son grows curious, abandoned, fractured . . .

I am a black woman of a certain age, time and place, breaking the system of silence I was born into, writing this book as a means of healing. Here and now, I write for myself since my mother could not have written such a book for either one of us. I use a cis-gender language with its many power inferences, although in my elder years I still learn to identify as gender non-conforming. Since I learned to be a woman growing up in the Missionary Baptist church where the teachings left me denying and losing myself, I have long since decentralized my worship and formulated my own restorative practice of spirituality. I am a Baby Boomer, belonging to that Americanized generation named for war, but that genuinely tried to change the warring world only to discover that war was built into the design.

I cannot write anything about my life without including the music of my people, the music that made it possible for us to survive, to dance through life's passages with a golden sound track. Music that marked the times, occasions, moments worth remembering. Music is my reference point, and I use it to mark the stories I share here.

The voice in the stories varies according to growth, speaking from a most interior place, speaking at once as Observer and as Observed. Through the stories I come out of hiding, gradually leaving the shadows and standing in the morning light at last.

The idea of intersectionality is helpful in describing, locating, marking the places oppressed people occupy. I write my life stories from the simultaneous, complicated experiences of religion, class, gender and race, also describing the ways in which I learned eventually to live, heal, and formulate a work to help myself and others.

My stories were written standing alone. There may be slight overlapping of timeframe from story to story, but each one contains a life-shaping lesson and experience. These are my secret stories, but not all. From writers I greatly respect, I learned in the end to hold something back for myself.

* * * * *

I never trusted the word "normal." As a first grader I learned to read from the book about happy, golden haired children playing with a perfect red ball and a frisky brown puppy living in a sweet little house with their Mom and Dad. Were they normal?

They were nothing at all like me.

Where I lived, there was always so much going on, so much that had gone on, adjustments being made, so much that would never go away because this stuff was in the air we breathed. I cannot recall a single time when I could use that word "normal" to describe us or me or the life I knew. It's true, things would get easier for a while, and then it would seem as if the worst part was over. These times were choice, wrapped in a feeling of possibility, the kind of relief that you have on an open, smooth road. As if coasting on a beautiful, sunny day in your brand-new car. But soon the weather changed, and, rather than complain about that, you learned to accept it, to accept the variable, unstable nature of this life.

Besides the absence of so-called normal, there was never time to get over, to fully notice, or even discuss the hard things, so we held onto them and went through life in this way, stumbling over our own dreaded bruises, as if we were ashamed of them. Ghostly feelings we never discussed got in the way all the time. That is, except for when we sang songs about them or danced or prayed about them. Maybe it was these ghosts that made our music and our prayers so powerful and enduring.

Otherwise, time and space didn't lend themselves to any real letting go. No one taught this skill, we had nothing tangible and relevant beyond the sweet Sunday school lesson on forgiveness. What is more, if, God forbid, we ever did forget what had happened to us, we would go through life in America like sitting ducks, and we knew that sitting ducks in our neighborhood did not survive.

So, especially when we sought and worked tirelessly for our share of the joys in life, for the things that made life worthwhile, (because the joy just ahead was our hope) beneath it all, we kept a kind of vigil, a stance of readiness for the coming fight. So went life, our way of resistance while we worked hard to pass on the joy to the next generations so that they could take care of themselves. This was how we loved. Because, regardless of what the outside world thought of us, whether or not it recognized or even cared about our oppression, we remembered it always. It was our responsibility to remember what has already happened, and while most of us remembered without words, remembered it in our waking dreams, or just carried it in the marrow of our bones, we held it deeply, down where we might need it later, as others of us remembered it on the surface of our skin, living at the ready, like war veterans, every minute of every day.

PART I

GIRLING

1950s & 1960s

Being Little

Since I was the first brown child born in my family, they couldn't pass anymore after me. I settled all doubts. I was brown and quiet in a loud, stormy sea of white, and from the beginning this made my skin feel strange, as if it and I didn't really belong. Not at home or at school!

One of the first words I learned to read was M-I-L-K with the pictures of the white milk man wearing his white uniform, driving the white truck, and carrying the crate of clear glass quart bottles of pure white milk. And I tasted the pure white milk on my tongue every time I saw that word and those pictures in my reader. I tasted the pure white milk from the milk carton during milk break and in my secret world I tried to get the milk as I drank it with my classmates, to help me belong, but even in my secret world, it couldn't help me. But that didn't stop me from trying.

One of the first words I learned to spell even before I went to school was chrysanthemum. Grandmother taught me that. She put some rhythm and smiles with it. Chry-san-the-MUM, as if she wanted to sing it. She was the world's best teacher! My dreams were always with me, and because of her, I had good dreams.

Oh, I had waking dreams from another time, reminding me of old, familiar places that I loved, like the forest, and a log cabin. The look, smell and feel of wood comforted me. Smells like sawdust on the floor at the A&P, and fresh cut trees, reminded me of my love for wood. Then the feel and shine on the rocks that I collected, and all of this — the woods, the wood, the rocks, all kinds of rock — reminded me who I used to be and who my real people were.

Somehow, I knew about other places. Like a place where people weren't free, and how they had to keep many secrets... And then there was another, beautiful place where people *were* free and where they ate ants, and I wondered how the ants tasted. I would think about this when I sat still outside and watched the ants going everywhere, and then, when I put my hand in their way, they would just walk on my hand and keep going. I felt their tininess and watched how they didn't stop for anything but would go on anyway. In Ant World — the world I thought was smallest of all — they were big and black and it tickled when they walked on my skin. The tickling was nice, and I sat in the quiet with them, just watching. This was my special time outside, and I thought Outside was the biggest, best world of all.

The only one in all the world that I could share this secret time with was my brother, Joey. I thought I knew how little I was, but he was even littler than me. And I had to take care of him. My mother said I did. And she would tell us all the time, *"All you have is each other, so, you'd better stay close."*

* * * * *

Now, when I went to Mrs. Johnson's second grade class, my mother gave me a key to the house on a silver chain to wear around my neck. She said never to take it off and never to tell anyone that I had the key to our house. The strong chain was nice to touch because of all the tiny balls on it. I saw one just like it in the closet at our old house where we had to pull the chain to turn the light on. But now that I was in the second grade, Joey started kindergarten. And, I had to take him to school with me every morning. But kindergarten was only in the morning. So, at lunchtime, I had to find him where we would meet and take his hand and we would run home. I used my key to let us in.

I would make soup for us from the can Mom left on the kitchen countertop. Campbell's soup, either cream of mushroom or chicken noodle or tomato or cream of celery or cream of asparagus. I hated that last one. Ewwww! Anyway, I opened the can and heated the soup in my very own saucepan on the stove. I poured water in the can one time, poured it into the pan and stirred with the wooden spoon until it started to steam. If I waited longer than that, it would be too hot. Then I poured it in the cups, one for Joey, one for me, and got the milk bottle and poured us a glass of milk and we both had a piece of bread. Sometimes we would have a sandwich, too. But we had to hurry and eat because I had to take him to the baby sitter's house and get back to school and I couldn't be late! So, we ate, and we left the house and I had to be sure to turn everything off, and lock the door, and then we ran there, and he would stay, and I'd say good-bye and then run all the way back to school. I was always out of breath at lunchtime. While I was running, my key was flying from side to side, and I would say to myself, "I can do it. I can do it."

Running back and forth every day all through our neighborhood, with the houses and flowers and fruit trees that I barely saw. It was so quiet, all I could hear were the birds singing, my shoes slapping the sidewalk, and my breathing. It was so quiet that a brown girl in the second grade could run around, out of breath, with secrets about ants and keys, that nobody ever asked about. But I loved more things. I loved the smell of the big, fat crayons when we took them out to color. I loved my little green rug on my skin at nap time. I loved feeling safe when I was in school. It was a really strange and quiet time there that I could feel but not understand or speak about.

I wondered about other things. Like fighting. Why did the bigger children fight? Why did they run to it and cheer and push into it? The fight was a horror, like Shock Theater, so, I would go away from the fight, not into it like the other kids. I didn't know why, but I wondered about this sometimes. These were my first questions. Why some kids loved fighting and making each other cry for fun?

* * * * *

And then, in the third grade I remembered something very big. I had learned how to read! Reading was a kind of power. From my waking dream I knew that maybe it was the strongest power I would ever have. And because of that, I wanted Joey to be able to read, too. So, I taught him how! Nothing could stop me. He knew his alphabet already, so I showed him his sounds and then his words and he learned it from me really fast and started reading, and I didn't tell anybody. It was our secret that he learned to read from me. That now, we both shared the strongest power ever. Now, we were both powerful, something like Mighty Mouse.

War, Peace, and Learning Big Words Quickly

My first memory of war's effects comes with the blue shadowy image of my father in an Air Force uniform. He had not been in war, but, beneath its false glamor, his uniform symbolized the "service of arms" which is about one thing. War. My memory of war's effects opens when I was three, with him leaving us for good, after much turmoil.

The effects of war continue with my stepfather, Daddy Maurice. In the U.S. Army he fought in the Korean War and had kept on fighting. He was 22 years old when he and my mother married. I remember his army boots and socks, his rough, pea green woolen army blanket pulled around his shoulders. At times, he seemed cold and contracted, wrapping himself in the blanket, soaking his peeling, souring feet in the zinc foot tub when he came home from work.

For him, there was always a fight to win. And each week, he would watch the Friday Night Fights with a vengeance. "Get 'im!" he'd holler, as if he was watching the fight at the ring. He read African magazines about Kwame Nkruma, and planned to take the family to Ghana to live someday. He poured his artistic genius into the intricate, exacting realm of architecture. Yet, he was an architect made to drive a bus for the city's transit authority, proving himself again before being offered a draftsman's job.

War, Peace, and Learning Big Words Quickly

It was during this time that he drew the plans for the house we would later live in. It was his and my mother's dream to build a redwood and glass ranch style house in Wheaton. While we lived in a tiny basement apartment, they counted their money down to the penny — to the point of rolling their own cigarettes, cutting his hair at home — and bought two double lots of land with the cash they saved. As a strategy for getting a bank loan, they used their land to secure a mortgage, since in those days, Negroes generally could not get mortgages without collateral. He used his plans, became his own general contractor, built the house, and moved us in.

* * * * *

I remember his rage. I saw and heard him repeatedly beat my mother and call her names. He was insanely jealous, punishing her with his fist whenever he *thought* any man on the street had spoken to her, looked at her, tipped his hat to her. He took aspirin by the handful for recurring, unbearable headaches. The rage, his jealousy, his tirades, the beatings, caused us to brace ourselves when he was around. He who trusted no one was a hard man to trust.

As his children, we learned life as complexity: to dance between the tirades and kindnesses, to treat these dangerous times as secrets. Secrets handled by our growing brains that filtered, organized and locked these times however, wherever they could. The only time it was any different was when Grandmother came to visit. She would show up at just the right time, just as the brutality teetered on the edges. She'd come and stay for a few days. Her presence, her love, her smile, her company made the difference. Any company made the difference.

* * * * *

He could be humorous, too. He played the ukulele and sang funny songs, songs he mostly made up, singing to Joey, and me. While he wasn't one for hymns, there was an old spiritual that he sang sometimes, *"there ere isa balm in Gil-e-ad, to heal the sin sick soul . . ."*

He worked on solo projects, drawing plans for things he dreamed of doing. He built things. A model ship with sails, and an air craft carrier. Both of these had many tiny parts to be put together and then painted. Then there were the tiny emblems and other accessories to be added. This was slow work and I remember how it brought a good sense of quiet and calm to the house.

He shared time with Joey building a Lionel train village, painting the boxcars by hand, erecting the model meticulously. I remember the smell of the glue, the drywall board he converted to a table to support the village, the little clear bottles of paint and the tiny brushes he used to paint the boxcars. The boxes that contained the boxcars and other model pieces, the tiny "trees," the train depot, the little black tracks with copper- colored railings. The good feelings of surprise, opening the boxes and seeing what he had bought. The sound of the whistle, the puffs of "smoke" from the engine, the red caboose. Joey was his buddy.

He bought me a tiny red bicycle with training wheels. It had plastic strings of different colors dangling from the handle bars. It was my first bike and I loved it. He took me outside and showed me how to ride with the training wheels, helping me up to the seat, showing me how to put my feet on the pedals and push. He was patient and kind, watching me ride, standing beside the bike while I learned to sit there, push my feet and balance myself. He made me feel safe in those moments. Eventually, he said I was ready to ride without the training wheels. So, he pushed them up and off the sidewalk and he walked behind the bike holding the seat while I rode. He did this and talked to me. "I'm here. You can do it." And I began to feel the bike changing under me, feeling more solid as I pedaled. And I called out to him, "You there, Daddy?" He had let go. I was riding on my own.

* * * * *

Then one Sunday as we watched a Leonard Bernstein concert on public television, something unthinkable happened. March 13, 1960, was a very cold winter day. We had planned a family car trip to Maywood after Daddy Maurice's bath. Mom, Joey and I were ready and waiting for him. But we never took the trip.

My mother began to call to him in the bathroom, thinking he had been in there longer than usual. There was no answer. She knocked on the bathroom door. Still no answer. Then she went and got a long nail and drove it into the doorknob hole, opened the door and went inside where she found him in the floor! She called to him and he didn't respond. Just as he was about to take his bath, he had died. He was 27. As she found him that way, she quickly dragged his body from the bathroom floor and into the hallway.

And as she dragged it, I never saw it. I never looked at it, because all I could do in that moment was just hear her and try my best to keep standing there. So, I just heard her screaming as she was dragging him, as she was helplessly, desperately screaming, screaming, screaming, melting completely into shock and grief.

* * * * *

I remember the neighbors coming to help, the family doctor coming to pronounce him dead. My mother calling Grandmother on the telephone, and saying simply, "he's gone," through her sobs. My mother quickly going somewhere away from us until the funeral. Whenever she was overwhelmed in her life, she would quickly go somewhere away from us.

The funeral. Seeing him lying there with a stocking cap on his head after the autopsy where they said he had died instantly. Died of a congenital cerebral hemorrhage and we had to learn that term. Quickly. Learn that congenital meant something he was born with. Cerebral hemorrhage meant that vessels in his brain had burst suddenly. The doctor also said that this had caused his headache pain, as well as his rage. Despite their report, I know now that his sudden death at that age was also partly due to the facts of life he faced while black in America. He was a war veteran and a college graduate treated with discrimination and disrespect in a structure of power not made with him in mind and there was nothing he could do about it. I did not understand this then, but I do now.

And of course, from then on, Mom expected us to get in and out of the bathroom quickly. That experience put her on high Bathroom Time alert. She had indeed braced herself well for the thing that had already happened.

* * * * *

I remember the brown and white dress I wore. Some man singing, *"Beyond the Sunset,"* a popular Christian song at the time, said to be his "favorite," but Daddy Maurice was no Christian, no fan of Christian music. I knew that much as I sat crying, wondering, bracing myself for what would happen next, for I knew that something surely would. Bracing, wondering, just as I always had when he was with us.

I remember riding in the long, black Cadillac car, sitting on the seat next to his mother, the woman we all called "Mama Nodie." The small, black pill box hat she wore, with a tiny black veil over her forehead and eyes, crying out loud, asking God why he had separated her from her son that way, as I just sat there, riding with her, riding with only the car's smooth, dull silence as her answer.

I remember sitting at the grave site in the Lincoln Cemetery, watching the soldiers fold The Flag into corners and present it to my mother. The loud, metal click, the sight of the gray cloth coffin lowering slowly into the deep, cold grave surrounded by snow, ice and black dirt, wondering how he would feel being down there all alone forever. The meaningless, continuous words of the preacher and everyone else. Grandmother coming to be with us. My teacher, Mrs. Johnson, sending a letter and so many drawings from the kids at school asking one by one what had happened to my father.

I remember the house growing still, silent, happy, and new again, after the years of rage, vigilance, and fear that had to have soaked into those yet unpainted walls. The bedroom lights coming on by themselves for the first few nights after the funeral, as it seemed he was somehow there and trying to contact us. Grandmother — who saw things in dreams — saying he told her this, "Tell my buddy I said good-bye." Aunt Sandra and her three boys coming to stay for a while.

My eight-year-old mind carefully tried to take in and to understand what had happened. While I loved and would miss this man, I also felt a deep, secret relief that the beatings and the name calling had suddenly stopped, once and for all. He had been the only real father I had known. He was all extremes rolled into one, extremes that challenged and pushed so hard at life and for so long until something had to give. And it did. Now, there would be peace in the house. Or, would there? As these thoughts and questions swirled around my head, I took the new quiet, and with it made some important decisions of my own.

First and foremost. No man would ever hit or curse me. No man. And, beneath this resolve was another, equally clear decision yet unknown to me until this writing. While my eight-year-old brain was busy doing everything she could to protect me, there was more on the horizon she could not foresee. More uniforms ahead. So, for now, I knew one more sure thing. I would never, ever let another stepfather anywhere near my heart.

* * * * *

One sunny summer afternoon, we ventured out and enjoyed a slow walk to the community Jamboree and back. At the Jamboree, there were clowns, free rides, cotton candy, and colorful things people in town made by hand. Back home, my mother filled the house with music. Loudly, she played Khachaturian's Masquerade Suite Waltz on her Webcor wooden box Hi-fi. And that's when my cousins, Joey, and I danced, danced like never before, danced freedom, danced wild, carefree, hysterical, danced ourselves drunk, danced in circles, danced until the world danced and everything in it turned to soup.

The king is dead. Long may he live. The Masquerade Suite Waltz.

Church Choreo

Once More and Again
"Brothers and sisters, right now I'm gone ask you to come to order, to cease your walking and talking, and let's get on one accord!"

The voices. Deacon Van Coleman, Deacon Earnest Shaw, Deacon Willie Myrick, Deacon Jimmy Coleman. There were many more seated on the left side, in the two front rows and whose faces will never leave me.

That greeting in the sanctuary on any Sunday morning meant that Sunday School was officially over. At the sound of the greeting, people would either make their way to the front pews or leave the room entirely, for it began the deacons' devotional, meaning that morning service would start within the next 15 minutes. Behind the deacons in one or two rows, sat the church mothers, all dressed in white, with sweaters or shawls wrapped around their shoulders. These were the grandmothers of the church, the pastor's mother and other elders who didn't say very much, but who would sometimes offer their testimonies. On the opposite side sat the church nurses, dressed in full uniform from their white hats to their white shoes and stockings, carrying nursing bags, wearing navy blue capes, filling up at least two rows of the front right pews. All these pews would fill up during the deacons' devotion.

* * * * **

This is the way it was. Our sequential, exciting order leading to the pinnacle of worship every Sunday morning that you could count on because it never changed. There was first this, then that, and, like a clock you learned to read and memorize, you took comfort in it. Like the God we learned about, it was always the same.

For our people, devotion consisted of a combination of five oral activities. Singing, praying, Scripture reading, reciting the ancestral chants, and testifying. There were certain common worship phrases. For example, in prayer, the petitioner would begin by saying, "This morning, Father God, I come once more and again before the throne of grace, with knee bent and body bowed, just to say thank you. I come gifting you all the honor and the praise." "Lord, it's not because we've been so good; not because we've been so kind, but because of your grace . . ." "You woke me up this morning, started me on my way, gave me food to eat, gave me a place to sleep," "You brought me from a mighty long way, and I just want to say thank you!"

After the prayer, one of the deacons would lead us in traditional songs from the time of our ancestors, nameless chants that everybody knew and revered. These had been handed down for hundreds of years and our people still sang and kept them alive in their hearts. If you were at a church in Mississippi or a church in Florida, a church in Illinois or a church in Missouri, these chants were there. Then there were the familiar Gospel Pearls like *"Shine on Me," "This Little Light of Mine," "Pass Me Not," "Woke up this Mornin' With my Mind," "Jesus is on the Main Line (Tell 'im What you Want),"* and *"I Shall Not be Moved."*

Deacon Willie Myrick sang *"I Shall Not be Moved,"* with enthusiasm. He was a brown skinned, tall and stocky man, able to occupy the space about him quite well. He looked like authority, like someone you could trust. I felt safe hearing and watching him sing us through the devotion and into the worship service.

In these rhythmic, humble prayers of deflection, the speaker would kneel and fold his hands in the same way my grandparents prayed. We deserved nothing, we may have very little, but in the tradition of our enslaved ancestors, we were wealthy in spirit and gave thanks for everything. This was our belief system. As if in this world of wrong and right, we, the lowly had done nothing right, and may even have flat out done wrong. As if whatever we had gained in this world where we were hated was either by accident, or through the gift of a blessing we had not earned. To have all we needed, it had come through grace. If we didn't, we kept asking and working. I couldn't make much sense of it. It didn't leave me feeling good about myself. What it did leave me with was the feeling that there was indeed Something powerful to believe in. No question about that. The power in the prayers and the hymns made that part clear. And I would feel better because of these prayers and the hymns we sang together. But my relationship to It was filled with questions. And these questions would persist well into adulthood when I finally found ways to begin exploring them.

"If you want more power, tell 'im what you want!"

* * * * *

When I was nine years old, on Christmas of 1961, Aunt Lucille came to the house, took me to church for the first time, and I didn't want to go! Of course, I didn't know a single soul except for her when we got there. She took me through those big, wooden doors, into the vestibule, down that short stairway and onto the cement floor of the church basement where the first person we saw was Mrs. Eunice

Little. Auntie introduced us and left me there with Mrs. Little. Pulled away from my familiar, right then and there, I cried! I wanted to run away. And Mrs. Little gently took me by the hand and smiled, and told me that I would remember this day, because soon, she said, I would cry when it was time to leave.

And in time, as I found a place there, Mrs. Little's words came true . . .

I will never forget her help that Sunday. Her little hat, little voice, her little hand to hold and the smell of her perfume as I first crossed that important threshold. Mrs. Little was one of the women leaders of the church, one of my elders who showed me love, made me feel safe and welcome, gave me an example to follow, and taught me, by how she looked and carried herself, what she said and didn't say, what she did and didn't do, how to be a woman.

Now I call the roll, and list that group of women who, along with Mrs. Little, held up a real-time example for me when I was so young but felt in such a hurry to be anything but a child. Mrs. Lois McKee, Mrs. Mary Baker, Mrs. Mary Thornton, Mrs. Beatrice Edwards, Mrs. Evelyn Thompson, Mrs. Ann Warren, Mrs. Cerlivia Johnson, Mrs. Juanita Davis, Mrs. Lubertha Wright, Mrs. Margaret Coleman, Mrs. Florene Dillard, Mrs. Annie Mae Shaw, and Walterene Jones, along with (Aunt) Mrs. Lucille Conway Loman. These women took their part in church leadership, along with the need to look that part, very seriously. Every Sunday without fail, beautiful women were on parade, with their hats, hair, make-up, perfume, jewelry, their suits or dresses, their purses and shoes. I'm talking about mink stoles, hats of feather, wool, or woven straw on their heads to accessorize the finest ensembles, and, of course, the ritual it took each week to put this style together.

At that time, women created and embodied their church elegance, wanting to be unique, outstanding, from the short net to the calf skinned pocket book with the strong, gold clasp, to the matching shoes, to the nails, gloves and the anklet to accent the beautiful legs dressed in sheer stockings.

These women did not play around, and I was their attentive audience member, missing nothing obvious and everything not so. This part of churchgoing, paying attention to the women, what they did, what they had on, was essential. It was important to emulate as much about how they carried themselves as I could get away with. And I did. That is, until my mother reined me in.

* * * * *

I took my time before joining, wanting to be sure my heart was in it. By the time I did, it was. So, on Easter Sunday morning, 1962, I was baptized in Sunrise service at Tabernacle Baptist Church. Rev. John Connor, our Assistant Pastor, stood in the pool with me, as our pastor stood on the platform and said the words over me. Then, in the following Sunday morning service, I received the right hand of fellowship from the deacons after the doors of the church were opened and the new members were received. It was my rite of passage, showing I was now an official member of the church.

Rain or shine, winter or summer, every Sunday morning was a celebration! Before long, my mother had joined this group of women leaders in the church. And she joined not just by the work she did there, she joined the fashion plate, too. Her church work and mine meant we would go a few times during the week. Sunday School teachers' meeting on Wednesday nights, her Senior Choir rehearsals on Friday nights, my Young Adult Choir rehearsals on Saturday afternoons. Joey had joined and become a Deacon in the Junior

Church, serving with Joseph McCray, Mrs. Little's son, under Rev. Kelly the Minister. By Sunday, we had caught the momentum of yet another completed week and were very happy about going to church.

The "combined choirs" sang together every Sunday. The Senior, the Inspirational, and the Young Adult choirs. There was always something special going on or being planned at the church, so that the excitement was both continuous and contagious. As the Deacons sang their last devotional song, the musicians would chime in and the choir would be in place, ready to march in at exactly 11:00.

The music of the church was one of the most important and exciting elements of the service. Our master musicians channeled the sounds of the spirit, irrepressible, old, willful as life itself and straight from the heart of Africa. The witness of special moments presses the "play" button in my deepest memory and enjoys such moments so plentiful from that time. Like a drill sergeant directing the choir, Rev. Milton Brunson often slapped his thunderous hands together, lunging forward, drawing the powerful sound from our bodies, knowing it would be perfect. *"Jesus' Love Just Bubbles Over In my Heart," "Rise Up and Walk,"* and *"Walk On By Faith Each Day"* were among the many songs he taught us. Even during rehearsal, sometimes these songs took hold, brought us to our feet, and sent chairs falling over.

Like it was yesterday, I remember Mahalia Jackson singing with us. Sometimes we had guest singers like The Hutchinson Sunbeams, Rev. James Cleveland, The Staples, and The Caravans. Just as memorable were our own. Larry Clay, who sounded just like Sam Cooke. Stanley Keeble, who sang with enough fire to burn himself. DeLois Scott, with her own special style, the tiny velvet bows pinned to the side curls of her short cut hair, and the moment she closed her eyes, stepped to the microphone, placed her hands at both sides of the rostrum, leaned in, and simply . . . sang.

Most of the time I felt affirmed, encouraged, as if there was plenty of room in the church for me to grow up happily there. One Sunday when Grandmother visited church with us, the three of us sat together and she squeezed my hand during a high point in the service, and I saw Joey with his eyes closed, crying, saying only, "I'll go, Lord, I'll go."

* * * * *

The church basement had been my first encounter with this place. I still can't quite explain it, but something happened in that crowded, long, bustling room to make us all feel so connected, so completely alive. You could find all kinds of free, nourishing food for the soul tightly jammed in that space. Things like shelter, belonging and hope so powerful that sadness could not survive there.

In the far back was a water fountain and a small walk-in closet for choir members' coats and robes. The teenagers hung out by the coat racks at the right corner. Along the back wall were pop machines with wooden cases of empty bottles Mr. Hamb had stacked by the wall. The caretaker of buildings and grounds, Mr. Hamb walked with a slight limp, chewed gum with his mouth open, and had the world's biggest key ring laden with keys of all kinds hanging from his side pocket. And he had tools, mops, buckets and hand trucks, too. On the left wall in front of the kitchen, was Deacon Frasier's hot dog stand with tempting snacks like Jay's potato chips and a tall jar of dill pickles on the counter.

Just beneath the activity, the kitchen situated in the back far left infused the air with invitation. In the front left corner, there was an old upright piano and somebody — a soloist or a trio — might be practicing with a musician for a song to be sung in a program later. Right by the entryway was the nurses' room equipped with a thin bed dressed in white linen, and supplies used to care for those who fell out during service. The trustees' office was on the opposite wall, and you'd see the men in dark suits with serious looks on their faces going in and out. Further down that wall was the church office where there was another door. You'd go in and there were other offices inside where the important folks could be found. In the far back were the washrooms, and you'd pass through a hallway and furnace room to get to the ladies.' In the corner behind the kitchen was the concrete back stairway leading outside.

In the midst of all this were long wooden tables covered with oil cloth, and folding metal chairs, lining both sides and down the center of the room. There were still more chairs lined up along the side walls where people sat and talked and drank coffee and pop and laughed. Thick magic covered us all like a bright afternoon rainbow. When you needed air, you could stand outside the back door or sit on the stone bannisters of the front porch and take in the sprawling, green view of Fuller Park stretched out across the street in front of you.

After service we would either go home or line up in the church basement for a homemade soul food dinner. Church dinners cost $1.00 then. A piece of cake was fifteen cents or so, if you wanted dessert. If we were staying all day, then the time after service was when the fun began. After dinner, we palled around with our friends until the 3:30 service. I had friends from Sunday School and the choir, girlfriends like Brenda and Cheryl that I went to school with, but my best friends at church were the gay boys. Jerry and Billy. I wasn't absolutely sure they were gay, they just never had any girlfriends that I saw, they were easy to talk to, and they were inseparable, so, I made that assumption. This wasn't something you would mention, you'd just feel it and go with it. We would sometimes meet up outside of church and take trips together, like go to the museum of Science and Industry on the bus. They were always at the church, I loved them both, and they loved me, too.

*****

Sometimes we had visiting ministers or choirs. They would share with us at the 3:30 service which dismissed by 5:00 or 5:30. Baptist Training Union began in the Community House at 6:15 and until about 7:00 or 7:15 we would learn more about our denomination, its structure, its rules, its history and such. As young people, we had special discussions in BTU, sometimes called BYPU. After that we would rush back to the main building and prepare for whatever choir musical was scheduled. On the first Sunday, we had communion service. On the fifth Sunday, there was no musical. But, for every other Sunday, the 7:30 choir musicals brought folks back into the sanctuary to prepare for the radio broadcast, starting at 9:00 P.M. and lasting until 10:00. That service was where the excitement lived. We sang our hearts out at the broadcast and put our best voices forward since that service was tightly planned and required perfection.

And so it was, in these assorted ways, that for a very special time, the church of my childhood became my second home.

Fifty Cents Short

Life in 1966 was about discoveries. Just the year before, I had graduated with honors from Elementary School, that perfect world of order and silence. Now, a survivor of my freshman year and a proud, rising sophomore, I was fast approaching the time when absolutely everything would be funny. Until that day, life was still seriously organized into two great, unequal parts, the school year and summer vacation.

Vacationing now, Justine Johnson, Meryl Moore and I were busy planning another new discovery. We would attend the National Baptist Sunday School Convention at Charlotte, North Carolina as church delegates. In different parts of the South Side, we were all proud to have finished the school year intact. We three usually palled around between Sunday services, and were happy to be growing up together.

*   *   *   *   *

There was a really hip song out that summer about being in with the "in crowd," knowing what it knows and going where it goes. The in-crowd at our church was a set group. You had to be 16 and beautiful to be "in," and I was two years too young. Like bees around honey, the in-crowd gathered in the back corner of the church basement, laughing out loud about whatever they had been up to. Always laughing it up, drinking the fun of their time, I envied their explosive teenage life on full blast. It was the life I craved. Being in the Choir put me in the vicinity of the sounds and sights of the "in crowd," but observing them was as close as I'd ever get.

The Temptations had a smash hit that summer, *"Ain't Too Proud to Beg."* Whenever it came on the radio, we'd scream it out right along with David Ruffin. Walking down the street, sometimes we'd fall to our knees,

> *"I know you wanna leave me,*
> *but I re-fuse to let you go . . ."*

Listening to the words, you could hear that it was a really sad song, but the beat of it felt happy and made you dance. But, I didn't know about pride or beggin' for love. Not yet.

"Ain't Too Proud to Beg" became the theme song for our trip down South. There were other hits too, like, *"Open the Door to Your Heart,"* by Darryl Banks, *"This is a Man's World"* and *"Money Won't Change You,"* both by James Brown, *"Let's Go Get Stoned"* by Ray Charles (that mostly made us laugh), and, *"When you Wake Up,"* by Cash McCall. Now that last song was so smooth and mellow for boppin,' it felt like the music picked up your feet and moved your body for you. Rev. Cleveland also had a record out that summer, *"Without a Song,"* that everybody was singin.' And even though it might have been a little out of style by then, *"Just Ask the Lonely"* by the Four Tops was also orbiting our trip.

With this background music we laughed at life, laughed at the contradictions right there in plain sight, laughed at the tension between the way things really were and what we were being taught. We laughed hilariously, because that's what you do when you are so young and growing, learning and still so desperately needing to trust the ones who are raising you, when you believe with all your heart that everything looking so very beautiful all around you is real, and that surely you will figure it all out someday. You just play along and you laugh.

* * * * *

A common practice among girls at that time and place, Justine, Meryl and I decided to dress alike for our plane trip. We'd be flying together to the Convention City, all of us for the first time. For me, it also meant going South for the first time, since I had been no farther south than Indianapolis. Dressing alike seemed the best way to mark and announce these firsts. I suggested blue dresses, Justine suggested blue shoes, and Meryl suggested dark blue fishnet stockings. Justine already had her shoes, and told us where to get ours, so we would match exactly. We would get our fishnets at the shoe store, too. Justine told us about some boss shoes for three dollars at Bakers. This was exciting, because there was a Bakers Shoes store on Sixty-Third and Halsted. She said the shoes were flat, powder blue suede, with a pointed toe, an ankle strap and three flower petals cut across the instep. We were so excited!

* * * * *

For us church kids, looking good was important. And, following the example of the women in the church, a good plan for looking good made it foolproof. Our good plan was to be dressed alike, dressed to the nines going on a church trip to the South. What could be better?

I would need money for this. Three dollars for the shoes, one dollar for the fishnets, maybe another quarter for tax, and fifty cents for round trip bus fare. For less than five dollars I would have my shoes and stockings for the trip!!! I already had my dress. I couldn't wait!

* * * * *

A woman's grooming practices began in her teenage years. Being beautiful involved many things. Dressing and grooming oneself always required lots of time and effort. We were expected to look perfect, to be girdled, held in place no matter where we were or what we wore. This practice was regimented, reinforced at school, and we quickly grew accustomed to it.

* * * * *

Every week, for gym class inspection, we stood silently on our Assigned Numbers while our teacher walked down the line carrying her clipboard and pen, making note of how you looked. Inspection was part of your Gym Grade. To pass, your plain white gym shoes had to be laundered and polished, your light blue one-piece cotton gym suit had to be laundered and starched, and you had clean white sweat socks on. But there was one more thing. Many of us wore long line panty girdles, so, there would be tight elastic extensions of all colors, past the leg hole on our uniforms holding our hips and thighs in place. Except for the rainbow of girdles, white, orange, pink, red, black, we stood in uniform. If you dared pull the girdle leg up to hide it under the gym suit, the tight roll quickly cut off your circulation.

With mandatory uni-butts, we had long forgotten how it felt to breathe and walk free. But I figured it was worth the sacrifice once I developed the habit. In school, I mostly wore shoes and socks because of all the walking and running I had to do. Then, of course, we had stockings for special days, that extra transparent skin covering your legs like a kind of make-up. I loved full fashion stockings, and by then had switched to cinnamon. I watched my legs for new hair, really wanting the hair to grow so that they, too, would be so sexy with the hair held down underneath the stockings.

But, dressing up in one's Sunday best required these multiple garment layers. Panties, girdle, stockings fastened to your girdle, and for that Special Week of the Month, you added The Belt.

Insulating you like wrapping paper over all of this was your slip. Either half or full, you went nowhere without that slip for warmth in the winter and, in the summer sunlight, your half-slip was insurance that nothing under your dress was visible to curious eyes. Our bras were made of cotton, easy and comfortable to wear. But they were pointed, adding a sharp angle to your shell, blouse, or dress, two cone tips sticking out of your chest like rockets.

Back then, clothes were cut to fit the shape, curves, length, and landmarks of our bodies. We had waistlines, hiplines, shoulder lines, necklines. The spirit of our clothing was to caress, cover and accentuate. Clothing reflected size, posture, and confidence. Like extra layers of skin to reflect well-being, clothes were like bright sun rays, a source of happiness and warmth, and with all of this in mind, you carefully crafted your outfit every day. But in church, inscribed your Feminine Signature through the layers of your outfit with extra special care. You learned to walk upright and flow with the imaginary breeze, your body was part of nature's garden. Your head a blossom, your torso and legs a stem, your arms and hands the leaves, your feet the roots.

But, where was I in all of this fresh picked, beautiful fuss?

* * * * *

My dress for the trip was a one-of-a-kind deep blue-green color. Actually, it had a tad more green than blue. It was an empire style number with three covered buttons down the bodice and a tiny bow stitched at the front center. I loved the empire style, with no waistline, but a ribbing sewn just under the bra line, to bring attention there. We all wore virgin pins, big, plain metal circles pinned to the heart side of our collars, thinking this identified us even more as virgins of the hip and mature variety.

After I packed my bag, all I had left to do was to shop for my accessories. I had calculated my expenses. Five dollars would be enough. I asked him and my step dad, Mr. Latimore, gave me the money. Right away I headed off to Sixty-Third. The vertical silver poles on the bus extended from floor to ceiling so you could hold on while you rode. I was so excited about the trip, how I would look, all the fun we were going to have, that I held that pole really tight, tight enough to make my hand sweat, while I sat there daydreaming. I couldn't get to Bakers fast enough.

I got off the bus right in front of the store. Although I never saw them before, the shoes Justine described were right in the front window, standing out like a sore thumb. And now, there was a problem. When she said they were "on sale for three dollars," she had left out one detail. They were Three Ninety-Nine! This left me short of enough money for my shoes and fishnets by about fifty cents! Three ninety-nine means four dollars! I believed Justine when she said "three dollars," so that's how much I brought. I knew nothing about "extra."

Nobody taught me the concept of extra. I'd never heard of it. I brought what I needed, no more, or less. Now I was short and pretty mad. The fishnets were ninety-nine cents. Altogether I would need six dollars, not five, including bus fare, with enough for tax, which would leave me a little bit of change. So, I got the shoes, and planned to get my fishnets later. To save myself a quarter, I walked the two miles home.

I didn't tell Mr. Latimore what had happened because he always kept a really long lecture handy, and I wasn't in the mood. Mr. Latimore was older than Mom, and they had married in a hurry on the 4th of July 1964. They were both Sunday School teachers and choir members at church. He was a very experienced man who had come to Chicago from Birmingham. I could tell that he loved Mom very much and was proud to be her husband.

But out of the blue he'd only talk angry about how I looked. He would say things about my attitude, insist that I was "fighting something." Then he'd say my legs were pretty, and with a red face remind me that I "wasn't dating!" I hated when he looked at me with his beady eyes and talked to me like that. Whatever I was fighting probably had to do with him! It was a safe bet that he wouldn't want to drive me back for the fishnets. Besides, he had worked all day and was tired for sure. "Just forget it," I thought. I'd find another way.

* * * * *

At fourteen, it was important for things to work according to plan. When they worked, I was relieved. Relieved of some of the awkward feelings that came with being fourteen, not knowing why I had them or why they hurt so much, feeling almost invisible among my friends some of the time, more like a ghost from somewhere far away and less like just a regular girl.

Girling meant preparation. Getting ready for better days, smoother times, safety and more power over what went on in my life. Girling meant looking ahead, focusing, even hurrying for the chance to be GROWN.

I called Justine and told her that she had given me the wrong information. She didn't see the big deal. The difference between three and four dollars meant nothing to her. Then I put the shoes with my dress. Bad color combination! I could see why the shoes were only three ninety-nine. It was too hot for suede. They weren't even real suede, and I did not like them at all. Now, with the shoes and dress together, clearly, all blues do not go together just as all reds don't. If only I had the dress with me when I got the shoes. But this was the dress I had, these were the shoes we would all wear, and it was too late to change anything.

* * * * *

My mother and Mr. Latimore gave me a good talking to about being down South for a week. Mom added that if she detected anything in my attitude before time to leave, then, I could keep my "ass at home." I was to mind my P's and Q's and listen to Ms. T. and Aunt Lucille, who would be going with us. No problem. I loved them both, and would do whatever they said. Mom never talked to me that way before, and that kind of talk made me hold my breath, giving her no reason at all to cancel my trip.

While I held my breath, the adults agreed it would be best that we spend the night at Meryl's and go to the airport from there the next morning. So, we did. Once there, I was able to breathe. I was even more excited than before, so I rolled up my hair to look so good in the morning that the clashing colors wouldn't even matter.

Experimenting with make-up, my plan was to wear a Marilyn Monroe beauty mark on the side of my mouth. Hoping the beauty mark would divert eyes from the slight case of acne on my forehead, I put it there with a dab of dark brown eyeliner. Hoping against hope the foundation would cover up the blemishes on my forehead, but it never did. Skin problems added to the awkwardness. Excitement or no, nothing was working. That sweet spot where I could hum my way through weird moments still eluded me. To make matters worse, I had rolled my hair too tight. And, without my fishnets, I showed up for the trip barelegged, which Aunt Lucille frowned upon.

Chicago Negro girls had a thing about shoe size. Everybody wore a 7-and-a-half. Except me. I wore an 8-and-a-half. If I told, they'd call me Big Feet. So, not only didn't I tell, I bought size 8 thinking it would make my feet look smaller and my legs look bigger! So, the shoes hurt my feet. I hated pointed toe shoes, these had slick, hard bottoms that stuck to the soles of my sweaty feet the more we walked in the hot sun.

This stuff that didn't work made the awkwardness feel endless. My personal cloud, awkward sometimes melted a little, letting the sun peak through, like when I sang or laughed. But mostly awkward was just there, the film over my eyes, something I was conscious of most of the time, something I hoped nobody noticed. Although I hadn't given up, I mostly felt powerless to change it.

* * * * *

There we were, together on an Eastern Airlines Boeing 707 jet. *"Fly Eastern, number one to the sun!"* Once we put on our seat belts, we giggled and started holding hands. We all had our Bibles. So, we took them out and started praying sincerely, pleading with Jesus for safety.

Once we were in Charlotte, everything seemed twice as slow and twice as funny. We could get some of the same radio music there, which was a nice treat. The weather was very hot, though. Hotter than anything. So hot we didn't say more than we had to. So hot we talked about frying eggs on the sidewalk and being down in Africa. So sun baked sweaty hot that the houses and cars were all air conditioned. So hot and wet it created a Negro girl's worst emergency. Swollen hair! Curl Free did not protect against moisture and heat. My hair swole up so big, all I could think to do was to put extra grease on it when I rolled it, and to tie it up even tighter before I went to bed.

In Charlotte, we went everywhere in "courtesy cars," and stayed that week at a "courtesy house" with one of the local Baptist families. This much courtesy protected us from Jim Crow. A fact that nobody mentioned. We didn't even realize it at the time, but for our whole trip, they loved us so much that they personally kept us sheltered from mean old Southern bigotry.

And we laughed at the way the Southerners talked. Once we were settled in, I tried calling home, collect, like my mother told me to. But the telephone operator's slow, drawling talk tickled me so, that to keep from laughing in her face, I hung up the phone.

* * * * *

We laughed the whole time. That time had come and I loved it. Laughing time. And, to keep people from laughing at me, I got really good at keeping them laughing about everything else. At night, we talked about funny times at school. We passed gas and laughed ourselves to sleep.

We found a mall near the courtesy house, one with koi fish in a pond just outside the door. It was the only public place we were allowed to go on foot. At our eating place in the mall, I ordered a cheeseburger deluxe with sweet pickle slices, a chocolate malt, and a slice of cherry pie. Every day.

* * * * *

All week, we met kids from other cities. Kids from Milwaukee, Peoria, and, couples quickly began to form. I met Beverley from Milwaukee who had the same birthday as mine! She and another girl from her church shared our room at the courtesy house. Beverley found a really cute boyfriend named Craig. I had enough "boyfriends" at home, and didn't need another one in Charlotte.

Every day we rode to the church conference center by schedule and rehearsed our music. A woman named Evelyn something directed and taught us. There were classes, too, with material similar to what we learned in Baptist Training Union at home — What Baptists Believe, etc., — only now I was learning it with people I didn't know. In our Friday night closing ceremony, we marched in, holding candles, singing in three-part harmony...

God of love, God of power, God most holy and divine
From this hour, by thy grace and power
Make us wholly thine.

We packed and flew home early Saturday morning. Then, back for church on Sunday, we had to speak. Aunt Lucille, Dean of Christian Education, cut Sunday School short that day so there would be time for the Assembly AND the Deacons' devotion. We each gave reports of our time in Charlotte, said what we had learned, and offered thanks for the opportunity to represent the church at the conference, but couldn't tell it all.

* * * * *

For a while after that trip, I blamed Justine to her face and in my head for making me buy those awful shoes. But, best of all, I was able to borrow a pair of comfortable sandals from my new friend, Beverley, whose feet were the same size as mine. She had packed an extra pair.

Imagine. Extra, foot-feeling-good shoes in just the right size . . . in hot Charlotte.

Imagine.

Extra.

Imagine.

Code Pintac

In July of 1965, we moved to the eighty-two hundred block of South Emerald Avenue. *"Shot-gun! Shoot 'em 'fore 'e run now!"* Junior Walker and the All Stars echoed yard to yard as we settled into life on the first floor of Grandmother's house. For our noticeable boundaries, an auto pound extended east to west across 83rd on the south end, and train tracks ran raised above the unpaved alley behind us. As I studied both sides of Emerald's face south to north, its looks held up at least until 80th. Emerald's face was a hodgepodge of small, two- and three-story old frame houses, lined with bright green hedges and young leafy trees.

Half a block west was Halsted, our main artery through town. Not just a street, but a people magnet, Halsted was jammed with storefront windows dressed with neon. Whatever you wanted was within walking or running distance. So, once you learned where to go for what, you could have little bits of Christmas all year round.

Black and white, many of our elder neighbors sat on their porches, overseeing the block's comings and goings. The blacks thought we lived far enough south to think of our neighborhood as nice. To the whites, there was nowhere else to go. Yet. For us kids, with no park nearby, we played in the street or on the sidewalk. After we had been there awhile, and on those days when nothing else was happening, we sometimes collected change from the kids on the block and then fired up what remained of our backyard barbeque pit. I'd take the change around to Auburn Foods and buy a whole chicken. After I cut up and washed it, Joey would try grilling it. Then we'd serve the meat on bread, with cups of icy Kool-Aid to wash it down.

We had moved abruptly to the Auburn Gresham neighborhood from Chatham, now a world away. And in the fall,

I would begin high school at Calumet. Joey was in the 7th grade and would attend Gresham Elementary.

*****

Rollo Perkins and Lloyd White would show up on the porch most days after school. Rollo was in my grade, but, since school just wasn't Lloyd's thing, he was a year or so behind. Just the sight of these inseparable guys packing loads of fun, heading my way made me happy.

Rollo was tall, dark, sometimes even handsome, depending on his outfit. He and his older brother lived with both their parents on the second floor of the corner house. Rollo was cool and really quiet, so when he *did* say something, we listened. His jokes were the funniest because he wasted no words. You held your breath awaiting their stinging, sidesplitting reward.

His buddy, Lloyd, lived around the corner in a small house with his mother and little sister. Lloyd was short, cute, and used great big body language — the hip dip, quick spin, talking hands — working hard for his laughs, practicing and dancing the feelings he didn't have words for . . . practicing for something, some contest he expected to win.

*****

In those days, our past-times required keen imagination, something we had plenty of. Our competing impatience and imagination made for some crazy moments. And since time in the nineteen sixties moved like cold honey, by force of gravity, we often gave time a collective nudge, took it into our own hands, and *made* things happen.

Among our people, joking was a skill, a craft to practice and master. Here's an example. We'd sit around the living room and watch the television with no sound, as Rollo and Lloyd would find hilarious words to match the facial expressions of the white people on the screen. And then, after our parents divorced, they would ask for a snack, knowing we didn't have one. One of them would walk to the kitchen, open the refrigerator door and stand there, speechless, because all that was inside was ice water.

* * * * *

Thankfully, though, we never ran out of music, a thought I shudder to consider. Joe Cobb's voice woke me up in the mornings! He was the disk jockey known as "Youngblood" on "WVON, 1450." And, as a freshman that year, I'd walk to school to the rhythm of *"My Girl,"* and *"Papa's Got a Brand-New Bag!"* playing through the ear piece on my transistor radio. We had the music, the music for love, for joy, or any mood at all. We had a song for whatever way you found yourself. And we needed that music, because without words for much of life, we let the music do the talking. And talk it did. Many a conversation took place then, with just our hearts and the music. Talking.

Heading west on 82nd Street, my morning walk to school was serene. Most days I'd stop at Mrs. Brown's grocery store for a Payday bar. She'd ask about me with a smile and wish me a good day. I loved every step from home to school, not knowing what this chapter of my life would mean. I loved crossing Halsted, Green, Peoria, Sangamon, Morgan, Aberdeen, Carpenter . . . arriving at May.

Eighty-second Street was extra wide, but with hardly any traffic, the street was lined end to end with chiseled red brick buildings. These buildings never changed, some were even accented with clay tile roofs and stained-glass windows in the front. So sparkling crisp in spring, so warm and inviting in winter. I'd wonder about who lived there, and guess how rich they were.

Sometimes there were other students walking, too, but we mostly kept to ourselves. This solitary routine, enjoying my music and candy, looking, thinking, carrying my books, prepared or not for the day, shaded in my own temporary world, walking in the shade of giant maple, elm, oak growing skyward on both sides, then sideways, meeting in the middle, and forming a lush bouquet of green umbrellas covering me, was like meditation. This routine, these years of slow, quiet walking, years at one school, years soaked with so much action were the most stable I had ever known.

* * * *

By then I'd figured out that I wasn't an "in crowd" kind of girl. I probably could have tried, perhaps with a bigger smile or more pep. What if I dared trying to fit in, even without long hair or light skin? Who knew? I only knew this. I had to resist all the ordinary things that kids did to belong. Competing, joining, striving to gain entrance. Shouldn't it be enough to know everybody and have everybody know me?

Something was wrong with school. If you weren't careful, high school could be like a really big mouth that swallowed you up. There is a roll I could call for the swallowed up, disappearing kids ... It was a place where white students were graduating or leaving by choice, where Negro students slowly became the majority, where you won respect and fame according to the rules of the game. So maybe this really big mouth could be like a football field. And maybe some ambitious kids made the team.

This put The Players in front of everyone. Their rookie teammates sat on the sidelines waiting for their chance. Meanwhile they suited up, with their names on the backs of their shirts. Fewer folks knew them, at least until they got called up and ran out to prove their stuff. Then, a select group of Smart, Pretty Girls led the cheers. They wore uniforms too, and moved in unison, more like dancers. They had clout, but not as much as the Players. Everyone else sat in the stands. The nerds and special kids sat down front with their teachers. From there things went strangely downhill. The higher up on the stands you sat, and the less noise you made, the fewer folks knew you were even alive. This game plan put me at the top row, with the parents. And somehow, in the midst of the game, with its regular practices and plays, in the short span of four years, you were expected to perform a miracle. Grow up! Enter girl. Exit woman.

* * * * *

Anyway, it all started in the 10th grade. I'm talking about the pressure from Rollo and Lloyd's little codes. "Oh, trust me, you look like you could handle it," and, "I can tell by your eyes, Girl, that you could reeeeeeeally handle it," they'd say over and over. Capitalizing on my hooded eyes, they were talking about reefer, and, to "handle it" meant to take and try the reefer without losing control, and, to keep the reefer secret. I would find ways to change the subject, but they kept on bringing it back up.

* * * * *

By the time I made it to the 11th grade, Joey had gotten to high school. So, to keep from being called an L-7, or a "square," Joey and I came up with the first part of a strategy. We started giving basement dance parties on Saturday nights. Our exciting parties — quarter parties, talent parties — hurled us practically overnight into the mainstream of high school life, on our own simple terms.

These exciting, yet unauthorized parties worked most of the time since Mom was rarely home on weekends anymore.

Now, with our house as a hangout on the block, from the front porch to the living room, back yard to the basement, our parties quickly became a regular thing. So popular around school were they that people would automatically show up for "that set on 82nd Street." To prepare, we swept and mopped the basement floor, opened the windows, turned on the music, put the blue light bulb in, had a bowl of potato chips and dip or warm tuna mac salad with crackers ready, and unlocked and cracked open the back door. Everybody knew to come around back, to keep from upsetting Grandmother with that pesky, wind-up doorbell, especially after we taped a **Come Around Back** sign to the front door with a left arrow pointing to the side walkway.

One time, she got wind of the party anyway. Trying to be subtle about it, she came quietly down the back stairs on her tiptoes, turned on the bright lights, stood elegantly in the center of the room, and read her sacred poetry for about 15 minutes while everyone respectfully listened. Then she left . . . and the party continued.

These parties cracked a hole in the old social stratosphere and let us in. The parties were our time to shine, break out the latest music, sing out loud, dance like crazy. Just when James Brown came out with *"Cold Sweat,"* we played it one afternoon, hanging out in the living room with Rollo and Lloyd, when Billy from Green Street took the floor, entranced by the loud music, pulling his pants up high, forming a scarf around the banana floating in his pocket. We felt it, too, and laughed as we watched while he danced wildly, like he couldn't help himself, he danced just like people did in church.

Then at one of the parties, when Sly and the Family Stone came out with *"Dance to the Music,"* on the part with the seven booms, I let my body have her way while my mind looked on. And our friends backed up, gave me room, watched in disbelief as the shy girl, yeah, That Girl, danced like crazy, danced her behind off, all by her lonesome.

* * * * *

Meanwhile, as if the parties didn't matter to them, Rollo and Lloyd kept up the pressure. In fact, the parties may have signaled even more that we really could "handle it," especially with all those bad records and those blue lights . . . So, I decided the time for a plan had come. Long before I knew how to drive a car, this decision came close to that thrill. Like moving faster now with the help of spinning wheels, shifting up into high gear, letting the clutch go and pushing down smoothly, firmly on the gas pedal! Action time.

Truth is, Joey and I could out-think anybody around. We used our minds to figure things out. We made up our own dances. We kept handy codes to communicate with, in case we needed to say things nobody else should hear. Sometimes we used numbers; sometimes we used symbols. While I knew I shouldn't try to "handle it," I knew as well that school was already hard enough, that I couldn't, on top of everything else, afford to be called un-cool.

Back to the plan . . .

We had cats around the house. In a neighborhood like ours, cats kept the mice out of sight and, if you paid attention, would teach you what they knew. So, I did. And I remembered that something called catnip made them act almost like drunk people, except that they got happy and snappy. They didn't beat one another up, their eyes didn't get red, they didn't gain sudden insight into the world's worst problems, and they didn't seem hung over the next day. In high gear, I started wondering, imagining . . . Catnip . . . hmmm. I kept thinking as I walked to the Pet Shop to price it. "Oh," the man said, "Got a half-pound bag here for forty-nine cents!"

With this news, I ran home, told Joey, we scraped up fifty cents between us, and hurried back to the Pet Shop. One half-pound bag of coarse cut catnip was a whole lot! Cigarette paper was too small and soft to hold it together! So, while we walked, we decided on the cheaper alternative. *Newspaper.* We had tall stacks of newspaper at home. Joey had an idea about what we could call the stuff. The party would be that night. Our plan was set. We got home, grabbed some newspaper, went to the basement, rolled up several Really Big Cigarettes, and twisted them at the "other" end. They were bigger than cigar size — they'd be comparable to today's "blunts." Then we stacked them on a serving tray and put all of it off to the side where it would sit and settle until just the right moment.

Once the basement was full of kids, and the party got going strong, we walked slowly and plain faced all the way to the back. We pulled out a couple of the big cigarettes, and lit them. They burned slow and strange, extra smoky, like clothes or something. *Tighten Up!* by Archie Bell and the Drells played in the foreground, people danced at the front end of the basement, while Joey and I dealt Pintac for free in the back.

The stuff gave off a wild, choky scent that attracted Rollo and Lloyd. Trying to look hip and mysterious, I took one, and so did Joey. The Pintac was exotic, thick, too strong to inhale, but, going through the motions, we offered both the guys a drag and they took it! Once they inhaled, they looked at each other, and passed it around to some of the other guys, too. Lloyd said, "Man, that's some baaaaaadddddddd shit you got there; it's startin' to turn me onnnn!!! Oooo-ooooooooo wweeeeeeeeeeeeeee!!!" "Where'd you get that bad shit from?"

"Oh, that," I swallowed, trying to hold back my cough, tears, and laughter all at once. I told him, "It's something new, Man. Just came out. Called Pintac!" Turning my mouth upside down, I elbowed him in the side and whispered,

"Sheeeeeee-iiiiiiiiiit, Man, don't tell me you dudes hadn't heard about Pintac!?" Lloyd smiled and exclaimed as he and Rollo slapped a hard, mean five, "See! You got to *watch* these quiet types. I *knew* you could handle it!" Lloyd said, laughing, looking at me while Joey and I exchanged innocent glances.

* * * *

Just between you and me, I never felt anything much from the Pintac. The way it burned and everything, I figured it wasn't meant for smoking, that it must really, truly be meant ONLY for the cats. But, the best news of all is, after that night, Rollo, Lloyd, or anybody else, never spoke to me about "handling it" ever again.

Dance!

Part One

Nineteen sixty-six was packed with excitement! My first plane trip. My first telephone conversation with Daddy. It was autumn, my sophomore year, and a Young People's Cotillion would take place at Freedom Baptist in just a few weeks! Aunt Lucille asked if I wanted to be a debutante. Of course, I did. She said in that case, my escort had been selected. Forrest Young. My heart stopped, raced, then stopped again.

Yes, my elders loved me more than I knew, and saw through me, as if my short life was water, a clear stream running fast, running to the river.

Forrest T.M. — for "The Most" — was tall, slender, dark, with the brightest smile and the world's biggest, most expressive eyes. His eyes told stories. With just one glance, they said how he felt, and then, he had this special, powerful way of talking. He hurled the killingest words he could right into your face. He loved to laugh, and could make us laugh, too. If you got confused and Forrest knew it, he would say that you were confused over nothing. It's "the same difference," he'd insist, to show you how stupid it was to feel worried or confused. About anything.

He lived only a block from my house, so his uncle or cousin would sometimes drop me off from church. I didn't say much. In fact, I didn't say anything, but I really loved Forrest. It was my secret. I couldn't say anything because it seemed as if he didn't even know I was alive. Not really. Oh, we'd see each other in school, and he'd speak or smile and keep going. It was okay. We'd see each other in church, too, so, I felt an advantage over the other girls at church, since I got to see Forrest almost every day. He didn't seem nearly as popular at school as he was at church. At church he was a magnet, drawing and holding everybody to him just the way the caramel on my Payday candy bar drew and held those salty Virginia peanuts right where they needed to be.

Now with the cotillion I had a new, very exciting advantage. But, when word got out, nobody thought of much of it. We'd be a local news item at church, but nothing sensational. Just a nice evening for two nice young people. Not even a real date.

Forrest had just gotten his driver's license, but wouldn't be driving that night. Deacon Miller, his uncle, would drive us. "Uncle D," was a gentle man who, among many other things, served as our youth chaperone at the church. They'd come to pick me up that night at 7:00 P.M. sharp, and I promised to be ready. Now, all I had to do was find a dress.

Sometimes our Augusts were very hot, then the cooling off began. But this year, it was mid-September, and the weather was still unbearable. Humid in the high nineties, with no relief in sight. Back then there was no air conditioning. Not in church, not in cars, not on the bus, not at home, or at school. We walked or took CTA everywhere, and learned to live with the weather, hot or cold.

* * * * *

Mom had allowed me to "go with" James Waters, another boy from church. James loved football. He was really nice, and talked with intelligence. It was hard to talk on the phone because of his work and football practice schedule. So, we would agree to talk in the middle of the night! I'd put the telephone by my bed and quickly pick up the receiver just as soon as it started to ring, and talk with my head and the receiver under the pillow, because we weren't supposed to be on the phone that late.

Anyway, we would talk for hours! James wanted to take me places, but I wouldn't be old enough to really date for a while yet. Once, Mom let him take me to a party. She thought this would be a safe party, that if I went with James, it would be all right.

James lived on the West Side, and didn't have a car. So, on the bus, he came to pick me up and we went to the party, in my neighborhood. What my mother didn't know is that even with James, this wasn't a party she would want me to attend. There would be almost no talking going on at this party. Rather than talking, there was slow dragging, not a whole lot of that. And, even though us Baptist kids weren't supposed to be dancing, kids were going farther than the dance. The lights were so dim you didn't know who was there or with whom, and you had to follow your arms like a blind person to move around the place.

I was scared to let anybody get that close to me. Scared of what I might do, of what it might feel like. I already knew what it was like to have a boy I didn't really "like" hold me close on the dance floor and breathe down my neck. Didn't seem quite right to be all hugged up that way just for play. Being that close to a boy let you in on his business. Stuff I didn't want to know unless he was special to me. I figured, since I was only fourteen, I had time to find out. Then, we were taught in church and at home that dancing was a sin. Mrs. Thornton, our B.T.U. teacher, had issued us a serious warning about sinful behavior that she called "seck," and she said that "seck" was something we'd better stay away from. Dancing was dangerous, tempting, she said, because it would lead to "seck." I'd heard Grandmother say something similar, and she said it enough times it echoed in my head, "Any man who gets *that* close to me has *got* to be my husband!" My elders' specific warnings added to my teenage awkwardness. So, when it came to sin, I figured it was easier to be obedient than sorry, so, I did what I could to avoid grinding and "seck."

James had tried kissing me. Really kissing me with his mouth open, and it felt weird. He was three years older than me, and interested in lots of things. He read books and planned to go to the Navy after high school. He was a youth leader in the church, and he admired my mother a lot. By then, she was a Sunday school superintendent. I was glad he wasn't my cotillion date; because he was so short, I had to bring flat slippers to wear between services just so we could stand together. Even in my low heels, I was taller than James. The one who'd steal my heart would have to be tall, then smart, then handsome. More like Forrest.

* * * * *

By then Forrest was at least 6 feet tall. He was pretty cool and would just take charge. My mother had given me the nickname, "Boobie," and I didn't know what that meant. She called me Boobie once at church where my friends could hear. After that, Forrest would call me "Boobie" with a grin, and I hated it. He had bucked teeth, and when he laughed, you could see them all. But Forrest was strong enough to have bucked teeth and still keep the upper hand.

Forrest could really sing. At choir rehearsal, you knew he was there, because his voice was clear and strong enough to carry the whole tenor section. So, if he wasn't there, you felt that, too. He led one of our songs, *"I'm So Glad,"* and did such a good job. I loved to hear him singing. He would joke about everything, except singing. That is the way we all felt about the music. Our music was serious, and we sang it with our whole hearts. When our voices came together, it was better than anything. As a choir, we were awesome. And we knew it.

* * * * *

Only after I had finished my seventh grade Homemaking class did Mom teach me what she knew about good fabric and sewing. I could sew, but not like she could. She used the very best patterns. She believed in making or buying the best. She taught me to shop in the best stores. When she *could* buy clothes, she shopped there, finding rare treasures marked down. For Mom, nothing but the very best was good enough.

With the cotillion coming up, Mom said she'd make my dress! We decided on gold brocade, accented with ivory elbow-length gloves, a pair of ivory shoes and matching bag. Mom found a beautiful Vogue pattern and got started. I knew the outfit would be perfect. She finished my dress just in time. Cousin Celesta was visiting from New York and brought along a soft ivory stole for me to carry and made suggestions about how I should wear my hair. Since Forrest was tall, I could wear it up, have my heels, and not worry about my height. The thought of all of this was so exciting!

* * * * *

The night of the cotillion came around. Right on time, Uncle D. pulled up in front of the house with Forrest who wore a fine black tuxedo with a white boutonniere on his lapel. He smiled and pinned the white corsage on my dress as my mother told him I had to be home by midnight and checked with Uncle D. to be sure. He gave his word that he'd bring me home promptly. Celesta smiled her huge, gummy smile and looked so proud as we left. She looked happier about the night than I did! All I knew was that we were going, and that the two of us together amounted to something extra special.

One song reminds me of that specialness. *"Since I Lost My Baby"* by the Temptations played over this whole event. Even now, the sound of it reminds me of how Celesta and I had talked and laughed about Everything Cotillion. It reminds me of the smell in the evening air, the feeling of being with Forrest, how the thick gold brocade covered my body and how the skirt stood out a little because of the special crinoline half-slip Mom made, and of the feel of pulling on and buttoning up those long, smooth evening gloves.

* * * * *

When she could, Mom would take Joey and me to dinner downtown for practice. At her favorite restaurants, she taught us detailed table etiquette, the proper use of formal silverware, and such. I was confident about that. Suddenly, my tension was all about the secret I was holding.

Freedom Baptist Church had a brand-new building, with a new banquet hall as the site for this year's annual cotillion. There were reserved places for Forrest and me at a guest table where our names were printed on little cards sitting in our plates. Mr. Young. Ms. Commerse. He was a gentleman, doing gentlemanly things. The things I guessed he must have learned from his brothers or from Uncle D, since his father was gone. He tried to make conversation, but I mostly felt nervous with him, nervous because deep down, I thought he was so much better or stronger or confident than me. I didn't know what to say, so I kept quiet.

This need to talk is something I hadn't thought about practicing. I was there, noticing everything, but falling completely mute. Something was sucking up my words. Like inside my throat was a concrete wall, an immovable wall, a wall nobody told me to expect, let alone, how to take down. How in the world could I take down a wall that felt bigger than me?

* * * * *

In cotillion rehearsals, our elders had explained that the cotillion meant we were being presented into black Baptist society. It meant we were now officially considered "young people." Christian young people, crossing an important threshold, well on our way to adulthood. It was our time to achieve and move toward the bright future our elders and ancestors had worked so hard and given so much to make possible. And I was crossing over on the arm of The Most.

We had practiced the cotillion procession. The band played, and the procession began with our promenade down the center between two rows of people. They would call our names as we began walking. We'd walk arm-in-arm and smile from end to end. That is all. It was over very quickly, but I remember how walking between those lines on Forrest's arm made me feel taller, regal, fairy tale proud. Something about walking beside him made me even happier than when we sang in the choir. This happiness would be short-lived, because the cotillion clock had started ticking promptly at seven and I thought our time would fly by.

After the procession, they served our meal in small portions. The banquet hall was cold, so, with my little fur stole, I tried to keep warm. After dinner, we waltzed on a crowded floor with couples just like us. And I wondered what the rest of the night would be like. So far, it had excited me and made me nervous. And, like something to treasure, I tried to hold the night in my hand for as long as I could. My evening with Forrest was confusing, because I wanted to have it, enjoy it, and I also wanted it to be over before I embarrassed myself.

Some part of me saw every detail about the cotillion and helped me never forget. Long before, I had learned to hold my breath to appear calm and peaceful, especially when I wasn't. I thought it was important to appear calm and peaceful, so that people would think of me that way. Little did I know, holding my breath would make my nervousness even worse.

* * * * *

When Uncle D. dropped us off at the church, we didn't know that there would be an After Party. When he came to get us, he and Forrest asked me about the After Party. Forrest wanted to go and I said I did, too. Uncle D. took us there, to one of the member's homes, and agreed to pick us up at a quarter to twelve. It was just after dark, just past nine when we got there, which left a couple of hours for the party.

It was in the basement of a small brick home. I didn't know exactly where, but we went in through the front door and through the house, out the side door, around to the back, down another short, steep flight of concrete stairs, and in past a screen door. I stepped carefully to be sure not to trip and fall. I wanted to protect the special feeling that those clothes gave me. Those clothes proved I wasn't dreaming. Those clothes covered my body and my dread as I entered the basement where just a handful of other debutants, and the After Party waited! Once I was there, I was afraid of everything, except for those clothes.

* * * * *

The cotillion was over now, and this was a simple, barebones affair with dim lights and a large house fan sitting in the middle of the concrete floor, blowing on low speed to keep us cool. Punch and chips had been placed on a side table.

Of course, *"Since I Lost My Baby"* played as we arrived, and I remember the sweet feeling I got as I heard the piano, the strings, and then David Ruffin's sad voice. As if I were light enough to float away on the music, as if the only thing holding my feet to the floor was the weight of the brocade, I silently savored those feelings.

I went in and took a seat on the sofa toward the back while Forrest went outside to shoot the breeze with some of the guys. This was a relief, although sooner than later, he came back in, and sat down next to me.

That's when they played the song. The song that poured itself all over that party and our two hours there, the song that soaked itself into my mind, like maple syrup over hot buttered biscuits. *"Ooooooo Baby, Baby,"* by Smokey Robinson and the Miracles.

Under one blue light, as if on cue, Forrest stood up, turned to me and extended his hand, knowing for sure I'd want to dance. And, I did. God knows I did. Here was that moment I've played back a thousand times, and each time it's the same.

Forrest The Most, strong, tall, and beautiful, sincerely asking me to dance with him, dance to a song that was sure to pull out all my secrets and take us to heaven. Instead, my feet froze. The concrete wall in my throat was now the size of a skyscraper. I shook my head, "no." He asked me again, smiling this time. "Boobie, come on, let's dance," trying to break through, making sure he had heard me right, not taking my answer. So, I said it this time. "No, I don't want to."

Stop. Rewind. Play.

"Boobie, come on, let's dance," he urged, truly still trying, sincerely extending his hand. "No, I don't want to." I never budged. I put my head down, leaned forward, tightly clenching the front edge of the sofa with the backs of my knees.

I'm not sure whether it was because they didn't have much else in the way of music, or if it was just so good already to everyone else, but they played that song over and over that night. "*OOooooooo ooooooooooo ooooooooo, Baaaaa-bay, Bahabay . . .*" I listened so closely to every word, and the line that felt so magical and important to me was when Smokey said, "You've made mistakes too."

Was this my mistake? I've asked myself that question many times, because truly, I knew that if Forrest held me close in his arms, I would have melted all over him, and we would have learned one another's secrets that night. The thought of this frightened me terribly and I didn't dare let it happen. And as I sat listening to the music, watching everyone, holding my breath, dressed in the finest clothes I had worn my entire life, I was seeing it all in slow motion, as eventually, Forrest put down his hand, and went on to dance with another girl, a girl he didn't know.

This was my *Splendor in the Grass* life shaping, girling moment. That night shaped me the way warm clay becomes a pot at somebody's turning wheel. And my elders turned the wheel, bending my life around cotillion night. But I sat frozen still in the chill of fear, fear of my flesh, my bones hardening as the wheel turned. *Still and hard, I reached the course of the river of my life now and saw it reverse itself. My silence had stopped time, stopped the river. And I stood at the shore, watching. Stood alone in my silence watching the river rush to the sea without me.*

* * * *

Soon, Uncle D. came back for us. Forrest and I bid good-byes to our host, and finally we left the After Party. We both rode in the back seat and Forrest held my hand. Having him so near, touching my skin overwhelmed all of me. My heart pounded. I perspired. I held my breath even more. Was he was going to try to kiss me good night? Oh God, no. As we sat there, I felt The Fire, a fact I couldn't let anyone know about! Forrest was ready to kiss me good night, and I was terrified. We pulled up in front of my house right on time, at twelve o'clock sharp.

Forrest walked around the car, opened my door and helped me out. He walked me up the stairs and to my door. He opened the screen door for me and we stood there, inside it. Although I had my key, I couldn't wait. I couldn't stand there, fumbling for the key, waiting. I couldn't look at him, or wait for him to step toward me or say anything. So, in that second, desperately, I rang the doorbell! And as soon as Mom opened the door, I ran inside. My body heat had begun to smolder, I was holding my breath to keep it all under control, and I was about to explode.

* * * * *

I never saw any pictures of us that night. But since we did stop at his house to let his family see us before we headed out, I'm thinking somebody there must have taken pictures of us. Not only was I glad that Forrest never mentioned that night to me, I also hoped he didn't feel too badly about it. I've thought about that night, and replayed it in my mind numerous times.

Forever, the sound of Smokey singing *Oooooooo, Baby Baby,* takes me back to Cotillion night, to my secrets, and to the terrible pain of refusing to dance. Dance with the fine boy, the boy I reeeeeeeeally loved.

Part Two

Three years later, we'd have one more chance.

By then, I had left the church and at the time couldn't see how much I had left behind, how big of a deal it was. I knew for sure that I could keep my faith, and just knowing this felt radical. I figured my issue(s) with the church would someday resolve. Later I'd realize that so much had happened to me under the church's auspices. That the church had been a major, influential character in the stage play of my life. It had been a parent, raising me without protecting me, teaching me without persuading me, and I needed time to come to terms with the contradictions and with all of the ways in which the church had helped, influenced, and failed me.

* * * * *

Maybe this is what growing up is all about.

Our senior year was a distinguished time. To mark this for us all year long, our school held a special tradition. We had a "senior campus" area, where we were admitted solely because of our twelfth-grade status. That beautiful, intensely green, serene and open area located between the north and south wings of the school was ours to frequent between classes. And to me, the status that came with this coveted area was a passageway taking us one step closer to the world we were preparing to enter.

* * * * *

Melvin was the coolest. So cool, in fact, that he announced right off that he wasn't into proms. He wasn't about to "dress up in a tuxedo and go to anybody's ballroom" with me. Instead, he would *give* me the fifteen dollars to get my shoes, gloves, and a purse to complete my outfit. Fine.

Mr. Latimore's departure that year had dramatically changed our lives. But while we adjusted, Mom insisted I not let Melvin talk me out of my prom the way my father had done her. I thought about it and realized she was right.

I wondered who my date would be. I had a couple of friend-guys I could go with, but they "liked" me. With friend-guys, there would come that dreaded moment when they stepped over the line to let you know how "unfair" it was to go on "just being friends." I didn't like feeling that kind of pressure from friends.

As it turned out, Forrest and his girlfriend, Cathy, happened to be on the outs, and prom time was just around the corner. He came to me one day at school, and asked if I had a date for the prom. I told him I didn't. He suggested we go together, "just you and me," he said, smiling that wonderful smile. I agreed, without letting him know how perfect this was for me. This time there was no tension, no breath holding, no concrete wall, because, by then, my secret had faded away, and I had almost forgotten about Forrest. I was committed and serious with Melvin now. The way I saw it, Forrest and I could go and really have fun this time. He was safe, we knew each other, and he surely wouldn't pressure me. For once, I could just relax and have a good time.

* * * * *

Our attire for the evening was outta sight! I'd wear a straight empire, turquoise satin gown. Mom and I put the look together, and again, she made the dress. It was simple, sleeveless, with spaghetti straps and a bolero with a hand sewn crystal trim. With Melvin's money, I bought a pair of black poi de soir pumps and matching bag. My corsage would be a black orchid dusted with a hint of crystal glitter. Forrest ordered the black orchid. I loved that about him. He was a first-class kind of guy and not only did he never make qualms about anything; he made everything perfect! He would wear black with a turquoise cummerbund and boutonniere. His surprise to me was when he pulled up in a turquoise and black Lincoln Continental! I have no idea how he arranged this, but Forrest had set a tone of perfection, of sheer elegance for our evening.

* * * * *

Forrest and I double dated with his best buddy Ted, and Bessie, his girlfriend, another couple from church. The four of us also went to school together. Forrest and I ate our food and danced a couple of dances. I think we took pictures, but didn't buy them.

At 17, I thought that feeling comfortable around someone made them safe for friendship, but that friendship made them off limits for love. Being in love meant you couldn't speak freely, that you kept your guard up and hid your innermost feelings. Being in love meant you kept the secrets that made you totally vulnerable. The ones you never admitted, not even to yourself. You just felt the emotion moving in circles, pushing you away from yourself, and I thought this was just the way things were.

After we left the class dinner dance at the Pick Congress Hotel, the four of us went to Kon Tiki Ports on the gold coast. There, we had drinks. My first formal drinks. Frozen daiquiris. They were so tasty that I had a couple. After the first one, I began to do something out of character. Talk. And laugh. An older white guy sang at the piano bar, really making me laugh without intending to.

Suddenly everything seemed easy and lots of fun. The four of us walked around the area for a bit, but all the interesting shops were closed. We hadn't planned for things to do after leaving the hotel. An after party at the hotel hosted by our class "in crowd," was taking place, but as "outies," we skipped it. So, Forrest walked us back to the car and drove to that part of Lake Michigan known as The Point. For the evening, he had an eight-track tape playing. Eight-tracks were the latest thing that Spring. Dionne Warwick was singing, *"I've Been Loving You Too Long to Stop Now."*

"Don't make me stop now . . . don't make me stop now . . ."

We got to the lake and found a place to park among the many other prom night cars. Ted and Bessie decided to go for it, right in the back seat. Forrest and I sat listening to the music, and a thought flashed across my mind screen, "If only he knew how I felt that night at the cotillion." He reached for my hand and held it. He tried to kiss me and I said, "no." He asked why. I reminded him that we both "belonged to another."

* * * * *

What Forrest didn't know is how much can happen to a girl in three years. He didn't know that Melvin had, some months before, pressed and made me his woman, taught me things that really relaxed my body, but never quite relaxed my mind.

Forrest interrupted my train of thought, reminding me that he had spared no expense for us to have a perfect evening, and that he wanted us to do just that. His words were as they had always been, respectful, gentle, yet, to the point. At the time, I didn't see that this may have meant something, that this moment could have turned into a real conversation, something of importance to me. I didn't ask him to explain or to say more. I didn't share what I knew or initiate that conversation. I didn't have enough voice for it. Not yet.

Then he asked, "Boobie, do you mean we're just going to sit out our prom night at the lake and watch the sun come up, while everybody else enjoys themselves?" I said, "Yep, that's what I mean." Forrest checked to make sure, "you're *that* dedicated to the cause?" I answered, "I guess I am." He sighed, clicked his teeth and twisted up the sides of his mouth, giving me his familiar "look." What more could I say? My idea of faithfulness was absolute, something I believed in and wanted to uphold. Yet, if he had pressed me on it, I could never have made sense of it, of my decision in my own words. But my mind was made up, and he was polite about it.

The natural beauty of the night, its full moon, and fresh lakefront breeze combed the shore making it feel so fine on my skin. The deep golden light floated on the water and reached all the way to the front seat of the car. The tape played, "*Take me to heart and I'll always love you . . .*" while Forrest honored my wishes, wishes he never pretended to like. With a perfectly romantic setting, he and I sat together like buddies and sang along with the music, watching the sun come up, and bypassing a prom night rite of passage when for many, course books, curfews, and virginity became sweet, precious memories.

Movement: Notes from the Lap of History

While still in the church, we witnessed much of the Civil Rights movement. Our pastor was a very strong supporter of Dr. King's work. Our church was part of his Chicago headquarters when he visited the area. It was a proud time for us to have him there, and to know that plans were set to open his Poor People's Campaign national office, to be called Operation Breadbasket, there in Chicago. Aunt Lucille was establishing that office.

After he won the Nobel Peace Prize, he came to a Jewish synagogue in Skokie to speak. What a majestic speaker. Eloquent, too, but to the ears of a young girl, very long-winded. I nodded off several times and each time, my mother poked me with her elbow. We also heard him speak at Friendship Baptist Church on 71st Street, and this time it was more like a service. The church was packed with people and Mahalia Jackson sang that day.

Dr. King's mentor, Dr. Benjamin E. Mays, then President of Morehouse College, came to town and spoke at a luncheon at McCormick Place. Mrs. Mary Thornton took a group of young people from the church, including me. I can still remember sitting close to the speaker's lectern and seeing him stand and speak so proudly about the history of the college, the needs of our people, his calling the youth to action. The church decided the what, who, and when we would receive lessons in the culture and history of our people.

It was such an important time in our city, in our community, in our history, and I grew up in the heart of it, literally in the center of a cultural unfolding, with change exploding everywhere around me. In a small way I noticed what was happening and knew that I was fortunate to be growing up when and where I did but mostly, I took it for granted.

I can draw from the memories now, from what I learned back then, and see things I missed at the time. Here is one more example. I was a member of the Young Adult choir in our church until I was almost 16.

At one such choir rehearsal a tall, very good-looking man with a big, cottony Afro, dressed in overalls walked slowly into the church. He seemed to be looking for somebody. He was driving an old VW Beetle and had two little girls and his wife with him. Turns out, this was the Rev. Jesse L. Jackson, relocating his young family to Chicago. He too became affiliated with our church and soon had a spot in the pulpit where he frequently spoke, and eventually became our "Associate Pastor." In fact, he and the Rev. Henry O. Hardy were ordained as ministers on the same Sunday afternoon. They were both just out of divinity school, and had bright, promising futures ahead of them. I was there on that day, too, knowing without doubt that I was watching history being made. What I did not know is that those two young ministers would continue to walk together as brothers through the milestones of their careers for the rest of their lives, walk all the way into the distant future, to two historic presidential bids, with one running, and the other supporting from backstage.

At about this same time, there was a large, powerful gang known as the Blackstone Rangers operating on the South Side. Rev. C.T. Vivian, from Dr. King's Executive Committee, was living in Chicago, working within The Woodlawn Organization, a non-profit agency addressing some of the needs within our community. Rev. Vivian decided to reach out and begin working with the Blackstone Rangers to teach them new, purposeful ways of being. Rev. Vivian also became active within our church. I loved hearing him speak. He was a fiery speaker that gave me hope. I admired him for his work in the South. He was the one who had stood on the Alabama courthouse steps and told Sheriff Clark to "arrest us if we're wrong; don't beat us!" He was the kind of man I could respect!

Our church was at the center of everything. Our choir and pastor were well known. On Easter Sunday, because of the number of people who would show up for service, we had Sunrise Service at the Tabernacle Baptist Church where Rev. Louis Rawls, the father of Lou Rawls, was pastor. In that historic church, other singers like Sam Cooke and Bobby Womack had been part of the gospel group known as the Soul Stirrers.

But, late in 1966, when something in her had changed, my mother decided to leave the church. I never heard her say this next part out loud, but somewhere I read that folks in the Black Power movement were beginning to distance themselves from the church and its teachings. They said that the church was now irrelevant, that it hadn't freed us as a people. That the church funneled sorely needed resources out of the hands of the poor and into the hands of pastors. That the church did not teach the truth and that the church knew better.

By that time the movement was as radical as these notions. My mother left it up to us to decide what we wanted to do about church membership. By 1967, after much careful thought, I decided to leave too, but I had to reason it out for myself, since everything that the church had taught me, all my Baptist training, had been something I had tried to accept as true, although some of it didn't make sense. I had also been taught to have "blind faith" when it came to the church teachings that didn't make sense to me.

I had begun struggling with the blind faith and was beginning to feel something more. I could tell that my elders were hiding things, teaching one thing and doing another. This left me disillusioned. Disillusionment was a heavy feeling that I could not shake right away, and I figured it might be a normal, but a big thing, too, like another awkward part of growing up that nobody told me about. The older I became, the more of these moments I discovered.

At around that time, and maybe to help myself, I remembered the old adage, "ignorance is bliss." I took it very much to heart and very personally. It seemed to mean that we have times in our lives when we must choose between holding on to what we know where things are comfortable, or, moving in new directions to discover and explore what we don't. I figured it would probably be easier and more comfortable to stay in the church. But, I also suspected that by then, so sadly, the church had probably at least in terms of training, taught me all it could. Or, so I thought at the time.

Already I knew for sure that if nothing else, I had to develop myself. I had to grow and learn, although I didn't know what form(s) this development would take. But for now, I understood, by Grandmother's example, that I could worship anywhere, even at home, and that I would take God with me wherever I went. It had been a huge and hard decision, but this was it. I would miss my home church very much, miss my friends, miss the routine and the belonging, the excitement and the spirit of the church, the fun parts of it, too, far more than I could ever predict.

But I couldn't deny the importance of these other things that were suddenly calling me elsewhere. So, that was it. I was done with my church way of life. Except for one thing that I wouldn't fully appreciate until much, much later.

My home church experience had lodged many things and memories — hymns, images, teachings, good times and Scripture — deep down in my spirit beyond the world's reach, and all of this would remain with me, like living treasure, for the rest of my life.

* * * * *

When I was a sophomore and Joey was in the eighth grade, Mom returned to college full-time. She said it would take forever to finish school at night while working full time. So, instead of being a full-time secretary, Mom was now a full-time student at Wilson Junior College! The thing with Mom was not just change as a matter of course, but it was usually major, sweeping change, change that made you hang on for dear life until you caught on.

My mother and Mr. Latimore had abruptly separated and divorced, after less than three years together. The year after that, we stopped going to church altogether. More than anything else, these two changes isolated my brother and me and opened up a new era of poverty. Meals became irregular. Mom began stretching what little she had even farther than usual. For example, to go along with her own homemade bread and mayonnaise, she bought potted meat, at the time just ten cents a can. These scrumptious sandwiches created a treat of treats, above and beyond a cherished meal at a time when the idea of our next meal was a question we dare not ask.

My mother stopped smoking, something she'd been trying to do for years. Soon, in one fell swoop, she also changed the family's diet. One afternoon, she came home and announced, "As of right now, we WILL eat no more meat, eggs, cheese, milk. We will stop eating refined foods: white sugar, white flour, white rice, white bread. We will read labels on the foods we buy. If you can't pronounce an ingredient, you don't need to eat it. This is better for us!" No discussion, nothing. That's it. Bam. Just like that. A whole new way of eating. That is, when we did eat.

* * * * *

She met a new friend at school, a young black poet named Don L. Lee with his own book of poetry, entitled "Think Black." The first time I saw him, I thought of the new song just released by Linda Jones. *"Hypnotized."*

With Mom, there was never any middle ground. She'd either be all in or all out. Don L. Lee was handsome, a tall, thin man with a crowning brown natural, and a gradual, partial smile. He seemed nice enough, but my mother changed a lot more once she started spending time with him. He didn't say much, so, I got to know him by watching my mother change. She soon started talking about "blackness." I can see now that blackness had begun with thinking more carefully and respecting the body, the community more, but Mom never said that. I just had to figure it out and try to keep up. It was important for me to keep up with her.

Soon she stopped wearing make-up. She changed her hair and instead of straightening it, like always, she started wearing the natural style and picking it. She changed her clothes, too. Her jewelry, everything about her appearance flipped. And I watched in awe. I couldn't keep up with this part. I had struggled so hard with my appearance already that this new way of looking would have to grow on me.

In a flash we went from doing everything to be beautiful women now to doing nothing. It upset the little balance I had just considering it, and I needed time to figure out how to join in. It wasn't that I didn't want to. It made sense to me that we should no longer conform to the white standard of beauty. I just didn't know how to stop conforming. It felt as if I had been addicted to the white standard of beauty, and could not figure out the sudden stopping, the going cold turkey.

This is one thing about our people that perplexed me. Communicating! I had learned that an explanation was not coming. They showed you a new behavior, a new dance, sang you a new song, made a sudden change, and, if you wanted to participate, you had to pick up on it and find your own way in.

But I couldn't figure this one out so easily. I thought I understood, but I needed to move more slowly and as I did, Mom ridiculed me now and again, even publicly in her writing, for not being black enough! Even Dr. King said it, "We know nothing of Africa." It was very sad, but true. And Mom didn't explain how we would move overnight from being Negroes to being black. I had learned and lived the habit of being a Negro all my life so far, and as an eleventh grader, I figured I'd finally gotten the hang of it. It was all I knew and it took all I had, being a clean-cut, well-groomed, proud, quiet Negro girl. I needed help making the change to black, more help than just sudden edicts and expectations, all of which challenged me to reimagine and meet myself anew, yes, reimagine and meet the self even I had never known.

Now, as if I didn't have enough evidence already, I soon saw that this would also be the year that Mom would redefine herself and discover her voice! That was the year that she, Don, Carolyn Rodgers and Sterling Plumpp bought a mimeograph machine, a saddle stapler, and together established a publishing company focused on producing the work of black writers in the movement for black liberation around the world.

In time it began to make sense. It felt as if the pores of my body began to breathe for the first time. I came out of my girdle. And my make-up. I cut my hair and little by little learned how to let myself be free and be black for the first time. Brown, black, beautiful.

* * * * *

Mom began writing Black Poetry. Their group of writers grew quickly, and she was in the thick of the Movement. She compiled her first collection of poetry, soon published by their new company. Her book was called, *"Images in Black."* Mom and I took the mimeographed pages, the stapler, and spread everything across our living room floor. We started by collating the pages, folding, stapling. I designed the front cover by hand, and together, we assembled her books, now ready to be sold for one dollar each.

As part of this group, she was mentored through regular writers' workshops by two very established authors. That is, Gwendolyn Brooks and Hoyt Fuller. For the rest of that decade and well into the next, my mother's activism shaped our lives, and in this timeframe, continued to change everything.

With these writers, came a whole new family. Walter Bradford, Anne McNeil, Carolyn Rodgers, Rhonda Davis, Angela Jackson, Mike Cooke, Jim Taylor, Amos Moore, Ebon Dooley, Barbara Mahone, Randson Boykin, Kathy Slade, Jim Cunning-ham, Carole Parks, David Llorens and others. Mom took me with her to these meetings, mostly conducted in the homes of Brooks and Fuller, but sometimes in the home of Margaret and Charles Burroughs, educators, writers, and curators of African artifacts.

This was my introduction to all things literary, beginning with the way artists treat each other. Outside of the workshops, these folks seemed like nothing but family. But, in them, writers read and received critique of all kinds for their poetry and short stories. This critique was sometimes heated.

Sometimes it went so far as to become a debate over the real purpose of black art... I listened closely. I learned to listen to the way people read, to really hear what they read, and to know deep inside that I had something, too. Thoughts, feelings, questions, imaginings. I had everything but a voice.

They were writing during a very unstable time, a time of complete change and bloodshed. An entire decade replete with assassinations from Medgar to Fred and Mark that we were expected to simply endure. How do you survive this kind of news, this kind of loss? We did it with the help of what we had. Each other, our community, our dreams and determination, our music.

The music of that time was tailor made to the feeling that was growing in and among us. This soundtrack set by select black musicians such as John Coltrane, Leon Thomas, Miles Davis, Pharoah Saunders, Les McAnn, Eddie Harris, Phil Cohran, Wes Montgomery, Nina Simone, Ritchie Havens, Edwin Starr, Roberta Flack, Curtis Mayfield, James Brown, Aretha Franklin and Terry Callier followed, welcomed and inspired us like morning sunshine, and could be heard blaring, echoing everywhere black people gathered.

* * * * *

I must crown the Queen of Soul in a personal way. I did not know her, but my pastor was a close friend of her father's. That fact connected us by just two men. Then through soundwaves, singing the meaning, the truth about black, grown womanhood in this country, she taught us all about it. Her music, piano, songs about love, loving, trying to love, love she lost, love she mourned, dreamed of, and celebrated with her soul. Love was her subject. She breathed deeper life into others' songs. She gifted us, helped us move our natural selves a little freer through this world. Protest, celebrate, worship, reflect, the music of our blood. Embodying, affirming our reality as she was called to do then, to be our voice, our heart, our grown woman royalty.

* * * * *

Actress Val Gray Ward established a black theatre group she called the Kuumba Players. She became part of the writers' group. One afternoon "Aunt Val" called when I was at home alone.
"Hey Baby!"
"Hey Aunt Vall!"
"Your Mama home?"
"Nope."
"Well, give her this message for me."
"Okay."
"Tell her I said y'all better get on over here at least by 6:30, because Jimmy Baldwin's in town and he's coming over to the house tonight and we're gonna eat and talk with him, okay? You got that?"
"Yes. I'll tell her as soon as she gets in."
"Okay, then. Love you."
"Love you too."
"Bye!"
"Bye bye!"
Just as soon as Mom returned, I relayed the message and she stopped and looked at me and asked, "Well, do you want to come?"
What? My mother generally offered me no options. If given a choice, I'd say "no," not because I wasn't interested, but because she actually gave me a choice and so I was now stunned. This is what happened. She went, took Joey and because this felt like grace for me, grace that I couldn't see as anything else, I passed up a chance to sit up all night with

black writers and actors chatting over pizza and beer with James Baldwin.

Mom had joined a women's organization called "The Black Women's Committee for the Protection and Care of Our Children." They rented an old brownstone in the Bronzeville neighborhood where they helped support young mothers and their small children. This was another group of less than a dozen women, trying to do good work on the inner-city South Side. Diane Bevel spearheaded this group. Sometimes I babysat her two preschool aged children, Sherri and Doug. Diane talked a whole lot about Vietnam.

As part of Dr. King's inner circle, Diane had been one of the Freedom Riders, had as a student marched with him, and helped to organize the strategies of that phase of the Civil Rights movement. Now she continued her work elsewhere, in other ways.

After Dr. King's assassination, Diane went to Vietnam trying to learn as much as she could about what was going on. She came back and gave talks about what she learned. Although there was an anti-war movement, I didn't understand the importance of Vietnam and its connection to our movement. I had friends being drafted and going over. I didn't understand what had happened to Dr. King, how his focus had shifted, and it took me decades to appreciate it. At the time, Diane was helping to educate our community about the war, about America's violent history, the bigger new issues Dr. King had, toward the end of his life, begun to understand and speak up about.

This was a serious matter, the part about Vietnam. The activism of this movement grew more and more serious as in a broader, more global scope. Eventually, some of my aunties and uncles mentioned hearing an extra "click" on the phone when they made calls. Some said they had even stopped paying their bills but that their phone service was never cut off. Some said that they suddenly found new antennae attached to the bottoms or the backs of their cars. But this never deterred them. In fact, they would mock the idea of surveillance and even holler out, *"Hey, did you get that?"* while they were talking! But Joey and I didn't think it was funny when by my senior year, unmarked cars and men in plain clothes followed us, inching along the street behind us as we walked to school, many times without lunch money.

* * * * *

Before long, my mother became well known as a poet, teacher and speaker. She finished college, went on to earn her graduate degree at the University of Chicago, and soon became one of the first instructors of Black Studies at the University of Illinois Chicago campus. She gave poetry readings locally and nationwide. Once, she took me to New York City where she read her poetry on a show with the Last Poets at the Apollo Theatre in Harlem. We stood in that historic backstage space, where all the signed photographs hang on the walls, and watched from there as Mom read her *Fable for my People.*

Earlier that night, an opening act before the poetry readings, The Five Stair Steps' performed their own music. They were now departed from rhythm and blues adopting a very psychedelic feel. After the event, we went somewhere in The Village to eat where we met actor Dick Anthony Williams, theatrical director Woody King, actor and writer Vertamae Smart Grosvenor. This was the same night as the first Ali-Frazer fight, and the sadness over Ali's loss hung overhead, over the whole city of New York, like an awful and very low fog.

* * * * *

By the early '80s, after another series of major changes in her life, my mother suddenly, silently left the movement, closed the door on that deep commitment she had kept and honored for so long. She transitioned to another career, another chapter in her life. It was, indeed, another, such stark change that one day I decided to ask her about it.

"What happened, Mom? Why did you leave the movement?"

She answered simply, " . . . because it was destroying me."

Unbreakable: The Longest Walk

One time I tried stringing popcorn for the Christmas tree, a fun, old-fashioned craft that didn't cost much money. It was slow going since at least half the kernels kept crumbling. Still, I stuck with it, hoping against these odds to eventually make a good string long enough to use. Little did I know that Life was the string that kept seeking our hearts to thread its needle into and keep us together, and that, my mothers — aunties, Grandmother, the women who raised me — they, their children, all of us, we were the kernels.

Even though they hid things beneath their jokes and crazy stories, I could always feel what they felt: anxious, unsure, strong, too, sometimes, and even smart, but, mostly just beautiful. They were all beautiful, and beauty mattered most when it came to being a woman. A woman could always depend on her looks, could fall back on her looks because her looks were the first thing anyone saw. And if she kept her looks up, the world would never, ever have to know about the crumbling kernels... and how hard it was to string them together.

* * * * *

That time when everything in my life was funny had by now come and gone. I was a senior. In our English Literature class, we read Margaret Walker's *Jubilee*, one of the first assignments that quenched my thirst for a great black story. Somebody had given me a cool drink of water. And now, I knew the main character, Vyrie, so well, it was as if I'd traveled to be where she was, had come to know her people, and could see them celebrating her, picking banjo, blowing harmonica, just for Vyrie. I imagined her dancing on the dusty dry dirt, pounding her bare feet, laughing, insisting on the happiness evidenced by her swelling belly, savoring these simple moments, drop by precious drop ... with me as her guest, celebrating too.

* * * * *

"Hey Girl! You, with the pretty little Afro ..." Not used to being approached that way by boys, I ignored his call from the back of our classroom. But in the fall of 1968, surely, Melvin was no boy ...

I'd seen him in the halls and as I walked home sometimes, driving by, smiling and waving from his 1966 lavender Mustang. But this time, rather than just another beep-beep, he slowed down, offered me a ride and I hopped in. He listened to jazz or rock turned up loud, switching back and forth between the two. He turned it down long enough to tell me he was 19. That was old, the oldest boy I had ever talked to. So, I said I was 17, since I didn't want him to think I was too young ...

* * * * *

After class one day, our teacher asked to see me. She talked about my *Jubilee* book report that had earned an "A." Her tone and glance all at once probing, caring, her surprise played down, twice she emphasized the words, as she encouraged me to "keep writing." Unsure if I'd heard her right, I thanked her and left, not knowing what else to say, not at all knowing what to do with her unexpected praise. Would I tell my friends? Tell my mother? What did it mean?

Something similar happened in Afro American History. Our assignment was to compare the life and work of abolitionist David Walker to that of Malcolm X. I did my reading, writing, turned in my paper and forgot about it. Until Mr. Stell described in class how his colleagues said that "these black children," had no potential, and then told us how he "read them a paper by one of [his] students." At a time when school was the last place I wanted to be, my God, *he meant my paper!* At the end of class, he pulled me aside, patted me on the back, told me to "keep writing . . ."

And I still didn't get it.

* * * * *

Now on my own, I only wrote love poems. Nobody *talked about love.* I wanted to know about it, to find, touch and wash my hands in love words. I wrote about its funniness and its strangeness. I'd fold and file the poems in my white envelope and slide them safely beneath my underwear and to the back of everything else in my top dresser drawer.

* * * * *

Melvin made me laugh. With his crazy sheepish smile, he asked me in a loud voice whether I liked The Beatles, or, Jimi Hendrix. He amused me, and when I laughed, he got even funnier. I tried not to laugh *at* him, but sometimes he was just so funny that the difference faded.

Melvin smoked. Steady, cool, already a Working Man at the A&P, his style qualified for an Afro Sheen billboard. Solo, mysterious, he walked like he had a secret. Long twin dimples framed his smile, his slender legs bowed slightly, his perfect height my canopy. He dressed so fine in soft leather shoes, silk tailored slacks and matching Italian knit shirts.

Melvin looked good. He wore his thick, black hair short with a bold part down one side. His smooth, clear skin was the color of cocoa. His forehead high, his eyes deeply black, accented by flowing brows and lashes, his sharp nose flared wide like a beak. His full lips below that bushy mustache, his arms and hands long and strong, and the hovering cloud of his musky scent filled me up. Everything about him overtook me and switched my thinking brain OFF.

Melvin was odd. Using the word "respect" often, he even had a respect checklist. He loved old people. He wouldn't eat "just anybody's" cooking. He wouldn't call anyone after 9:00 P.M., not even on weekends. He waited in the front room when visiting. Anybody who didn't keep these rules didn't know about respect. Melvin's strange rules came with safety lines he wouldn't cross. In a way this was safe to me.

With respect, he could often laugh at and enjoy the sport of life. Calling his uniqueness "indifference," he did things other boys didn't do — like work every day — and he didn't do the things they did — like study, go to football games, plan for college, and belong. His style, rhythm, boundaries and scent were predictable, time on the clock, and so the entrainment began.

* * * * *

Soon after we started talking, he took me to the Fall Sock Hop.

We danced to *"Cloud Nine"* by the Temptations. Then, *"Soulful Strut,"* by Red Holt Unlimited with the beat and keyboards encircling his lengthy, methodical moves. Ever after, that *"Strut"* melody brought those moves of his back to mind.

At that time, to dance to a song was to agree with what it said. *"Cloud Nine,"* then *"Who's Makin' Love"* by Johnny Taylor were hit songs I wasn't comfortable dancing to. People were saying bad things out loud, about getting high, about cheating. It wouldn't be long before I'd learn the why of these popular songs . . .

With *"Runaway Child"* by the Temptations, I discovered there on the polished wood gymnasium floor that besides being equally funny and mesmerizing, Melvin Jackson could really dance! When we bopped, without thought or care, he sent me out to twirl while he just stood there and kept cool time.

* * * * *

He'd stop by before or after work, wearing black slacks, his white, long sleeved shirt with the open cuffs turned under and with the tail out, the black rubber comb slid upside down in his back pocket. He'd bring us a bag or two of groceries, or a dozen Wimpy burgers. He'd buy Italian beef sandwiches for everybody. He'd feed me Oreo cookies and milk, help Joey with his geometry homework, give him money for a haircut, give us money for lunch. If he *thought* I needed something, he'd bring it. Melvin's thoughtfulness nourished me and by now, I was full of him.

When I'd ask how he was feeling, he'd always say, "tired and sleepy..." We'd hang out but didn't talk much. He really liked for me to oil his scalp and would ask me to. I'd take the Sulfur 8 and his unbreakable comb, part his hair in skinny sections, and start oiling. He'd either go to sleep, or we'd kiss.

Before long, it happened.

He must have assumed — since I was "17" — that I'd let him go all the way and when I wouldn't, he asked why. I said I wasn't sure he loved me. Sadly, slowly, he repeated this, *"My girl thinks I don't love her,"* as if to a third person, as if he'd surely earned my love by then. Without another word, he slipped his jacket on, ran the comb from front to back through his hair then packed it down, lit a cigarette, and left.

In that moment I felt thrown away, like a piece of trash, a hurtful feeling I just filed away in silence like so many others.

Next time, he said, "I love you." Since he'd never even asked me to be his "girl," and since by then I loved him too, his soft words reassured me. Giving in slowly, cautiously, I asked if he'd ever leave me. He whispered, "No, I'll never leave you" breathlessly into my ear, and just like in the movies, I heard music as I lost my skin to his.

He coached me, letting me know when I wasn't "responding." Like a dance, he helped me relax into his flow and join in. The next step was to "take *everything off* this time." After that, just the idea, the feel of his smooth skin on mine sent me flying. Drunk and dizzy, I was the dancer who'd twirled too many times as Dr. Melvin blew my mind like a hand harp and chased those dreaded monthly cramps away for good. And, I put a secret mark on my calendar to keep track of each occasion. Melvin was bringing me step by step, happily into an unknown world.

"Oh, oh, black is the color of my true love's hair . . ."

Just as Nina Simone, Tony Bennett and other grown-up singers had their way of saying what love was, it seemed with Melvin, I very suddenly had some deep sense of it, some knowing all over myself, just what it was that they were singing about . . .

Sometimes we'd watch television or listen and sing along with *"My Cherie Amore," "What Does it Take to Win Your Love,"* and *"Where are you Going,"* by Stevie Wonder, Junior Walker and the Allstars, and Jerry Butler. One pesky song that played on the radio constantly, needled me, like someone I didn't like sitting behind me in class. *"If I Could Turn Back the Hands of Time"* by Tyrone Davis, marked the winter of 1968 like the side of a dingy bank of yellow stained snow encrusted on any street corner.

"Leaving would be the last thing on my mind . . ."

In a different way, another really grown-up song turned out to be important. Melvin sang along word for word with Lou Rawls' *"World of Trouble,"* as I half-heartedly listened . . .

"... *They are both such a treasure, 'cause they're both so sweet...*"

* * * * *

Living out of this part of my life was new and strange because of the sense of freedom and power it gave me. I was 16 now and wanted a part-time job. I didn't need a work permit by then, but I checked with Mom for permission. "Young ladies need to focus on school, not working. No job for you!" It never occurred to me to just go get a job after school. Mom would never have missed me.

Sad with Melvin gone, sad in another way with him there, my sadness was too thick for words. I tried talking with Mom one time about my sadness when it had become difficult to bear. I didn't want to cry so much since people would only say, "oh, don't cry," like crying was something I wanted to do or tried to do. My sadness had become embarrassing and I didn't know what to do about it. So, I brought the subject up to Mom and when I did, she didn't seem to hear me. She just stopped me from talking, and said something I will never forget.

"The only thing wrong with you is that you're my daughter."

I didn't know what she meant by that, and didn't want to know, so, of course, I never brought that subject to her again.

That Christmas, Melvin brought me a giant, stuffed teddy bear. I never cared about stuffed animals and so, never had any. He could have given it to anybody, which made me hate it even more. But since he gave it with that big smile, I took it. Then, right away, he left.

In February I turned 17 and didn't make much of the birthday, although he did get me chocolate candy for Valentine's Day.

By next summer, the end of senior year, a full six months

after he'd started spending the night, I was pregnant. I could have marched with my class, but didn't. I assumed I had failed gym. I'd skipped it because a really big girl I didn't know, who "liked Melvin," was bullying me because of him. I didn't know I hadn't failed, that my English teacher had put in a good word with the gym teacher for me. I didn't know, because I never asked.

Once my rarely-at-home mother discovered my condition, she clamped down. The summer before, she'd so forthrightly announced her decision to "resign from motherhood," stating she had things she wanted to do. I interpreted this news to mean that I was on my own. Now, to escape the awkwardness and confusion of such great change between us, change that would be hard to figure out for quite a while, I decided to go and stay with Bubba. I called Melvin, packed my things into a shopping bag, and he drove me there.

"Is that all you have?" he asked me.

Being away from home indefinitely, I felt more alone. I missed my brother. My mother never called. When I called, Joey said he and Mom got along better now. I tried talking to Grandmother who I felt closer to, but that was no good, either, because whatever I told her she always told my mother. Instead of family, this felt more like Swiss cheese, just a thin square full of round holes.

* * * * *

What a summer. Glued to her daytime game shows and to the endless baseball season, Bubba wasn't good company. The astronauts landed on the moon. One by one I played hundreds of games of solitaire, a game I hear the English call, "Patience," something I needed a whole lot of. Isaac Hayes released *Hot Buttered Soul,* with *Walk on By* ricocheting on and off the burnt pavement.

"Just do me a favor, and walk on by . . ."

Playing cards to pass the time, I pondered two mishaps that could have been deadly, but had turned out otherwise. The first was a mishap if only because Melvin had actually talked. Really talked.

Not long after the teddy bear Christmas, he came to me and said he'd realized some things. He said I was "too good" for him, that he had "changed a lot" since we met, that he "didn't like" the changes, that his "friends had noticed" them too, that it was time he returned to his "old ways." He said he had "a life to live," that he wanted to do his thing "while it could still be done." Then he told me about another really smart, nice girl whose parents had never liked him. When *she got pregnant,* he said, they got rid of her baby and told him to stay away. It broke his heart. He didn't want that to happen again. This was more than he'd said to me in the whole time I had known him, and as I listened through my surprise, his words so rehearsed, so matter-of-fact, so clear from his point of view, so heartless from mine.

As he spoke, I suddenly got this falling sensation. My brain started working hard, searching for answers, for mistakes I'd made, and the stream of tears ran. I felt worthless and used. Grandmother's funny saying came to mind, *"It's not the fall, but that sudden stop that hurts!"*

I had given myself to Melvin, he was dumping me and this sudden stop felt fatal. I had been serious about my love. How could he promise to be with me and now change, like it was only make-believe? Was it make-believe from the start? With no answers, and no other way to understand it, I felt like giving up. I went to the medicine cabinet looking for something I could take. There was only aspirin, so, I took a handful, wrote a note that I folded up into tiny pieces and gave to Joey, then fell on the sofa in my room, and closed my eyes, expecting not to get back up.

Joey read the note, cussed Melvin out, put him out of the house, got me up, made me drink milk and walk the floor until I could get myself back together...

* * * * *

Was my life really ruined, like they said? I didn't think so, but how could I be sure? I locked the questions inside. Then, when Bubba asked if I "*really wanted that baby,*" I really resented her question, resented her asking me as if it was nothing. Didn't she know, how could she *not know* how important my baby was to me, that my baby would be mine? Pretty, smart, loving and that together, she and I would be so happy! My baby, my little family, mine. All mine!

"*How can I be sure,*
  in a world that's constantly changing..."

The second mishap occurred just after Bubba asked her question. Expecting him to understand, to stand with me now after all we'd been through together, I mentioned this to Melvin and unsympathetically, he simply repeated the question, this time taking me to the next step, careful about the wording.

"*Let's do something to help you have a period, since it's still so early.*"

"Oh," I thought... and then I, too, wondered... consenting with a bit of reluctance, to take that next step and "do something." I asked around and found out from my friend's older sister that some women used quinine and gin, four capsules and a single shot. I told Melvin this and when he asked, I said I'd take it. He brought the brown paper bag, stayed for a bit and left. I took it, soon went to sleep for a long time and awoke with my ears ringing. That was all. I looked and looked for the bleeding. He called just to ask what had happened. Pondering this as if for the first time. About what we had done, what I had done, I rubbed my belly, told my baby how sorry I was, and promised not to hurt her again.

Funny, remembering these mishaps I see the guilt I felt over hurting one of us, but not both.

* * * * *

That summer's broken record, *"Jealous Kind of Fella,"* by Tyrone Davis, pushed my nausea past its limit. Sick and tired of that stunted sound, I grabbed onto something else, familiar yet still unknown. I started seriously listening to jazz where the deep, comforting love songs were plentiful. Sergio Mendes' and Brazil '66's, *"Pretty World," "Fool on the Hill,"* and *"So Many Stars,"* Eddie Harris' *"Listen Here,"* and Les McCann's *"Compared to What?"* But most of all, Peggy Lee's *"Is That All There is?"* gave me an uncanny feeling, like she'd asked me life's biggest question, like somebody was eavesdropping on my life, telling the whole world, and laughing at me.

With just the good music for company, I waited and waited for Melvin to remember me during those endless weeks. These songs filled my days, as the sadness I'd always known grew and changed colors along with my body.

And there are oh,

so many stars, so many stars . . .

Sadness, like a zillion popcorn kernels piled mountain high and now bursting. Sadness always there in the stillness, now bubbled over. July and August when the heat of my very life reached its peak, I felt that popcorn — what Isaac was *really singing about* — each kernel popping, filling up the vacant spaces of all my dream. These kernels defied stringing.

Whatever would I do?

First, I had to shield my baby from the sadness. I figured if I could only put it out of my mind, she'd be all right. So, I swallowed it all down as far as I could, beneath the thick wall around her, keeping her free from it. It was harder with some of the music, though. Like Roberta Flack singing the last line in *"The First Time Ever I Saw Your Face,"* my tears flowed as I remembered, him.

"*. . . Your face, your face, your face, your face.*"

* * * * *

What about me? Aimless, alone now, I wondered if I, too, wasn't still in some kind of womb.

But, to take steps and get on with things, I enrolled in summer school and took a gym class at Harlan High, where my cousins went. I needed money, so, it was time to find my very first job. I was hired at Spiegel's order department, making two dollars, thirty-five cents per hour. When I went to apply, they asked the date of my last period, and I wondered if all jobs ask that question.

It was late July, I couldn't give them the true, early June date without spilling the beans. So, I said July, since I wasn't showing yet. And, along with the others hired that day, I filled out my forms and got my start date. On my start date, I got up, got ready, and vomited my breakfast before I could get from the porch and onto the sidewalk. Dizzy, I went back inside, fell back into bed. Couldn't eat the right food, couldn't settle my stomach, couldn't get enough sleep . . . just couldn't.

If all that wasn't enough, that same night while Bubba was out at her club meeting, her boyfriend, Calvin — a giant man with a steel plate in his head — quickly moved in, too, and soon began bullying and threatening us both . . .

* * * * *

For the few days he ranted, Calvin kept the phone off the hook to be sure we called nobody. During that time, I learned that Calvin beat Bubba and that she never cried out, never complained. This shocked me. I kept watch on the phone and as soon as I could, called Sonny who immediately came and took me back home. I could always count on Sonny. At home, life felt like a slow walk down an endless staircase. Forced by life, my mother was available and even kinder now. We talked. She said since I was pregnant my bone ends would close and that I wouldn't grow any taller. When she said that, I was relieved to know I had reached my full height, but didn't consider what else my mother might be trying to say about my life using my bone ends as a metaphor.

Later, after it turned cold, Mom and one of her best friends, Mama Adilisha, took me out with them one night. We went to a small club on the near North Side to hear Terry Callier sing. I will never forget that winter night. All the songs he sang he had written. The one I liked best was *"Ordinary Joe."* It made me feel happy. I sat there listening to him, sipping a Seven Up on the rocks, pretending to be a worldly woman.

* * * * *

As the season turned into short days, becoming an icy gray winter, I went to night school and took Typing II. It was dark when I got to class, so, Joey walked with me in the cold, on the ice and snow, making sure I didn't fall. I didn't need the credit. I hadn't even needed the summer gym class, but I had to take a class to graduate in ceremony. I did, and simultaneously turned down my full state scholarship to Southern Illinois University at Carbondale, as a strange, new Beatles' song got my attention. And I was the only one who didn't know that I had officially graduated already.

Come together, right now, over me!

* * * * *

By then, Melvin had disappeared. I knew for sure when I'd called him at work one day and he never even came to the phone. Until I finally hung up, I imagined the receiver just hanging from the pay phone, idly twisting around its cord. Soon, the bully from gym came to our house! She said she and Melvin were getting married! She wore an engagement ring and said she, too, was "pregnant!" She said that she would need tests to be sure my baby was his before allowing him to help us! Grandmother personally delivered this news. Hearing it that way doubled my shame and embarrassment.

Afraid, stunned, but mostly just ashamed, I couldn't talk that day. Back in school when I'd asked him about her, I'd believed him when he said there was nothing between them. *He* had betrayed me, and all the words I wished for now were sucked up. I had to gather myself. It would take time to figure out and move through this mess. I had more decisions to make than energy to act. There was nothing I could do about this, her meanest bullying yet.

When I thought of her or saw her, her wide size reminded me of trucking, tackling, beef eating men. Maybe an iron machine built to bake tar onto the street when they repave it. Like Melvin, she was always well-dressed, but as thin as he was, I never imagined him in any remote way attracted to *somebody that big*. I never considered it possible. But his song, the one I didn't hear, had said otherwise. *If it was a snake . . . Well, wasn't it? Wasn't I silently suffering from snakebite?*

Who would protect me from life's snakes and bullies? That was the question I spent days asking myself as my belly continued its slow swell. And, if *this* was what they meant by "wild oats," Melvin had dropped his *all over the place!* Now, *I* was going to have a baby, that other "nice" girl had gone on about her business, the bully was gloating, and meanwhile, I thought I had *an image* to protect. With ten dollars, I walked to Woolworth's and bought a silver-plated wedding band to wear in public. That shiny symbol *of the idea* that somebody loved both me and my baby helped me walk proudly and keep my head up.

* * * * *

I walked into the storefront medical center on 79th Street and signed in. They took blood, examined me and said I was surely pregnant, as if I'd been in doubt. They told me my bill would be $84.00. I said I thought it was a free clinic. They asked me to leave. Later I found the right clinic, just around the corner from St. Sabina. They said I'd deliver at Cook County Hospital. I called the Chicago Maternity Center. Their fee was $250 for the pre- and postnatal care, including home delivery. I could make payments as I was able. *That's* what I wanted.

For the remaining months as I walked the longest walk of my life, heavy, alone, in the wind, on the frozen pavement, wanting things to be different, counting the days until my baby would be born, I sang to myself,

"... *Cryin's not for me, ... 'cause, I'm never
gonna stop the rain by complainin,'*"

When I wrote the poem about my feelings, some of the popcorn disappeared. I felt good about it. Before filing it away, I showed it to my mother. She read it and asked if she could show it to Gwendolyn Brooks. I said "yes." Soon, she said Ms. Brooks wanted "to publish" my poem, and had asked her to see if I would agree. "No," I said, and socked it into the envelope with the rest of my writings, and, like a hot potato, my mother

dropped the whole thing, and never mentioned it again.
*"... and I grasp to know again the poison love ...
that left me here in bloom ..."*

The last line of that poem is all I still remember, and, even though my teachers had said it, too — which now made three people in all — although three of the most respectable people I knew had said otherwise, *I could not see nor connect these dots in my head. Deep down, I believed my life wasn't mine, not about me. My voice barely a whisper, I had no right at all to say what I felt or what had happened to me, it didn't matter anyway, and this had always been true. Who cared? Besides, I didn't feel permitted to speak in this world alongside my mother. It was her turn now, not mine.*

* * * * *

Silently, quickly, and with a grunt or two I had found some words and funneled my feelings into that little poem. Rather than mope, I kept Melvin's memory, thoughts of needing or missing him, being abandoned and betrayed by him, all to bare minimum. As to when I'd see him again, what I expected of him, those were extra hot potatoes I could only drop. I didn't want my baby swimming in my anger toward him. So, I poured it all into that short poem, cried the tears, rejected the help, and called it a day.

To survive, I took a few deep breaths and started to think of myself, to see myself as unbreakable. Kinda like the comb, able somehow to untangle any kink or snag. Determined to move, I banished his memory to the farthest corner of my head and then packed this into an imaginary cardboard box, sealed and carried it up to my mental attic for permanent storage where it would remain stacked with the rest of the old things I needed to forget.

Then, three things happened. First, Lena, a friend from school, gave me a baby shower. I invited a dozen or so of my friends from church and my best friends from school. Nobody came, except Joey.

Next, before I got too big, I went one Sunday night to the radio broadcast at church and took Juanita from school, with me. I tried to hide my pregnancy, making sure my coat was big enough to cover us both. I stood in the basement talking and somebody said in my ear, "You look pregnant," as if that was surely all that mattered since they hadn't seen me in so long, and now this meant I had had sex before marriage which meant I was a ruined sinner. This hurt. And, since pregnant really was how I looked, I didn't reply. I simply left and stayed away.

* * * * *

Finally, within the next few weeks, one by one, all of my sweet guy friends from the block — Gerry, Sonny, Rollo, and Lloyd — each came and proposed to me . . . Soon, one Saturday night that winter and by much coercion, Sonny and Gerry came and took me to a house party. My condition made me reluctant to go.

My condition put me in a different status from any other young person I knew. I was single and pregnant, which put the Great Unwritten Rule into play. I would remain untouched until my child was born. That rule was written deep inside me, oozing from the pores of my skin, my eyelids, my scalp, like some kind of oil, sealing me off from the outside world's influences. The oil accompanied the pregnancy, triggered by his abandonment. The oil mandated a kind of sacrificial shutdown. That is what I would endure, to keep my baby and myself respectable. One more thing never to discuss.

As for the party — something more immediate — what would it be like? Would I dance? Who would dance with me? How comfortable would I be if I saw somebody there that I knew? What would I say? What would I do but just sit there and watch everybody else have fun? But Sonny and Gerry kept saying how important it was for me to get out. I was still young, they said. So, that was enough. I went, and the song for that night, a new song by Marvin Gaye that felt like he was singing to me. So that's what I did at the party. I sat in the car and then I sat at the party and I nursed a pop, and I sang that song over and over.

"that's the way love is, sho 'nuff how it is . . ."

* * * * *

My body changed. Not having monthly periods for the first time in five years was a nice vacation. My engorged, sore breasts were melon-sized. There was no bra sufficient for me, not one that I could afford. The dark circles around my nipples grew really dark, and black stripes appeared on my hips and stomach. Sometimes I looked at my body and thought about zebras and other mammals with multiple lines and colors on their skin. I suspected it would all go away, but it was strange to look at, so, I didn't, no more than I absolutely had to.

I starved for the joy and comfort and love that I thought went along with having a baby. Having Melvin's hand touch my belly with love, having him show interest in the baby or in what was happening to us both was so far-fetched, I never even dared dream it. So, again and again whenever this or any desire for him came up, I swallowed and dismissed it. I gained weight, up from 110 pounds to 155. Always hungry, I wanted much more to eat than what we had. Trying to fill my stomach for the remaining time, I ate Chef Boyardee's canned spaghetti and beef ravioli.

My mother kept two-pound bags of whole wheat pancake and muffin mix. I made hot, buttered muffins at least twice each week and ate most of them. As my blood pressure rose, my hands and feet swole. The folks at the clinic warned me about the "hidden sources of salt" in my food. This was frustrating because my food choices were few, confined to how far I could stretch the little money I had. I expected that once I had my baby, my body would, like a rubber band, simply snap back to her agile, strong, slim and healthy state, and that things would just return to "normal."

By then Melvin had started sending me ten dollars each week by his sisters. I knew that the doorbell would ring every Friday, we'd say "hello," I'd say "thanks." We didn't mention the obvious, that they saw him all the time and that I never did. They did tell me just after Christmas that he'd gone to Tennessee "to think." Meanwhile, that little ten dollars went for baby supplies and food. More stuff to keep silent about.

One afternoon as I sat watching the ABC After School Movie with my play sister, Jean, I felt a flutter. Bloooop, bloooop, there, then gone. Again. My baby kicked! When she did, my whole belly moved from side to side, and I rubbed my belly and talked to her.

I told her that I loved her, that I couldn't wait to see her. I sang to her.

"*Wanna say, wanna say, wanna say,*
Someday, we'll be together."

I made maternity clothes, baby clothes, sewed colorful borders around her cotton diapers, crocheted baby gowns and blankets. Besides sewing, I went to the store, to the clinic, came home, cooked, ate, listened to music, watched movies and once I graduated, enrolled at my mother's insistence at the newly named Kennedy-King Junior College. With winter almost gone, just another day, my eighteenth birthday quietly came and went. I was a woman now, with the help of Brazil '66, singing another Beatles' song.

"... *The man with the thousand voices talking perfectly loud*..."

* * * * *

I sat watching ABC's *Thursday Movie of the Week* as my pains began, a feeling similar to monthly cramps, only far worse. I wasn't afraid to give birth. Nobody could predict this experience, so, I hadn't thought too much about it, except that it would surely come. Except that I didn't want knives or drugs. I told my mother it was starting.

She wrote down how long each pain lasted. She called the Maternity Center. They said to wait until my pains were five minutes apart, then to call back. That I should not eat anything, but should take an enema. I did as I was told.

It was after midnight before the pains were five minutes apart. Since I wanted to look nice afterwards, I thought. There was no telling what this would be like, how much time it would take. So, I rolled my hair up and tied it tightly in a scarf.

My mother called her best friend, Ms. Bonaparte, the nurse, who came. She called Mrs. Lewis, Melvin's mother, who also came. She visited sometimes to check on me. She told my mother that Melvin didn't marry the bully, that she wasn't pregnant after all. She said she'd "get on him" for not calling me. As if it was that simple, as if her scolding would make everything dandy. She'd only mention helplessly that, "men sure do act funny when a woman gets pregnant." I had never heard anything so ridiculous, but it seemed strange that she got by reducing and brushing away the most painful experience of my life with such simple wisdom, such a lame excuse ... I wasn't angry at her. She was just trying to help. She had been kind to me. She introduced me to her friends and sister as her "daughter in law," which made me feel like part of her family, accepted just as I was. She asked if I needed anything and I always said no.

At my maternity center visits, they asked me personal questions, too. They said they had a social worker I could talk to. It was hard enough to give up all sense of privacy, dress and undress in a room with nothing but curtains around it, a room heavy with the smell of pregnant women and our hormones, as if some patients hadn't showered before coming in. It was hard enough then to get up on that table and let somebody just look and feel all around inside and outside my body. How could I talk to them, to strangers, about *what I felt?* What did they know? I refused the social worker interviews, the visiting nurse, all of it. I was not a statistic. I could take care of myself and my baby. We would be all right. All I had to do was to get through this. My resolve for my mind and body felt certain and strong by now.

Dr. Tucker was very old. Still, she was known to be the best at what she did. She and her nurse arrived, spread newspaper, sheets and towels on the kitchen table and moved me there. With an open safety pin strategically placed at the tip end inside her glove, she popped my water bag during the exam, which sped up and sharpened the labor pains. I forgot about everything as Bonaparte and Lewis each held one of my hands and mother and nurse each held a leg.

Out of nowhere, demanding to know their plan for "that afterbirth," Grandmother busted in through the back door — the window had already been removed — almost making this scene laughable. And the pain squeezed harder, vacuuming my body, making me delirious, so in that state, I told them to "Get her out of here!" The pace and pain now unbearable, I took that quickest of exits, as natural and easy as breathing. My eyes shut tight, I floated over my own body, up, up over everything. Going away, to anywhere, and with the power to watch from there, I floated, remembered, waited, recounted those mishaps, wondered if I'd ever forgive them, knowing I'd never forget, as I heard Bobby Womack singing,

"oh baby, why ya wanna leave me . . .

why ya wanna go?"

And finally, in one swift, sure motion, she slipped into the world headfirst like somebody sliding into home plate without a second to spare! With the sound of her huge, first gasp of air, I felt enough relief for us both! Once they shined her up and placed her into the bassinet, I took a peek. She was beautiful. At three-thirty in the afternoon, on Friday, the first day of spring, this new mother of an eighteen inch, seven-pounds, 12-ounce baby girl, breathed again. Then, my melon-sized, striped breasts burned with fullness. Within a few hours, my breasts now engorged like pumpkins about ready to burst. I was miserable and didn't know what to do. I tried feeding the baby and she tried to eat but with no success. I didn't know much about the importance of breast milk to her, and so, I wasn't determined to keep trying. People gathered, family and friends partying, celebrating the birth of my baby. I asked my mother-in-law for advice. Here is what she told me.

"You take a red brick and let it sit in the sun until it gets hot. Then squirt some milk from each breast onto the brick and the milk will dry up." I wanted to laugh hard and loud at the sound of her words, so loud and hard now in my partial relief, loud and hard since this made no sense at all to me, but, I didn't. I restrained myself. By then I had just about become a master of restraint.

Yes, I wanted and craved sleep. I needed rest from the longest walk we had just finished. I also needed a moment to inhale and consider the even longer road up ahead. But first, I thought about something else, so I took off my scarf, took out my rollers, and combed my hair.

PART II

MOTHERING

1970s & 1980s

Angel and Me

Soon after her birth, I bought a Kodak Instamatic camera, film cartridges and flash cubes, keeping these on hand to capture the moves, looks, and moments of my growing baby. This precious little family member was such a sight. By then, she stood about two feet tall, with a pure, smooth, brown complexion. Her large brown eyes were most expressive, and she looked like she expected you to speak to her. According to Grandmother, her studious forehead boasted a capacity for knowledge. Her button nose and tiny mouth punctuated her bulging, baby fat cheeks.

* * * * *

In the summer of 1970, a time of new beginnings, the weather was great, and the music was even greater. It was all a celebration of Angel's arrival! *"Diamond in the back, sunroof top . . ."* by William Devaughn, The Jacksons' four smash hits, *"I Want You Back," "A-B-C," "The Love you Save,"* and *"I'll be There," "Smiling Faces"* by Undisputed Truth, *"Drowning in the Sea of Love"* by Joe Simon, *"If I Was Your Woman"* by Gladys Knight, *"Sha Na Boom Boom Yeah"* by the Staples, and *"I Found Love on a Two-Way Street,"* by The Moments. It was all for her, every song, every smile, every new dance, all the joy, and all the pain. That's the part I almost forgot. And it was easier to forget the pain when you looked good. Like a rubber band, I was able to snap back to my pre-pregnancy shape and weight. Well, almost.

I saw an advertisement for a new magazine just for black women called *Essence*. They wanted charter subscribers. I rushed to fill out the card and send in my six-dollar money order. *Essence* was an exciting, elegant, gift. It offered us images, beautiful images of ourselves! It was our time to browse, read, and think in detail about black womanhood. *Essence Magazine* was my first official grown black woman mail.

I started my first full-time job as a summer intern. It was a government job, in a regional agency of the Office of Economic Opportunity, downtown, for two dollars twenty-two cents per hour. I would prepare the baby and her bags, gather everything up, and we'd walk to the bus stop, ride to Mrs. Lewis' house, where I'd drop her off for the day. Every two weeks I'd have a paycheck just shy of one hundred fifty dollars. By the time I cashed it at the currency exchange, I'd have one hundred forty-two. I'd pay for babysitting, buy two cases of soy milk formula, whatever clothes she and I needed, and other foods. I even put a canopy crib suite on layaway and managed to get it delivered before she had outgrown her bassinet. This spending plan would usually leave me with just enough for bus fare back to work.

But the job ended in August. Now I was back in school, picking up where I had left off, finishing my first year. My mother wanted me there, much, much more than I wanted to be. It was a hopeless "conversation," with her telling me to get my education and me wanting to know why. School. With a good education — not realizing I had also been home schooled — school had left me sorely wanting, left me without a voice, without a sense of direction. Soon I would stop, and it would be five years before I would want to study anything more. I never thought about studying so that I could write, not even with my teachers' encouragement.

* * * * *

She had shocked me that day she turned seven months old, stood up by herself and, as if it was nothing, just took several quick steps toward me. I gasped at the sight of it, and stunned, she sat back down. She did not walk again until the day she turned nine months, and from then on there was no stopping her, no sitting back down.

By then, Angel was already speaking, not only in complete sentences, but holding conversation. One evening, my mother served one of her best and most affordable meals — spicy hot chill from the pot she had just made. She served it to us as we sat around the table. Grandmother had her bowl. I had mine, and Mama gave the baby a tiny cup. Grandmother scooped up a spoonful of hers and made her eyes touch mine as she blew her food and tasted. I smiled as they warned, "Smokin!"

Mom customarily made "inferno" chill that everybody loved. When she served it, it was usually piping heat hot and piping pepper hot, too. Angie touched a fingertip to her food and waited for a signal from me. I tasted mine and exclaimed, "Ooooo, Mama, this sure is good." Then the baby guided her fingertip to her mouth, tasted the sauce, started blowing with her mouth, opened her eyes wide, shook her head up and down, and agreed, "it's good; too good for me, so you eat it!" and as she shoved her cup over to Grandmother, we all screamed with laughter.

* * * * *

Now it was Christmas, and I had done the impossible. Put aside ten dollars for gifts. Everyone else would understand. This was my plan. I'd walk the three blocks to Jupiter and buy some Fisher Price toys. They last. They don't cost much.

Jupiter had taken the place of our neighborhood F.W. Woolworth at the corner of Seventy-Ninth and Halsted. All along the south wall of the store there were items for children, with bright sparkling toys right in front. I stood there, looking for items I could afford. One dollar ninety-nine. I found and grabbed three toys at that price, took them home and wrapped them for my baby. Once I had them wrapped, it seemed like a nice little Christmas. The tree wouldn't seem so bare.

The wooden toys were all brightly colored. One xylophone with each key a different color and note, with a wooden stylus. One bumble bee on wheels with red wings that moved around when you pulled the plastic string. The last gift was a puppy with brown and white floppy ears and legs that moved from front to back as he walked. I had change left over, enough for a little food.

So, there we were, Christmas morning. As if by clockwork, it had snowed perfectly the night before, a soft, Christmas Eve blanket. It was just cold enough for the fresh snow to stick. I had retrieved, put up, and decorated the small, three-foot plastic green tree we had left from the year before. It stood in the middle of the front of the living room just beneath the window. We tenderly declared gift-giving as not important this year. So, the only gifts underneath the tiny tree were the ones Santa left for the baby. The baby, now more like a miniature old lady, imitated Grandmother a lot, having just begun to walk earlier that week.

I sat beside the tree with her in my lap, and told her that today, we would have Christmas. I said that we give gifts to one another every year to celebrate the gift of Perfect Love God gave to us. I sang a carol for the world's most precious baby. O Little Town of Bethlehem. Wide eyed, she listened with all her heart, sitting there in her long white cotton gown and booties, like an old soul, attentive, wistful, unspoiled.

Then, I gave her her gifts to open. She looked with amazement. With her tiny hands, she took them, one by one. With just a little help, she joyfully opened her gifts and began to play with the xylophone right away. Tink, tink. Tinkle, tinkle, tink.

Those delicate sounds stirred me to wonder, wonder where Melvin was, what he could possibly be doing at that moment that was more important than watching this miraculous child open her life's first Christmas presents. Tinkle, tink. As quickly as they rose, I put those thoughts away, for they were sure to take me back to tears.

This was Christmas here and now, the Christmas we had. I needed to be grateful, and happy with her, for her. It was Christmas, and I was, in some way, teaching her what that meant. She was Christmas, pure, smiling, happy. Happy with the little bee, the puppy, the xylophone, the tiny tree. Just Angie and me. Ready with our holiday slate, fresh and clean. Ready to begin with whatever we drew upon that slate. Beginning. Christmas. Simply.

* * * * *

For her first birthday, I bought her a white fur coat with a matching hat to teach my child that she deserved the best in life. On that note, I never bought or accepted any second-hand clothing for her. I would shop at thrift stores and the Goodwill for small appliances such as a waffle iron or a radio but never clothed my children from those places, although I very well could have. I wanted them to have what I did not. The messages of change that year for her would come fast and furious. By the end of the year, we lived upstairs with her father, and her brother was on the way.

* * * * *

One day, this curious baby picked up a long fingernail file from somewhere, and before I could get it away from her, stuck the end of it into an electrical outlet. Zing! She was stunned, dropped the now burned nail file, and of course, never did that again.

I decided to potty train her just before her second birthday, figuring she could handle this next step without much of a problem. My young mother's mind would not stretch and imagine changing diapers for two. So, I picked up a training pot and some Carter's training pants for her and we got started. I told her to sit on the pot after eating and to let me know when she made something. It worked! I'd come, clean her up, clap my hands and celebrate her success each time.

Sometimes she would wet herself. There must have been something in my facial expression then, because she wanted to explain what had happened. "Mommy, I try to be a good girl." I'd stop everything then. She communicated like she was much older, telling me so much. And, at her age, I did not want her feeling like she couldn't make a mistake! I wanted her to know that making a mistake is natural when we're learning a new thing, and even after we've learned it. That the fact that she tried was good enough. But I must have been an impatient mother in the early days, until I learned better. We were both learning.

In the mornings, our routine included a little bit of early TV. I would exercise with Jack La Lane. And then she and later she and her brother would watch Romper Room, and the New Zoo Review.

* * * * *

But I was a mother *and wife* now, two distinct, connected relationships, both needing my attention. Getting close to Melvin was a slow undertaking. It happened on its own, but it felt like watching water boil, or awaiting the sunshine after an endless rainstorm. There were things he liked. MacDonald's Fish Sandwiches with extra tartar sauce. Or any sandwich at all with extra Miracle Whip and salt and pepper. He liked to watch cartoons and would sit and laugh at them, especially Tom & Jerry. He liked for me to make ice cream floats out of Dad's Old Fashioned Root Beer and vanilla ice cream. He taught me how to drive a stick shift on the streets of Chicago as if I knew what I was doing. He would talk about work and how much he had to do there. Unloading the trucks, breaking down the pallets, stocking the shelves, pricing the items. Inventory. And then, as he moved farther into management, dealing with employee situations, scheduling, communicating with area managers and with customers, keeping the store clean, opening, closing. Retail Clerks Union. Union Dues. Union Benefits. We were covered if anything ever happened. He made friends with folks at work. Kenny, Laverne, Evelyn, Harold. He slowly introduced me to them. I liked them all. I would visit the store and see him in action, wearing his red apron, playing the dozens, "signifying," as we called it. Talking about people and making them laugh, his preferred form of communication. He had Charlie, a ventriloquist's doll he would sit on his knee and, with his hand inside the back, make the doll's mouth move while he talked and everyone laughed. Mostly he did this at his mother's house. He liked certain songs he'd sing a line or two from, never the whole thing, and would break out singing at any time, for no apparent reason. People still did that in the '70s. Singing out loud, I mean.

> "Oh, I'd like to get to know you, yes I would."
> "Hey, little girl, comb your hair, fix your make-up . . ."
> ". . . Cold, now I can't believe your heart is cold . . ."

"Just a little lovin' early in the mornin'"
"Mother, mother, there's too many of you cryin'"
"Hey, Joe, where're you goin' with that gun in yo hand?"

He told me sad stories, too. About playing on the train tracks at age 11, being hit by a train and spending months at St. Joseph's Hospital with a "split liver," having surgery, and how his mother would come to visit him every day. About how he couldn't stand "heavy drinking," and so, trying hard not to end up like someone close to him who did, he did not drink. And when wistful, he'd even talk about his father, who had a stroke and died when he and his siblings "were babies." And I could feel how much he missed having his father around. We had that in common. Otherwise, he played with his kids, tickling them, making them laugh, just like the kid he was, too. We were all just kids then. He had pet names for me. "Paddlefoot," "Blockhead," and of course, "Bunzel," the other nickname Mom gave me that he heard her call me once and picked up on. Other than this, he had a couple of elders he would visit and tell me about. He would play pool at the end of the week to let off steam. And sometimes he'd take me to a movie or out dancing at a club. I loved to dance. It was fun dancing with him since he was so good at it. I loved to dress up and go out on the town with Melvin.

* * * * *

Because of the way things had been when I carried my daughter, and then in the time when it was just us two, among the biggest things I felt I owed her, was humor, something funny to laugh about. Making her laugh was important, seeing her laugh was a treat like nothing else. As she grew, I learned to buy children's books, the "Little Golden Books," at the grocery store, books from toy stores, and most especially, books by authors like Dr. Seuss and Beatrix Potter.

Beatrix Potter's books, published in the early part of the century, were timeless stories and illustrations. This author created them both, and so I began collecting her books. Whenever I would read to Angel at night, she snuggled up tightly and listened until she drifted off. It didn't matter what book I was reading from. This is the way we would bring the day to a close.

But when I read a particular Potter story, "The Pie and the Patty Pan," one that didn't make much sense, I read it with a kind of disbelief, and Angel began to pay close attention. Soon she began to giggle. And then, there was a point in the story that was flat out funny, she hollered with laughter and so did I. From then on, whenever I read that story to her, we knew that it would be just as funny to both of us. And it always was.

* * * * *

She was embarrassed on those days at school when I would show up unannounced at lunch time to make sure she and her brother were eating their homemade natural food lunches I packed each day for them. Sometimes I would find that they had traded with a classmate, a piece of fruit for something from the school lunch menu. This was not acceptable to me and we would talk about this at home. She said she felt like a "unicorn" child being so different from the others.

As a girl growing up, Angel seemed to like school and was a very good student. She always got lots of attention from her grandmothers. In fact, since she was the first grandchild, my mother doted on her throughout her childhood with a completely affirming brand of doting, as in "ask and ye shall receive." This brand of doting carried multiple benefits. As in after-school employment during her last years of high school, as in a satin, hand-made senior prom gown, and more. Her great grandmother had doted on her for much the same reasons, and bragged without ceasing to the rest of the family about baby Angel's doings and sayings, not knowing the resentment this caused.

* * * * *

Mothering was something I mostly did by instinct, but it required everything, all I had. I gave it without blinking, for it was my responsibility. But even at that young age I was starting to feel tired, needing time away, and I remember these secret feelings, similar to claustrophobia and fatigue at once, as if something was squeezing the life out of me. That's when I learned about the Chicago Health Club's membership special. I joined and began visiting once a week to spend time melting down in the steam bath and feeling like a queen, not for a day, but for just an hour.

Thinking back on the early years, the first decade of her childhood, I start by remembering that she lived in her birth home for almost four years. We moved into our home on Seeley where we lived for six years after that. Those were my tumultuous years, the years she describes now as "foul." Let me only say that our little house could not contain the invisible and sometimes visible fires raging between her young parents. Fires we knew little about recognizing let alone managing. But something happened then that I suspected at the time carried a message, one that rings clear only now.

* * * * *

I heard a tiny crunching sound in the middle of the night. A slight sound, just loud enough to keep me awake. I found ways to sleep anyway, sometimes putting my head under my pillow. This happened during one of those times when Melvin had moved out. So, I had to figure it out on my own. One night

I made up my mind to deal with it, to follow the sounds and solve the mystery...

I got out of bed and listened. The noise was definitely coming from somewhere inside the house. I couldn't see anything, but it was close, somewhere in my bedroom! It seemed to be coming from the doorway. I moved closer but still couldn't see anything. I listened more, and it was by the door. Nothing on the door. I moved toward the door and put my ear to it. Bingo! The crunching was coming from inside the door, but what could it be? I moved the door on the hinges and looked at the floor. Sawdust!

The doors in our home were solid wood, with a few tiny holes punched at either end. I got a can of Raid and sprayed at the top and waited to see what happened. Big, black ants came out. They chewed so loudly that I imagined they chewed with their mouths open! They had gray thoraxes and looked bigger than any black ants I had ever seen.

I wondered if the rest of the doors had ants, too. I walked around the house and listened to the doors. The upstairs doors had ants. I called Melvin and he came to take a look. It was a mystery to him, too. Meanwhile, we figured these ants were of a less common variety, and that the best thing to do was to take all the doors in the house off the hinges, and to move them into the basement, spray them all, put newspaper down at both ends, and to call the Orkin man.

Those doors were pretty heavy and it was good to have him there to help get them unhinged and carried away. The Orkin man came in and told us that these were carpenter ants. We had never heard of carpenter ants. He opened one of the doors for us and showed us where the ants had dug roads through the insides! Their work was so precise, it looked like they had used tools! The Orkin man said that these bugs were in the bee family. That made sense. He said that they eat the wood. He would need to come out on a regular basis and treat not just the doors, but the whole wooden structure of the home to be sure the ants destroyed nothing more.

We signed a contract for Orkin services and for quite a while, learned to expect to see dead carpenter ants on our floors. And, from that time on, I was able to sleep at night without the crunching, burning little sound begging my attention.

Sometimes, Nature has a way of stepping in and reflecting our situations, helping us understand our lives at times when we might have otherwise sat there scratching our heads. Nature's medicine eliminates the need to blame or shame ourselves. With Nature's help, we can accept certain painful chapters in our lives while we're getting a clue, without inflicting yet more pain. There was pain in our home during those times, pain trapped in the tight confines of our relationship. Pain eating away at the marriage, pain that kept us apart. This lesson makes me wonder if Nature always reflects our lives, or, if we've become so blind we can't see it.

* * * * *

As she grew, I counted on her to help take care of her brother for short periods of time. After school, she would meet and walk with him the block and a half from school to Mrs. Butler's house where they would wait until I came to pick them up.

At home, she and her brother had chores to do, more as they grew. Starting with cleaning their own rooms, picking up after themselves. I thought it was important for them as growing children to feel a sense of responsibility to help out around the house. They were never bored. There was always something at home to do. And when the weather was warm, if their chores and homework were done, they were free to go play outside with their friends.

And she did help me more and more. She told me early on that she "tried to be a good girl." My only daughter was a good girl, and I loved her. She wasn't just a good girl, she was a great girl, not because of what she did, but because of who she was. She had a tender heart and would let her feelings show.

When she was little, she loved animals and said she wanted to be a veterinarian. She loved them all. Horses, dogs, cats, squirrels, birds, everything. She loved them so much that, when we were in the car, she would cry anytime she saw a dead animal in the road. Her heart was so tender that she shared the animals' pain. As her mother, I thought about this and wondered how I could help. So, as I drove, I scoured the road ahead, looking for anything suspicious, and thought of a way to distract her attention until I could pass the area.

By the time she became a teenager, she changed her plan. By then, she wanted to be an artist. Meanwhile, in 8th grade, she played the flute in the school band. I joined the PTA that year trying to be of extra support to her but those meetings were long and drawn out at the end of my work day, so, I stopped going. She and Richie helped me with their baby brother when he was born, that same year.

Entering high school, she stepped into new growing, learning from books and about herself. Doing her own hair now, how to straighten and style it. Short hair accentuated her bright, beautiful smile. Style was very important now. She hung Prince posters on her bedroom walls. Purple Rain. Designer jeans were all the rage. "Guess" was top drawer.

Step-by-step, at her own pace, my daughter crafted her own look. And, thanks to the lay-away plan at my favorite stores, I was able to support this part of her self-discovery. She sang like an angel, too. A lot. Sometimes, we danced and sang together in harmony. Sometimes.

She always had nice best friends, and, as she grew, brought home respectable boyfriends. She became interested in photography in high school and in her senior year, had some of her work on display at the High Museum of Art. Because of her artistic talents, I tried steering her toward what she excelled in, what was part of who she was, Art. And so, I enrolled her in Art School in Virginia.

After her first year away, Angel decided that she didn't want to go back. "I'm not emotionally ready to be so far away from home." Able to articulate exactly what she felt, I admired her for that, despite my disappointment. And the music in my ear helping me through those tough moments with my daughter was Sade Adu's *"Love is Stronger than Pride."*

We struggled as she went her own way, struggled as our mother/daughter relationship changed, struggled to communicate adult-to-adult rather than adult-to-child. Something happened after she turned 19 that tipped the tables a tad too far for us both. She disrespected me and used my car after I told her that she could not. She would not admit that she had, and I only learned she had through her friend's inadvertent admission. Then, when I took a switch from a tree in our yard and whipped her legs, she promptly moved out.

* * * * *

During our years in St. Louis, I remember one morning phone call with her. She was very excited and asked me to listen to a story. She said that she had just enjoyed something nice for the very first time. What's that? I asked her. "Mom! A strawberry Nestle's Quick, just because I could." And she chuckled with delight, as we both learned something new.

It was indeed, her life. And she grew as our family grew, as we all grew, as times changed, and, ultimately took her in a direction all her own. She grew into a successful professional woman, a wife, mother, and homemaker in her own right, and with her own *Essence* subscription. Watching her move through these milestones was amazing. Minutes after her baby boy was born, she exclaimed as her face beamed with pride, "If I can do this, I can do anything!" I celebrated her strength with her, and felt so grateful as she proclaimed it.

Unbreakable indeed.

I arranged to provide the first month of day care for the baby when she returned to work. She marked the occasion with a dozen roses. Not long after that, shortly after my divorce, in fact, as I visited her one day, she offered this, "Mom, I know you're going to need a lot of support going through this now. But I won't be able to give you that."

The love I have for my daughter is such that although I notice and admire the clarity in her messages, even when they disappoint, I know that something else is going on. My mother was also there that day and Angie made her declaration so that we both could hear. This was embarrassing. Yet, I remained silent, yielding to my daughter's voice and self-expression. I have by now spent enough time pondering the feminine dynamic to not continue accepting whatever she says regardless how it lands. I deserve better. And my love refuses to surrender to her silence and distance. It maintains some reasonable form of contact . . . this love asks, calls, sends cards now and then, has even come to the house unannounced and sent a special gift box. In response, she has said only that she was "just busy" but that she loves me.

That's all.

Smiles for Manman

On Saturday, July 3, 1971, I married Melvin, a man just like John Shaft, "the private dick who's a sex machine to all the chicks." These serious guys shared a strut, a style, the black leather, and, except for John's stinging one-liners, were both painfully wordless in the love department. What does John Shaft have to do with Melvin? The film was released Friday, July 2, 1971, the night before our wedding, and at the time I did not make the connection, but it's unmistakable. They could have been twins, and to this day, I remind my children with a smile when they want to know more about their non-communicating father. "Watch any John Shaft movie."

* * * * *

I found my wedding dress in the basement of Chas. A. Stevens, my favorite store, and the layaway plan made the thirty-five dollar price tag affordable. My most important, most expensive store-bought dress to date was an ivory sheer Victorian, with its high collar and cuffs that included an opaque ring of lace at the top and bottom. It was an elegant midi-length with a sash, a semi-full skirt and slightly puffed upper sleeves.

Melvin didn't want anyone to see him get married, so, with our paperwork in hand, we rode to the church on 43rd and Cottage Grove, the church of Rev. Marvin Yancy, and stood there, just the two of us, with the Justice of the Peace and one witness, in a private ceremony taking our vows, while the organist and somebody in the background practiced a gospel song.

Papa — Mom's beloved boyfriend at the time — took me to the side a few days before and said something unforgettable. "I don't know why you're doing this. You're bound to fall in love so many more times. You're only 19 years old! Don't do it . . . ! You can finish school, *even with* that baby" he begged. His pure, loving words dropped rough and hard on my ears, but my heart was determined. I told him so, said I wished he hadn't told me what he did. For, despite the signs — I'd been having bad headaches, had fainted at the Plaza just outside the jewelry store, as we got my wedding band, and, really heard the lyrics of Carole King's *"It's Too Late,"* — I defied every bit of it, put my backbone straight and moved headlong into my plan.

On our wedding day, my mother cried. She had gotten my patent leather shoes and bag for me. She cried as we drove away, thinking I didn't see her tears. I did, but I needed to be married, to be loved. I needed to discover and explore my domestic longings, to believe that my marriage would last if only I tried hard enough.

After the ceremony Melvin drove me home and we changed clothes. It was late that hot afternoon, and I remember seeing people on the street as we drove home. Our neighbors, just sitting on their porches, were mostly old people whose exciting moments had probably already come and gone. I waved, they saw us and smiled. This was my moment. Didn't they know? I wanted, needed for them to know, to show them my newness. My new ring, my new smile, my new husband. My new legitimacy with two last names to show for it. The names of the two men who claimed me, my father and my husband. But I couldn't say these things. The deed was done, and in my body, I felt exhausted, dazed, a little bit strange, secretly strange about the things I didn't understand yet. The things

I didn't know yet. And, just a little, I let myself wonder what would come next for us. For Melvin, Angel, the baby on his way, and me.

That summer, Joey graduated from high school with honors, and a full scholarship to the university. He was focused and determined to meet his goals.

As for me, just weeks after Joey's special day, it was as if the things I knew for sure about my life on my wedding day were the negatives I was willing to overlook. We wouldn't have a honeymoon. We wouldn't have our own place just yet. We wouldn't talk much. Melvin's voice jarred me back into the moment.

"Hey! D'ya wanna order a pizza?" "Yes," I was really hungry. I called and placed the delivery order. Once the pizza arrived, Melvin paid the man, opened the box, and we sat on the side of the daybed and ate. Then he kissed me on the cheek, said he'd see me later, and went to shoot pool.

* * * * **

I took mental inventory. In addition to so much else, I secretly began our marriage on a note of forgiveness. In marrying him, I forgave Melvin for betraying me with the bully, and for deserting me without so much as a word. I did forgive, and vowed to myself never to throw these things up in his face. If I was still angry about this, I didn't realize it at the time. This vow of silence was easy to keep because I wanted our life together to be good. I thought this was the best way to handle things, so this is what I did. Now, I was pregnant again. He said he would make things right this time, and, giving him another chance, I believed he could. I believed I loved him.

* * * * *

Melvin wanted us to start by living with his mother, perhaps thinking it would ease his transition into marriage. I couldn't agree. If we had nothing else, I insisted, it would be a special space of our own. So, after Joey moved to campus, Grandmother took his room on the first floor, leaving the upstairs apartment for us. The old house had settled, the wood floors seemed to slant a bit, and they creaked a little when you walked on them. Our apartment needed an overhaul, cleaning, decorating and a fresh look.

We were both artists, but only one of us admitted it. Melvin. He could draw anything he saw, especially cartoons characters. Instead of doing his art and leaving it somewhere for people to admire, he became his art. His car, his clothes, his music, his walk, the things he left unsaid. The things he said. It was all art. To me. I just wish I had been a better interpreter at the time.

Meanwhile, coming up with a way to create our space was a fun, shared project. With our blended imaginations, we worked, happily transforming the space. After weeks of cleaning, painting, carpeting, and hanging new window treatments, it was ready. The living room, small bedroom, larger bedroom, kitchen, bathroom and enclosed back porch. Our first place together.

The walls were white and blue. Grandmother left us an almost new blue and black tweed sofa, a bed, and her small writing desk. In the living room and small bedroom, we installed black carpeting and hung black and white drapes. The kitchen was blue and green with new furniture I had made to order. A white Formica table, blue and green chairs, with matching blue and green curtains. The large bedroom was already papered a peach and white floral. I hung a single tufted lace curtain in the window and covered the bed with a white furry spread.

We painted the bathroom blue. The bathroom had an old clawfoot tub and sink, and was a real room with a built-in closet in one wall. Just beyond the bathroom and kitchen, we converted the enclosed porch into a bedroom using an electric heater, covering the linoleum floor with a gold and rust area rug, hanging a sheer curtain with a dainty, golden pattern.

Our place cost us $86.00 per month, including utilities.

Once settled in, we gradually figured out our weekend family routine. Saturday was generally busy, but Sunday was for family. Soon, one Sunday morning after breakfast, the three of us stood in the kitchen, Angie and me in pajamas and Melvin in his undies. I noticed Angie looking up at her father and smiling, pointing to the bulge in his briefs. Then, she pointed up and asked, "s'that, Daddy? s'that?"

Starting out with my tiny, new family, despite what it took me to get to that place, I thought I knew nothing about life. This was what I thought. Yet it seemed that the things I needed to learn would reveal themselves as we went along, like on-the-job-training, and I was committed, paying attention, because I wanted to do a good job as a mother, homemaker, and wife.

I used the writing desk for planning. Each week I sat there and wrote meal plans. I had learned this in school. From that came my shopping list. I thought about the things I needed to do for the children, chores around the house, and listed them, too. Homemaking would keep me busy for a while. I could really get into it. It was easy to create and perfect a routine. I tried not to lock myself into anything rigid, but I did keep up with the housework well. We had breakfast together and after their father went to work, we enjoyed a little morning TV until it was time to get the day started.

* * * * *

One day, a lengthy, in-depth generations-of-women conversation with Mama and Grandmother cost me embarrassment when Melvin came home in the middle of the day, looking for something. My hair was a mess, Angel was not bathed, and, everything in the house was in piles, a pile of swept dirt, piles of sorted laundry, I had started cleaning out the old refrigerator, had containers everywhere, and, when he walked in and saw it all, oh well.

Melvin wanted to do a good job, too. It would be years before my husband told me how much money he earned, and I didn't think to just ask. I wondered about it sometimes. It seemed like something he would want me to know. Still, without fail, he would bring home money for bills each Friday when he got paid. We didn't talk about money, except when he asked what bill was due. He gave it, and I thanked him. Besides the bill money, he gave me money for food. If I needed clothing, it was something to discuss. Since I was pregnant, I requested just a dress or two for when we went somewhere. I tried not to ask for much more than he gave.

I stretched my weekly $30 over groceries, laundromat, and carfare. I loved homemaking, planning meals, shopping smart. For our first Thanksgiving, when Melvin gave me the VIP treatment of $35 just for food, and took me to the store, I felt like a queen. I would also collect and save S&H green stamps, and go to the Redemption Center on Western Avenue once I had enough books filled. I'd find something useful for the house there, like an iron, can opener, or toaster.

Money was not the only thing we didn't talk about. We didn't talk much about anything. There weren't words for what we had. Not for our kind of love or knowing. He knew me, inside and out, like I was a book he had studied or even written from cover to cover. I thought I knew him in much the same way. When we looked into each other's eyes, we could see inside. He was 23. I was 20. We didn't appreciate the kind of seeing we had; didn't know what it meant, or what to do with it. Most of the time it amazed us, but we never talked about the amazement or what was happening when we felt happy.

We each had strong feelings. When something went wrong, everything in our household would just go suddenly and completely silent, like a telephone connection gone dead. As if somebody had drawn an invisible line down the middle of the bed. No touching. No talking. These silent times with Melvin were torture, punishment, the Greatest Loneliness in the World.

And, I was going to have a baby. One more thing not to talk about.

* * * * *

Bubba came to teach me her Thanksgiving dinner secret. She was a little rushed because she said Calvin didn't like her coming to spend holiday time with me. With the twenty dollars she gave me for my wedding gift, I bought my first set of stainless-steel cookware, and my first set of dinnerware. Green and blue, indestructible "melamine." I still have a souvenir bowl remaining from it.

Her secret was to wash the dishes as we cooked. By the time we finished, everything was washed, and we had a fresh, delicious dinner made from scratch. I had roasted and dressed a duck, without a rack. She made my favorite, her sweet potato souffle. When we were finished, she left in a hurry, and I thanked her a lot. My meals were as different as I thought I was. I made it a point to create new combinations, healthy meals, interesting foods, new tastes, new food memories.

Bubba had also taught me about money orders, something I needed to know about and use until I had enough money of my own to open a bank account.

* * * * *

But I was going to have a baby, a beautiful baby boy. Yes, I already knew that. His room was all prepared. We were proud of our new place. We bought a French provincial bedroom suite for Angie, placed it in her room out back, and used her crib set for the baby. For the first time ever, there was enough. Everything we needed was on hand. Everybody had space of their own. I was all prepared for another home delivery.

Melvin brought his sister, Bebe, to stay with us the last weeks of my pregnancy. This way, he could hang out at night without feeling guilty. I liked Bebe. But, he didn't talk to me. Was Bebe supposed to talk to me when he didn't? Bebe was quiet, and, so was I. It was hard to keep her entertained when I was busy trying to figure things out. She was supposed to keep me company, keep an eye on me while he was out. Meanwhile, having Bebe there forced a certain politeness, exposed and made her a party to the awkward silence we were already keeping.

Television was another important family member. Sometimes we'd all sit around and watch together. Sonny and Cher. The Smothers Brothers. Back then, television was family time.

After work, he'd sometimes hang out at a place called B&M Auto Repair, where the owners closed the shop at night and hosted gambling. I wrote down the number to B&M Melvin gave me in case I needed him. Wrote it down and, whenever I called, he'd either be there, or at the pool hall at the corner of 72nd and Halsted, owned by the same folks.

Music was another member of the immediate family. When he figured it was time, Melvin bought and put together a "component set." We'd listen to Jimi Hendrix and to the other rock music he loved. Sly and the Family Stone's *"Family Affair."* Al Greene's *"I'm Still in Love with You,"* George Benson's *"Breezin'"* were some of our favorites. But in a class by itself, Marvin Gaye's *"What's Going On,"* had come out the year before, and, like a staple, we played it endlessly whenever the mood struck. Melvin and I agreed on music. Mostly.

One day Mom knocked on the door and when I opened it, there she was, standing on the other side with an armful of books. They were books on health, maybe a couple dozen or so, paperbacks she'd read. Natural foods, natural hygiene, natural healing. She handed them to me and said wisely, "you're going to need these now." I took them gladly and when the time came, began learning. This new information would be subversive in the marriage because Melvin usually wasn't interested in things he hadn't heard of. He became interested over the years, though, when faced with a health issue of his own, but that time was off in the distance. For the time being, I got myself a basic blender and figured out gentle ways to introduce healthy eating to him while using it to raise our healthy children.

The more I learned about healthy eating, the more change became necessary. I needed to shop at more than one store. I needed to get good bread, good juice, but I had to shop very carefully. It would be easier once I learned how to drive. Until then, I just read the labels and did the best I could.

For the time being, I looked like I had a basketball in my blouse. To assure this pregnancy was easier, I was eating only fruit and vegetables, and by this time, I had learned to make my own soy yogurt. I couldn't get enough of it. I took vitamins. Ate wheat germ. Drank lots of juice. In one of my new books, I had read that having healthy babies was as simple as eating well during pregnancy. My baby was healthy, and, compared to the first, so far, the pregnancy had been easy. At least it was easier for my body. Not knowing about lending support to me, or anything else about his role at those times, Melvin also said lots of wrong things. He even said it had "better be a boy this time." At the time good health seemed to mean eating right but it would take time for some of us to get on board the Eating Right train. As for me, as I learned more about eating right, and took better care of my body, the rest of me began asking for attention and better care, too . . .

* * * * *

I had kept in close touch with my friend, Bev, in Milwaukee. Melvin took Angie and me to visit after her baby was born. Her baby, Carmen, and Angie, were about 6 months apart. Bev and I had had some of the same experiences, and, because we shared the exact same birthday, would tell people that we were sisters.

I had had "false labor" a few weeks before the baby's due date. Hard pain, coming and going. As my due date drew near, Bev and I talked. I reminded her of the long labor I had with my first baby. She suggested I take castor oil. Castor oil? She said to take one tablespoon stirred into a cup of orange juice to eliminate the waiting and false pains. She had tried this with her labor and it had worked. I sent Bebe to the store for the castor oil.

Never a worse drink was made. I drank the orange castor oil and went to bed. Serious labor came within minutes. I called Chicago Maternity Center and the doctors came right away. I knocked on the radiator pipe — the agreed signal to alert my mother. She and Grandmother came upstairs, cleared the bedroom, called Melvin's mother, who also came right away. Within a short, three hours my son, Richard, was born. Exactly one month and one day before his sister's second birthday, he arrived. Although at birth he looked exactly like her, his birth was very different from hers.

I was in a hurry to have Richard born on time, and he cooperated. The only problem had been his head. The size of his twenty-inch, eight pound, eight ounce body was surprising to Louise who had warned me repeatedly that he would be "anemic" because of my diet. But his head, his round, apple-shaped head seemed to get stuck in the birth canal and had required all the breath I could muster to push out. Once he broke through, it felt as if my whole life had cracked open, and he cried, cried, cried, and cried more. His cries were so loud and constant that I forgot that I needed to cry too!

* * * * *

The birth was so quick that it wasn't long before everyone got back to normal. Louise went into the kitchen to rustle up some breakfast. "You want some grits and eggs?" she called to me out the side of her mouth, knowing I was still exhausted from the labor. "No, thanks," I assured her. All I wanted was quiet, affection, and some sleep. None came. My husband ate his grits and eggs, said he'd see me later, and went to work as Soul Train played on the small, color television. With everyone finally gone, I drifted off to sleep, but my nap was soon broken by water as I awoke drenched with sweat.

Another knock on the pipe. My mother took my temperature. It felt like flu. She called the doctor. They came back and examined me. I had retained part of the afterbirth. While the doctor was with me, Angie, not sure what was going on, cried fearfully, "Mommy's all right; the baby's all right!"

The doctor massaged my abdomen, the material expelled, they gave me an antibiotic, and told me to continue nursing my baby. After this, I was fine.

Richard. Melvin Richard. These were the details surrounding his birth to a very young black couple trying to establish a new black family. Named for his father and mine, I started to name him Richard Melvin, but didn't want to hurt Melvin's feelings. I figured these names would give him a strong sense of self and purpose, a sense of connection with the men who had brought him here, and we called him by his middle name, "Richard" rather than Melvin, Jr., June Bug or Little Mel. Richie for short.

* * * * *

Richie was my crying baby. Melvin would scream at night, telling me to, "Make that baby shut up!" Twenty inches, eight and one-half pounds, and one extra nipple on his chest. He had been born with a full head of coal black, curly hair, with a creamy brown complexion everywhere on his body, except for the deep purple bruises around his hips, thighs, and the dark brown borders at the outer rims of his ears, showing us his smooth, permanent color.

I fed him, sang to him, walked with him, massaged and bathed him, talked to him. Still, he cried. Cried eternally. A cry carrying a message my ears could not decode. But, once he settled into his skin, into his new life and surroundings, the cry slowly faded. Once he knew where he was, he stopped crying. He began to look around, and smile.

* * * * *

Just after his birth, I stopped eating all poultry and seafood. My good health improved more as a result, and I needed to share this with my family. Vegetarianism became the greatest bone of contention between Melvin and me. He was not prepared for whatever it meant to eat and live without meat. Whoever heard of that anyway?

I fed Richie fresh vegetables and soy milk. As a baby, he was robust and very responsive. He quickly began to laugh and develop a hearty appetite. I gave him Swiss cereals with fresh blended vegetables, and he ate so much so fast that, that to feed him, I had to lay him across my lap with his head down. He would eat and eat and eat, as fast as I could put the spoonful in. When I saw how much he loved food, I learned to keep it handy because, when he was ready to eat, the food needed to be ready. Feeding him was an emergency. Although he was never an overweight baby, he grew quickly, and gained weight rapidly during his infant and toddling stages.

He would play and laugh. Melvin wouldn't play with him much while he was tiny, but, once he began to sit up and walk, everything changed. The rough housing, wrestling, tickling times began. By the time he could stand, he was already dancing. Mandrill's *Fencewalk.* Dr. John's *Right Place, Wrong Time.* This was the music that made him laugh and dance. Standing and bouncing on his legs made his diaper look heavy even when it wasn't. He'd bend his knees, bend his body at his waist, swing his arms from side to side, twist his torso and sometimes pivot around in a circle on one foot. He'd smile when he danced. And, when Melvin saw him dancing, he'd laugh, and we all laughed.

Richie got us talking by getting us laughing, with his tiny self, knocking down the walls of silence. Before he came, there hadn't been a lot to laugh about, and we spoke just the bare essentials. Angie was beautiful, dainty, intelligent, precocious, quiet. Melvin admired her for her words and sense, but couldn't horse around with her. With Richie, Mel let the kid living inside him take over and be the kid he really was. He could see himself again in small form and be there for himself. Richie had a raspy voice, the same as Mel, but you had to listen closely to hear his subtle rasp.

Sometimes Richie would want very much to say something and begin trying to speak faster than his words, too fast to keep up with himself. At those times, he would stutter. I'd come to him at those times, look into his eyes, hold his hand, and ask him to slow down. When he slowed down, he would not stutter. This made him happier, helped him say what he needed to say. We had lots of names for Richie. Apple Head. Little Man. Manman.

* * * * *

When Richie was two months old, my mother arranged for me to meet my father in person for the first time. I left Angie with Grandmother while we flew to New York. We'd be gone for two days. I took the baby with me, and, when we put them together, the resemblance was clear. Daddy and I looked just alike, too. I had to squeeze the lifetime of trapped emotion I felt into that visit of just a couple of hours. So overwhelmed to be with both my parents in the same room at one time, for the first time, to see my father and touch him, the place I had come from, I didn't know what to say. Daddy kept asking me about myself, and all I could do was smile. My mother smiled her biggest smile, Richie smiled his biggest smile. All of us just smiled . . .

Wherever I took Richie, people would admire him. They'd stop, smile, point, and say, "look at that little boy!" and I'd smile, too. He and his sister looked exactly alike to me. He refused to ride in a stroller, he demanded to be held. He refused to be left alone in his crib, he demanded to be with everyone else. He wanted to be touched, to be in the thick of things, to be surrounded with family, to be the center of attraction. His bright light lifted all our spirits. A very strong, determined baby, he made sure we saw him dancing, saying funny things, laughing. He was always smiling, even when he didn't want to smile. Whenever he was sad, I'd look at him for a second, deeply, straight into his eyes, and he couldn't help but smile again.

For fun, we'd go to the movies. I'd pack the children up and walk to the Halsted bus stop and ride to 63rd. We'd go to either the Empress or the Kim theatres. Both these places cost less than a dollar for adults, and small children were admitted for free. I'd make grilled cheese sandwiches, pack a few pieces of fruit and take newspaper to put underneath our feet so that we could sit down without them sticking to the floor.

Both Richie and Angie were born there in Grandmother's house. Angie, in the kitchen. Richie, in our upstairs bedroom. By then, we were busting out of the upstairs apartment. Now we needed more. I wanted us to have a home of our own after Richie came. This meant I had to return to work.

When I told Melvin about my work idea, he didn't like it. He said he hadn't married me to be any professional woman, just the mother of his children. Then he asked me, "Well, what can you do?" as if I had no skills he had noticed. I reminded him that I had two semesters of typing in school, had worked as a Clerk Typist in a government law office, and could do office work very well. So, when Richie was 9 months old, I took a job working as the first paid employee of the publishing company my mother helped to found. I eagerly went to work and began saving money. First for a family car, then for a house. For this to work, I needed child care for Angie and Richie.

My neighbor across the street, Mrs. Manuel, agreed to provide it. Taking them just across the street was so convenient. Sometimes Grandmother would go across and visit.

By that time, she was too old to do any more child care. Mr. Manuel, fell in love with Richie. He called him "My Man." He didn't say much about Richard, or talk to him using words. Just called him, "My Man!" and beamed whenever he saw him.

At work, I met two new friends, Linda and Pambanisha. They would visit us at home sometimes. They both loved Richie and enjoyed seeing him dance. Pambanisha would sometimes come over unannounced, "just to see Manman."

Melvin and I wanted something for the four of us that neither he nor I had had growing up. We found a home in the Damen Park neighborhood, at 78th and Seeley. We needed two thousand dollars to close on our loan. He figured out a way to get some of the money gambling. Then we pitched in, he took out a small loan, and soon we had it all. It was Christmas 1973.

We went shopping for a few things at Evergreen Plaza in the family car, our new Maxi Blue AMC Sportabout wagon. Feeling like real participants in the American Dream, at least as beginners, we had been approved for our loan and the closing date was set for just after the holidays. We were excited. Among the throng of shoppers in the mall, we planned to stop for something to eat before going home. I went into the Ladies Room before we left and somehow, lost the envelope containing the checks and cash, all our money for the closing. I didn't know it until I got home and looked for it. I told Melvin I couldn't find it. I looked again. He fussed. I retraced my steps and figured I must have lost it in the Ladies Room, where I saw it last. I felt stupid and sad. As he kept fussing, I didn't know what to do.

The next morning, we got a phone call. A woman at the mall had found our envelope. She gave me her address and said to come any time to pick it up. She said she saw the envelope on the floor in the Ladies Room, looked inside, got our number from the deposit slip, and called. I told her it was for the closing costs on our new home. She was my angel. I wanted to hug her but I didn't. I sent her a Christmas card, though, expressing my thanks for the blessed gift of her honesty. All the money was intact. We had been protected. Melvin converted it all into a certified check, and we had a successful closing.

Our mortgage payment was $256 per month, a real leap of faith for us, but by then I had a better job. The house showed no sign of dinge or neglect. In fact, I felt happy whenever I stepped inside it. It was a good house, evidence that we had not only moved, but had moved UP. It was a brown, two-story brick Georgian, built just after World War II, rock solid along with every other house in the neighborhood. Richie was walking pretty well when we moved in. January 1974. He figured out right away that coming down the winding staircase would be easier if he turned around at the top and slid down on his belly. He was proud of himself when he did that and would smile.

In the new house, Richie had a larger room, with a small balcony beyond a single French door. He put his toys in his toy box. He loved animals, fed his hamsters and watched them grow. From the beginning he was proud of his room and kept it neat. He was frustrated whenever his cousins came to visit. He didn't want to share his toys, because they would not put them back in the toy box!

He soon found something else to love. The movie, "Rocky" came out and we went to the drive-in theatre close by to see it. To Richie, everything about Rocky Balboa was great. The story, the star, the victory, the song, it all made him so happy that for years, whenever he heard that song, he smiled his big smile, as if he himself was the star who had figured out how to become a winner.

* * * * *

Once we settled in to the new house and got used to it, we began to fix it up. We painted the kitchen and I hung new curtains. Melvin installed new tile on the floors in the kitchen, powder room and the downstairs hallway. He put a new vanity in the powder room. We painted the dining room, put up shutters in the windows and mirrors on the wall. We pulled up the old carpeting downstairs and discovered the beautiful wood floors. We put new carpeting on the dining room floor, up the stairway and in the upstairs hallway. As long as we shared a project, did something together, we were fine. His brothers would visit. Moe, who was older. Mike, younger, who would always smile. Joe, older, would help him paint. I didn't hang around when they came over. I gave them space for Men's Talk.

* * * * *

Whenever Richie would get into trouble, Angie would assert herself. "Whip me, Mommy, don't whip the baby. Whip me!" So, I would whip nobody. I soon started to learn about other ways to get through to my children. Effective ways to get and hold their attention and make a point that would stay with them long enough to do some good. Parenting came with its challenges.

Melvin loved his children, and wanted them to have everything. At Christmas, they would have so many presents, they would run out of breath just opening their gifts. I wanted Angie to have black dolls. Melvin didn't care. In fact, he'd buy her white dolls saying Angie *wanted white dolls*. I wanted Richie to have toys that would teach him to be peaceful. No guns. Melvin brought him guns. In fact, he bought a BB gun and taught Richie to shoot squirrels and birds for fun.

Richie got a Big Wheel one Christmas and couldn't wait to ride. He would ride back and forth from one end of our block to the other as Melvin and I watched. His best friend on the block was Jerry. Jerry would come to the door and ask if Richie could come out and play. This would make Richie happy. I would let him go out. Richie and Jerry would ride their Big Wheels together. I would sit on the porch and watch them. Richie was smiling the whole time, trying to win the Big Wheel race.

We'd go on picnics at Lincoln Park Zoo, visit the Children's Zoo, and go canoeing on the lagoon. I'd take the children to museums and to free children's events I'd find out about in the Sunday Sun Times. When I could afford it, I'd take them to concerts and to the Kiddie Disco, too. We would do as many natural and cultural things as possible. I couldn't get Melvin to join in. He would always say "no." "No" seemed to be his favorite word when I'd ask.

During these years I was learning a lot. School and work were big ideas clashing in my mind. It seemed my work enabled us to have the home we had. Yet, unless I took a day off each month to actually be there in it, I couldn't enjoy having it. I felt painted in a corner. School would make everything easier, but, meanwhile, work and school at the same time made life so much harder. Work and school for a mother and wife was the hardest.

* * * * *

On any given Saturday I would shop at a few grocery stores in our area for food. I'd shop at the A&P, Sunflower Seed Health Foods Store on 95th Street, sometimes at HiLo on 79th. I'd usually find the quality and value I was looking for. And I took my children with me and taught them to stay true to the shopping list, read the labels, how to shop and compare, and stay within our budget. But slowly by that time, things were changing in a way that we didn't recognize right away. I will never forget the day as I shopped at A&P on Racine, noticing that the shelves in the aisles weren't full, but something else was going on.

I saw an elderly couple, reading the price tags and just standing there. They couldn't understand why the prices were going up so fast. At that time, most of the items on the shelves of grocery stores were less than one dollar. Fifty-nine cents, sixty-nine cents, and so forth. Many canned items were less than fifty cents in the mid-70s. But when the cost of items began to creep closer to one dollar each, that drove the cost of food beyond what elders at that time could afford. I felt their dismay as they stood there trying to decide what to do. It was not a high-priced store we were shopping in. My heart went out to them as I wondered with them what they were going to do.

* * * * *

When Richie went to kindergarten, I asked Mrs. Butler, who lived in the house on the next corner of our street, to care for him and Angie until I could get home from work. What an amazing black woman Mrs. Butler was. She had suffered a stroke many years before, which left her with the use of only one arm. She felt pain some of the time. Still, she kept a garden and brought me fresh tomatoes. Still, she looked after Richie and Angie in the afternoons, and with one hand, had taught Richie to tie his shoe laces. Until she passed away, whenever I'd see her, Mrs. Butler would always ask about her "Richard."

One day Richie's kindergarten teacher, Mrs. Mary Nedved, called me at work. She said, "Mrs. Jackson, I wanted you to have this news." I heard her excitement. I liked Mrs. Nedved a lot. "Richard was among the children I chose to test for the new gifted program we're starting here at Barton. And, well, I wanted you to know that he scored higher than anyone else. Mrs. Jackson, you've got a genius on your hands!" I took a deep breath and smiled. "Thanks, Mrs. Nedved, for your call, good-bye."

Once again, when presented with the fact of a special gift, I could only say, "thank you." I called Melvin at work and told him what she had said. "Your son is a genius," I said. He was quiet. I knew he was smiling, too, and so proud. Richie graduated from kindergarten dressed in a white cap and gown with the rest of his classmates. They sang songs. One special song that I remember from that day was *"I Can't Smile Without You,"* that they sang to the parents and the sight and sound of them brought tears to my eyes. Mom came with me and took pictures.

* * * * *

We started seeing Richie differently after that, expecting things, expecting him to come up with something. Would it be an invention? A new, world changing idea? I would listen carefully to him to see what was on his mind. Maybe we shouldn't have expected anything. Maybe we should have just learned to guide and understand, to give Richie extra room to express himself however he needed. But when it came to regular child care, we treated him just as we treated Angie.

Soon, Richie had a loose tooth, and it behaved differently than the others had. I kept close watch on it, waiting for it to come out but it wouldn't. It was very loose and bothering him. So, I remembered something Grandmother did for me while I lived with her. And I took a string, tied one end to Richie's tooth and the other end to the knob of our dining room door, had Richie stand right where I needed him to be and before I lost my nerve, slammed it shut tight! No wonder the tooth wouldn't fall out. It had a tiny root!!! I cleaned my son's mouth in disbelief and never again performed oral surgery at home.

* * * * *

Richie and Angie were baptized by Pastor Henry Hardy at Cosmopolitan Community Church on Easter Sunday, 1980. Melvin came to the church with us to see his children baptized. It was a warm, sunny Sunday, and we felt happy and peaceful, like a close family celebrating something together in church for the very first time.

* * * * *

Angie was born the first child of her generation to a family of women, and Melvin and I were not together. My mother and I kept cameras loaded to catch every new movement and all her moods.

For Richie it was different. Now that he is a man, he doesn't understand why there are so few pictures of him when he was little and growing up. Pondering his question to me I started writing his story so that he would understand what was going on when he was born.

I can't be sure whether it has anything to do with this question, this feeling, but, when Richard grew up, his apple head got hard. He wouldn't listen. He did things that made his mother walk the floor at night and pray.

. . . Bless my son today, O Lord, and let me not deny his pain,
for he's been cryin' since the day he was born
a cry that only you and I remember . . .

My mother says that his newborn cries may have been

because of the castor oil, that he may have felt rushed into the world, put out of his safe place. If that is true, if my son felt evicted from my womb, I want him to know that I am sorry.

This story will explain something more to Richard, the man. When he came along, I had my marriage, my new family, two small children, a new household to run, so much to learn and before he was walking, a job to hold down. Sometimes, all of this was overwhelming to his young mother. I didn't have the free time I had had when Angie was born, time to think and fill with the single hobby of picture taking. I did get *some* key pictures of him. But this part about the pictures and how many or how few was not about him as much as it was about how much I needed to do — to shift gears, to take care of everything, to begin the business of family living and keep my bases covered.

As he looks through the family album, Richard jokingly says that perhaps, because he was "the middle child," he may have been less important. When I think what a bright light he had with his smile, his way of thinking, talking, and just being himself, when I think how much love Richie got from everywhere, how much his sister loved him and felt that he was loved more than she, I know that he feels this way because he doesn't remember those early times.

He doesn't remember the family nights, the family baths, the family talks, the family walks, picnics at the zoo, birthdays, happy dancing, family trips, how much love he had, how much he meant to so many people. In time, Richie became a successful businessman. He is also a very gifted storyteller, something he doesn't want anyone to know. And from his heart he is a devoted uncle and father, giving himself to the next generation in a way that will last. Now, in 20/20 hindsight, I ramble through my memory storehouse, my treasure trove of keepsakes, capturing the things he should know, assembling the words to paint the pictures of Richard, the ones I have with me always. Private pictures, important, vivid, and as bright and real as the ones in viewfinders. Pictures kept safely in a place where he can't see them . . . at least . . . not until he looks straight into his mother's eyes.

The Best of My Love

Our block. It was our own vivid Kodak snapshot of The American Dream. The red brick bungalows with tile roofing, the red and yellow brick Georgian style houses, the perfectly manicured lawns, beautiful trees, the quiet calm of our neighborhood aesthetic sparkled most in clear weather, and this day was especially splendid. The crystal blue cloudless sky, the gentle breezes and golden sunbeams held hands above our heads and encouraged us all to believe that it was really true. We were the first generation of African American urban youth to follow the hard won, ever-widening boundaries of our community this far. This entirely white neighborhood, that way since it was built, had recently been "busted" by a realtor with the sale of a single home to a black family in 1973. This realtor and others knew that since 1968, fair housing might be the law, but it took acts of deception on their part five years later selling homes to black families in Damen Park without repercussions or violence. Now, with the help of white flight, Damen Park was all ours. All black. This was the how and why of it.

As I inhaled this perfect moment, it occurred to me yet again. Even if we could only *truly enjoy and touch* our gift for just two days out of each week, I reminded myself again that *this was IT*, this was what we worked so hard for.

It seemed I was at home alone, as the children played rope and rode Big Wheels out front with their friends. For music,

I put on the Ohio Players' *"Fire"* album awaiting my favorite jam, *"I Want to be Free."* It was the summer of 1978, the summer that Grandmother died, just after Independence Day.

Sure, I knew it wouldn't be long, but it felt so sudden. I was still getting over the idea that I wouldn't talk to her or see her again . . . But this particular Saturday afternoon soon carved itself into memory for other reasons yet unknown.

With the last of the grocery bags in the kitchen, I relished that little bit of time to myself, to breathe, to sing, to dance, to think, to make plans. As a young mother, wife, homemaker, secretary I was hard wired and organized, knowing that above everything, I was always, as in perpetually, in the business of making plans. Meals, shopping, teacher conferences, special projects at work, car repairs, doctor visits, you name it. My daily busyness was endless and, gratefully, my energy was too.

* * * * *

Now back to my point. The week before, I had heard this most unusual woman talking with Pastor T.L. Barrett on WBMX. "I'm bad!" she exclaimed, as she talked with callers about their lives, answering their questions insightfully, suggesting that they make an appointment. I, too, caught the excitement over her spiritual gift. She gave her phone number and I wrote it down! Convinced, I did not hesitate to I make my appointment. She said she would come to me . . . I gave her my address. It was all set.

Today was the day. It would be another fifteen minutes or so before she would arrive, and we couldn't have picked a better day! My thoughts raced. Would we sit out back in the sunshine? How would it go? What would she say? Should I make lemonade? Then, I calmed myself. She'd be here before I knew it. The visit would go quickly. I wrote my question down so I wouldn't forget.

I put the groceries away and tidied up. I vacuumed the dining room. In the front doorway I stood straightening then cleaning the hall mirror. In it, I first saw and heard her as she pulled up in front of my house right on time. From her red on red in red El Dorado convertible with the top down, she blasted the Emotions,' *"You Got the Best of My Love,"* as, with the palm of one hand, she parallel parked her long car to the beat.

There were two of them. Both big, bold, black women on a truth-telling mission! I opened the screen door and welcomed them in. I directed them into the dining room as they walked past me. I offered them something to drink. They wanted nothing, they replied, as they each sat down. The Mother had brought along a bottle of blessed oil, which she handed to me in a tiny brown paper bag. The bottle was small and smooth and I held it tightly for a moment. I assumed that I would be speaking with the Mother. I paid my sixty dollars, hoping the blessed oil wasn't extra and it wasn't.

The Mother spoke about my life, and said that I'd been in some pain. Everything else was generic. Finally, I asked her my one question. I wanted to hear her take on that tumultuous, unpredictable challenge in my life otherwise known as my marriage. She became still and quiet for a moment, and then simply said that it was a lie. She said that I "had lied!"

Lie? What lie?

Looking at me out of the corner of her eye, she wasted no words dropping this bombshell so casually, *"Well, you really like women!"*

Wh, wh, what? What was she saying?

Nope. I had no more questions!

Thank you very much.

Could I get a refund?

Whhhhhhhhhat liiiiiiiiiiiiiiiie?

I felt as if I was hurled into a fight now. This revelation rolled inside my head seeking a stopping place, like a bowling ball with no pins at the end of the lane, it just rollllllllllled while her advice registered, with no place to stop. No pins to knock over. But I did not panic. This *couldn't* be right . . . No way!

Our session over, Mother and daughter quickly left my home.

Dazed and breathless, I wondered . . . how she possibly knew this. *Could I even know it? Have I ever even had such a thought? Had I dared?* No. I certainly had not.

What lie? What in the world is this, and what do I do with it? I would do nothing. It, whatever "it" was, was blinding, so far beyond surprising that the good little Baptist girl in me snapped back and recoiled in horror at it. She had no thought or room or energy to give it and nowhere to put it now, and so the adult in charge caught my breath, and let "it" float in midair for a while. Soon, I dismissed it, dropped it, treated it the same way I would treat something scalding hot that I had mistakenly touched, something that had seriously burned my skin.

My kitchen phone came with a ten-foot cord that enabled me to simultaneously talk, work and move all over the room. I threw myself back into my housework, I began to prepare dinner and called my girlfriend, Bev, the most spiritual friend I had, told her what this woman had said, and together, we laughed about the ridiculousness of this . . . whole . . . idea.

"I want to be free! Oh, yeah!"

Once

Saturday was our around-the-house workday. As queen bee, I loved making something new, having fun with my work. In addition to housework, this was the day for picking fresh vegetables. The children and I had been to my favorite U-Pik Farm in Crown Point earlier that day. I crossed the state line for fresh produce weekly throughout the summer. With the summer over now, we were picking the autumn vegetables and fruit. The difference in the smell and taste of farm fresh food compared to store-bought made the time, work and drive worthwhile. One more way to keep my family healthy.

We had just picked green beans, kale, cabbage sprouts, tomatoes, corn, eggplant, cantaloupe and casaba melons. I had washed and frozen the greens. What a productive day. I made sandwiches for the children. They had eaten and were outside playing. Ready to relax, I sat in the living room with my basket of beans. I could justify watching TV only if my hands were occupied. The sun was setting by the glowing color of Dreamsicles pouring past the tall evergreen and into my front bay window. I turned on the television, and there he was.

* * * * *

Freddy had been the lead singer in a popular R&B group. I had heard about him recently going out on his own. I had forgotten about seeing him once on Sammy Davis, Jr.'s daytime TV show. He looked long-legged, dark brown, with a full beard and glistening smile, donning a white cowboy hat! Who was this guy anyway?

Before this very moment, I didn't know. Knew the deep gravel of his voice, but now, they showed all of him, his face, his movements. Some kind of heavenly thunder. I was mesmerized. Freddy Wilder walked slowly around the stage and sang about love from his heart to a throng of screaming women. He sweated, carefully, slowly, took off his clothing, one article at a time, threw these items into the crowd and never missed a beat. His thunder belted from a sculpted, bearded, sweat soaked black body, standing straight, singing hard. Making love fully clothed through his music. At once, his voice was a loud smile, a loving, gentle command, rolls and rolls of thunder.

The seventies was a time of striped bell-bottoms, blaring sound, psychedelic color, Earth, Wind & Fire, dreams of freedom, protest music, jobs, brick houses, better days. There I sat, picking green beans the way Grandmother had, and I was lost for words, pulled into the screen like metal to a magnet, warmed by a man I did not know. Why? Because I had never with my own eyes seen a beautiful, loving, black man on television or anywhere else, decrying his adoration for me or someone who looked like me. Because the sight and sound of Him was both sacred and profane; I was in shock. His magnificence and urgency messed with me.

* * * * *

That night I had my first prophetic dream. The weather was warm. Freddy had accomplished the impossible feat of shooting himself in the chest. He wore a burgundy silk tank top and dark slacks. The paramedics brought him into my house, laid him onto my living room floor, worked on him, could not save his life. I stood looking on in horror, wondering what any of this had to do with me. Wondering why he would hurt himself, wondering if he would live. Awoke the next morning dazed and wondering still . . .

* * * * *

Soon, on Tom Joyner's WJPC radio show, word came that Freddy was coming to Chicago. I listened to Tom some mornings on my way to work as he laughed and joked. I got the information. The Mill Run Theatre. Early December. It was now late September 1979. Just as soon as they went on sale, I got a pair of good tickets for a few extra dollars at the Palmer House box office. My friend, Limmie, said she'd go with me. It was set.

Meanwhile, I began listening. I wanted to hear more. Mostly his songs were about romance, but some were about spirituality! I was into that. He released an album with an interview. His words flowed. His sentences were thoughtful. Not that he had a lot to say. Mostly, he talked about being proud of his career and himself. But the deep sounds of his voice, the combined rasp, raw feeling, truth he knew astonished me.

At 27, what voice I had came with the roles I had played. I had skipped the part of my education set aside for finding voice, the parts intended for learning who I really was, beneath it all. So, I learned these things and gained my voice through life experiences, gradually.

The idea of that night, the performance night, felt like an escape. As if I had pushed a button to the trap door I didn't know was there. That night was, perhaps, a magical trip back into the realm of some of those things I had skipped. On the performance night, Melvin agreed to take care of the children. Mother's night out.

* * * * *

I took off to pick up Limmie in my '74 orange Super Beetle. Living and driving in Chicago was fun. Black people then drove with style, drove to the beat of our music. Back then, only a few folks had tape players, so you could tell when you pulled up next to somebody listening to the same radio station as you. You'd be singing the same song or visibly moving to the same beat. Once, as I headed home, westbound on 83rd, and crossed the Halsted intersection, a policeman pulled me over to ask who was driving the car while I was dancing and clapping my hands so hard! I apologized and the man let me go. For me and my Beetle on the streets of Chicago, driving was a sport I enjoyed and I had only been in the game since I was 21.

When I first learned to drive, Sonny said that I drive "with authority." I smiled. Lydia said that if she ever got sick and had to be taken to the hospital, instead of calling the ambulance, she'd call me. We'd laugh about that. I was just a young Mama with plenty of places to go, and not a lot of time to get there.

My Beetle was my second car. In it, $4.00 filled my tank, and I could drive on that all week. Gasoline was 49 cents per gallon at the time. Although it was cheap to drive, the Beetle constantly needed work and, of course, Melvin kept it running.

* * * * *

Limmie and I had quite a drive that cold night. She lived in the Pullman area. The Mill Run was off the Kennedy Expressway in the northern suburbs, not far from O'Hare Field. We parked, went inside the theatre and made ourselves comfortable. We had both dressed up and were very excited.

When it came to the subject of Freddie, mostly, we stopped talking and just laughed.

The show was a velvety blend of red, white and black, with an orchestra, three back-up singers, standing off to the side in their gowns, looking elegant and so content. Then, there was Freddie. Pure. Firey. Loose. Like an escaped tiger, pacing, roaring in the night. His arms rippled, shining after he stripped down from his tie, his jacket, his shirt, to his tank tee. He stood like a giant, looking for his equal, bellowing out to all creation for an equal, a flame bright enough to match his own. He sang to us, and in a frenzy, someone ran to the stage and threw a pair of pink panties his way. He ignored this and kept singing, singing us into the night, deeper, deeper, until we fell fast asleep. Life's lullaby, songs for the life of a woman. Songs of true love, good love, affection, protection, adoration, promise, safety. The songs we knew and had all lived to hear, the songs we would all die for, if only we could believe, just for one moment, that they were really true, really ours. Really for us. Seven songs for thousands of black women lulled to sleep by just one man.

* * * * *

There weren't words. Just exhausted sighs of disbelief and laughter, as if we had just come off the world's most incredible roller coaster. We had planned dinner after the show, but our emotions were too high for food. So, we sat there, collected and cooled ourselves so that we could go out, return to the night air, back to life. As we drove home, we said what we could. The show sure was short. He sure can sing. He sure is fine. It sure was exciting. What about those pink panties???!!!

At the time I felt and realized something that I never spoke about. I felt sidetracked from the life I was supposed to have. Not cheated, not short-changed, just sidetracked, like until then my own life was on PAUSE, that I lived on autopilot, lived a life filled with things to do, responsibilities, and I still didn't know who I was. I was a working mother with the father of my children still in my life. By my own "choices," I was a woman taking care of home and family dutifully, with myself left out of the equation. Left out because Papa had been right. And I had managed to get this far bypassing the reckless, exploring, playful parts of my youth. Some of those parts, anyway. And that playfulness would show up from time to time wanting to be expressed . . . at times like . . . this.

Now, Freddy on the brain was a strange new attitude for a working mom with two small children. But, like anything else that came up suddenly, I squeezed it in, and made the necessary adjustments. I started by buying two more of his albums. Would have bought them all had my money allowed. But from these, I found buried treasure. I listened to understand Freddy, to let his real words come through. I remembered my dream, and wondered what, if anything, I was supposed to know or do now.

Talked to my friends about it. That helped. I knew there was more, more meaning in this thin string of events. "More" was my key word. To find this key, I wrote poetry. In these poems was the language of caring, knowing, questions. Who could deny thunder and lightning? Who could walk through that storm, that downpour, and expect to stay dry? When this began to feel confusing, I stood there, inside the confusion knowing that things would have to make sense. Soon.

Meanwhile, Freddy on the brain summoned the Teen Within. She jumped for joy at the chance to finally do her thing. Was this really my Inner Teen, or just the parts of my womanhood that I knew nothing about? I wasn't sure, but I was having fun. My children played along, singing the songs, laughing at me. Melvin, known for finding humor in almost everything, failed to see the humor in this. This was his typical response whenever I smiled or laughed for reasons other than the children or him. So, of course, he took action.

He had a California friend to call me and claim to know Freddy personally. She said he was known for "bizarre" ways of living. She said she and Freddy were lovers, and that he would sometimes send a personal limo for her whenever he was performing in her city if they had agreed to meet. I congratulated her. Then, to beat it all, Melvin said something that I rejected right away. He said that Freddy was gay.

For as long as I could remember, I had heard the "gay" accusation in my community rise predictably like the sound of the Tuesday morning air raid siren, whenever anyone black rose to a certain level of success. They had to be "gay," one of the worst things anyone in our community could be said to be. A sexual outcast, a pervert, the ultimate condemnation. As far down as anyone could go, it was maximum damage, maximum putdown. We would never say those words right out, of course, we would just shun that person, give them the cold shoulder, wag the Bible in their face, all for long enough to run them away. Freddy, the black storm, gay? Nothing could be more ridiculous. Pul-eeeeeeze, I thought, knowing Melvin was doing it too, now, making this up to discourage, stop, shake me up, put my Inner Teen on notice to get back in line, to go back into hiding and make me behave.

This encouraged me more. I knew it wasn't true. I kept writing. Soon, I got an idea. I needed to see Freddy for myself. One more time. I called around, found the number to his office, called and asked where he was performing. They told me. One Night Only. The Four Star Theatre in Houston.

Payday was coming up. From the very beginning, I had taken my whole check and paid bills. This time would be different. I cashed my check, got myself a plane ticket, reserved myself a room for one night at the hotel nearest the theatre, put aside enough for a ticket to the show, and a round trip airport shuttle ticket. I would fix myself up, do my hair, nails, and take my time making sure I looked as nice as I could. I would get a new skirt and blouse to wear to the show. I would have just enough money to get these things done. So, I had to take food with me. Nuts, raisins, fruit, and sandwiches. I asked my mother to take the children for the weekend, and she agreed.

It was a bitter cold Chicago January. Cold enough to freeze your breath, cold enough to burn your boots when you walked on the ice. And I was going to Houston, Texas to see Freddy. I wrote one poem on the plane. This gave me three. To go with the poems, then, to come up with a plan. I would re-write the poems on hotel letterhead and seal them in an envelope with a personal cover note. Then, I'd walk to the theatre early enough to get my ticket, find someone who worked for him, give this person the envelope to deliver, and my mission would be accomplished. I could enjoy the show, and wait for a telephone call.

While flying, I looked out over the clouds and felt like even they, those massive white puffs of air, were part of my trip, that I was stepping into a dream, a fantasy, one where everything was all right. Our plane landed on time and I realized I was in a strange place where I knew nobody, a place where I was alone.

Driving me to the airport shuttle, Mom said she would be praying for me. I told her not to worry. She had a look of disbelief on her face. She said that "those people in the music business" were not to be trusted. I couldn't believe that. I knew that I was supposed to make this trip. I knew that I would be safe. Every corner I turned, things worked as planned. I carefully measured my food, because there would be no more. Fruit and nuts had been fine on the plane, in addition to the meal they served.

The Houston shuttle took me to the Dunfey Hotel, just down the road from the Four Star Theatre. I had never been to Texas and, Houston looked a little strange. Not a pretty place, not a bad looking place, but, Texas brought thoughts of President Kennedy. If it wasn't for Freddy, I would never have come.

My room was comfortable and nice. It even had one of those tiny refrigerators. I put my food in there. Once settled, I sat at the little round side table and wrote my poems out on the thick hotel stationery. I was proud of my writing, proud of what I was doing. I sealed the envelope. I called for room service to bring me a pot of hot water. Sat and sipped the cup of tea I made. Took a nap. Woke up in time for a slow bath, and prepared myself for the show.

The bath would help me melt away some of the travel tension built up from the time I had planned this little escapade. This was probably my boldest move ever. I was nervous. Determined, but uptight to be stepping out, to be handing my poetry over to somebody I didn't know, let alone somebody famous. Heck, my poetry had been a something of a mystery even to me, and until then I had only shared it when there was no other way to speak. This was one of those times, one of those times when something had to be said.

* * * * **

My hair had grown a couple inches down my back by now. I used Curl Free and, before the trip, had really spent time fixing myself up. I would wear it in a straight pageboy with short bangs over a maroon velour v-neck sweater, brown wool skirt and brown boots. I dressed and checked myself. "Good enough to pass inspection," I smiled and thought aloud. I threw on my favorite coat, my brown faux Persian lamb, grabbed my gloves, made sure I had my room key, and set out for adventure.

It had snowed in Houston. I walked along the road, walked in the cold sludge left on the snowy rough road to the theatre. It was about a mile. With no sidewalk, I walked as close to the edge as possible to keep from being splattered. In light traffic and with what daylight remained, I walked briskly, the way I imagined a powerful woman would walk. Cabs stopped and honked to see if I wanted a ride. If only I could have afforded a cab.

While I walked, I worked up a sweat. The last thing I needed, but walking at this pace, dressed as I was, sweat was a natural, certain result. It was more important to keep a good pace than to worry about what I smelled like. There would be time enough to dry off and freshen up once I reached the theatre.

The theatre was just ahead and to my right. I was able to walk up to the window and purchase my ticket. Once inside I saw tables with t-shirts, albums, life-sized posters next to a wicker chair for a fake photograph, and other memorabilia with Freddy's name everywhere. There were a few people browsing, buying. I walked to the door and handed my ticket to the usher. I was stunned when he showed me to my seat in the seventh row. There couldn't have been more than ten people in the place. It was really early. I had the envelope in my pocket. I waved, signaled to the usher who had brought me in and he came right away.

"Yes, Ma'am?"

"Would you please give this to somebody who works for Freddy? I'm here from Chicago, and brought this tonight, especially for him."

"Certainly, Miss," he said, with a smile, as he took the envelope from my hand and walked away.

A sigh of relief left my lips as I sank into the seat knowing I had done what I came to do. Then I realized I could go, freshen up now and really relax. I found the ladies' room and took one of those hard, brown paper towels and wet it with warm water. I dabbed the towel to my forehead, careful not to mess up my make-up. Then, I took another one, put some soap on and washed under my arms. I was musty from the walk. Instead of checking it in the store, I checked the label of my new sweater just before putting it on. Polyester. Damn! Too late now. Hopefully the soap and water would help. I checked the mirror. Still good. Returned to my seat.

Welcome relaxation swept over my body like a cool breeze moving through a stuffy room. People were beginning to trickle into the theater, and, as I saw them, I thought, there's a big difference between Houston and Chicago. Back home, there would be no trickling, no chance to walk up and get a choice ticket a couple of hours before the show, like I had just done. I knew why I was there. The others would find out once the show began. Excitement crept in. I was going to see one more show, just a little over a month after seeing the first.

Just then, a man who looked very much like Rev. Cleveland walked over to my row with the usher who had taken the envelope. "That's her," the usher said as he pointed me out to the Rev. Then the Rev. said, "Freddy wants to see you." Disbelief. What? My heart stopped. "Okay," I said, sliding up as if it was nothing, and walking to the aisle to follow him. What was happening? I thought I could just leave the envelope, and maybe get a call after the show. But this?

* * * * *

We walked through the back door of the theatre, down the lobby and through a door. That door led to a long corridor, and with every step I felt more and more disbelief. One more door and once inside the clock stopped. Freddy.

There he stood and he stepped toward me and said, "I'm Freddy." I smiled and said, "I know." I introduced myself. He smiled. "This is Manny," pointing out the other man standing on the far side of the room. Manny said, "hi," and smiled. Freddy added, "So you are the lady who wrote that beautiful poetry? Manny and I had to get a dictionary to figure out some of the words . . ." I knew he was pulling my leg, but, "thank you," I said, as I laughed. "Would you care for a drink or something to eat?" he asked, pointing to the covered table with chafing dishes and warming trays. "No, thank you. But I will have some juice" I said, knowing some food would have helped considerably. Some food to break the ice, fill my stomach, help me talk. I told myself that they probably didn't have anything a vegetarian could eat. And, I didn't want to get into a discussion about food. Food, the one thing I could have talked about easily. Food, something I loved as much as anyone. And so, oh no! Here it was, another one of those moments, etched in stone, like the cotillion. Return of The Stone Wall.

He showed me to the couch at the side of the room, and I took a seat. He handed me a styrofoam cup and a can of pineapple juice. It was just the right moment for cooling juice. As I sat there, I looked at him. He wore jeans, cowboy boots, and a cowboy hat. Like a bronze statue, reading a magazine, standing there, humming a song that sounded like something the O'Jays would have sung. Two or three bars of the song, he sang softly over and over again. I don't remember the words. But I kept thinking, "if only he would sing more of that song." Today I would have asked him to. Today I would have asked what he was reading. Today I would have had some food, and asked to speak with him alone. Today I might not have made a trip like that to begin with. Today . . . But I was 27 that year, and even though I made that trip, I felt lost, lost for words, my words. That is, except for the ones on the page.

I sat there feeling embarrassed to have nothing to say, embarrassed, like a throbbing sore thumb, embarrassed to be silent in a room with people coming and going. A woman comedienne (from Chicago) who I thought I hadn't heard of before walked into the room. She was his opening act. Actually, she had a recurring part in a sitcom called "Night Court." There were other women, too. One walked over and introduced herself.

"I'm Melinda. So, how do you know Freddy?"

"Just met him today. Flew in from Chicago."

She grunted. "Well, I've known him for years. I live here, and we're having a party back at my place after the show, like we always do when he's here."

"Nice," I said, knowing what she was getting at, knowing I wouldn't be invited to that party. Knowing I hadn't come all the way to Texas to see Freddy, and go to a party. I came to help wake him up. I was really here, in this room, and really frustrated.

Frustrated to have no words. With the embarrassment, the frustration, and feeling perturbed by Melinda's remarks, I began to sweat all over again. All that emotion. All that sweat.

The sweat from my walk hadn't dried, and now, here was more, a whole new supply. After sitting another fifteen minutes or so, an eternal fifteen minutes watching Freddy stand so still just a few feet away from me, reading his magazine, singing a note or two from a song I couldn't quite place, I tried to think of something to do. Now and then as he read, he would glance down at my boots and then back up at me. "Yes, my boots are worn and stained with road salt. Yours would be too if you had just walked a mile in slush!" I thought. My stomach growled from hunger. Melinda walked around the room and glanced at me again and again. Manny and the comedienne ate and talked at the back of the room. Unable to stand it any longer, I had to break the monotony. I checked my watch. Suddenly, some words . . .

"Well, I'd better be getting back to my seat . . ." they dropped from my mouth by themselves as I scooted to the edge of the sofa and stood up. Freddy stepped toward me and took my hand. "I hope you enjoy the show." And he stepped toward me more, following me to the door, as if to hug or kiss me as I left. "No way," I thought, I darted past him and out the door. "Good-bye," I said, smiling. More sweat. I was wringing wet by this time. Back to my seat, I wrapped myself in my coat and slid down in extreme relief. Despite the disaster that had just occurred, I was still in for a treat. The show. It would begin in just a few minutes. "Maybe he'll call after the show . . ." I tried to tell myself. After all, I did put my number on the cover note . . .

The comedienne's opening act was blue. "This woman is the modern, younger version of Moms," I thought. "Must take a whole lot of nerve for a woman to talk like that . . . in front of a crowd, for a living. I can't imagine it. Her life is the opposite of mine."

Then the show began. Much like the show I had seen. I loved the part where he blew out the candles! I thought about what it must be like, going from city to city, doing the same show over and over again. How it might even be boring, because the moves were the same, the words, the songs, the beat, the musical cues, all the same. It wasn't like jazz where each take is different. This was like cutting cookies, so that each one looks the same. It must be hard for an artist to live this way, I thought.

That isn't art, is it?

Yet, for me, it was another dose of fantasy as I sat there smiling, knowing that I had been in his space, and he in mine.

Knowing that I had left something with him that brought "a powerful, positive ... message, a prayer for ... happiness and inner peace ..." knowing that this poetry had to be different from anything he had ever gotten before. Knowing that I mainly wanted a chance to talk alone for a few minutes, just to tell him to slow down, to check himself, to return to what is true and right, while there was still time.

I knew when the show was over, so, I left during the final number to avoid some of the crowd. There were people all over the vestibule and lobby, talking, mulling over the items for sale. I wondered if any of them were part of his entourage. Not one familiar face in that crowd. I opened the door and stepped into the cold. I retraced my steps on the gravel road, and this time, there was more traffic, folks leaving the theatre. The dark didn't matter. I knew I was safe walking that road at night. Safe. Safe as I had ever been before. Back at my room I undressed and realized, as I took it off, that my sweater reeked with musk. "No more poly for me," I decided in hindsight. Another cup of tea and, this time, a soy meat sandwich. Another bath. I waited for the telephone to ring.

Deafening silence. Watching a telephone makes its power grow. A black princess telephone gone completely mute. I checked the phone to make sure it was all right. Of course, it was. Thought about his songs, his routine, his life as it looks from here. What that life must be like behind his eyes. Got into bed. Requested a wake-up call to be sure to get my return shuttle in plenty of time. I had learned not to rush myself. Lights out. "What a day," I thought, as I pulled the covers up. Wondered how the party was going. Wondered if he thought anymore about the poetry or me. "Someday I'll be able to tell my grandchildren about this. Then again, maybe I wouldn't," I thought as I expected to doze off ... and the thoughts continued ... This had been one heck of an adventure of any sort, depending upon how I described it. I had come to Texas, delivered the poetry, even met the man, and that is what was important. If he really read it, he would get the message. An intelligent brother, he didn't need my interpretation, my urgings, I told myself, as sleep came.

And while that line of thought ended here, on this note, in my room that night, it would be a while before I would really understand what had just happened to me. It would be years before I realized I had been spared some pain, spared the shock of stepping across a line and into a realm I was ill prepared for. It would be years. Before I would be thankful for having been rejected that night because of the musk. Before I would realize that the chemical reaction to cheap fabric had been a form of spiritual protection my body knew how and when to provide, protection that cost me nothing more than a little embarrassment.

I loved him.

This was separate and apart from my assignment, I knew, but I could not escape nor deny loving Freddy. It was love. Love, based on an idea, on a sense of connection, based upon pure seduction, wild beauty and power, based upon serendipity, romance, the idea of actual tenderness coming my way. This love made everything confusing, made me behave in confusing ways, make decisions that were confusing. He was everything, stepping into the empty shoes, into the tall blue coat, if only in my dreams. He was a dream come true. This love contradicted the whole purpose of my assignment, it seemed. But, I would have had to be dead not to love him. I was far from dead, and I really wanted him, or, I thought I did.

I could not wait to get home and talk with my girlfriends about this! Thank God for Limmie, Beverly, Lydia, and for the ten-foot coil cord on the end of my avocado kitchen wall telephone. I could do everything but fly, with that phone. Lord knows, I had plenty to tell them now.

Once back downtown, I needed to call my mother. I didn't have enough money for a telephone call. I waited a few minutes at the corner where she said she'd pick me up. No sight of her. It was so cold. I tried calling collect to make sure she didn't forget. Her husband refused the call. No problem, after a few minutes, she pulled up with the children in the car. I had left my children only a couple of times before, to see my father, for a funeral. I missed my little folks, my Angel and my Man-man.

While we drove, I told my mother what had happened, and she was in shock, asking for mercy as I talked. I didn't tell her everything, though, just the general stuff. I'd save the details for those who wanted to hear. I'd become completely immersed, race into a high creative gear and compile a book of the poetry I was still writing. I'd do whatever it took to deliver my complete message.

*****

Within the next two years his fame and success skyrocketed, and I kept showing up with loving poems of warning. Anytime I showed up at one of his performances, if I could spot and catch up to Manny, he escorted me backstage. The last time I saw him in Chicago, it was on a bitter cold January night. Limmie went with me. This time, I sweetened the pot with a picture, a handwritten note, poetry, and a crocheted neck scarf with his initials in the corner. As we sat on the couch watching and listening to the people do what they do, Freddy made his entrance down the stairs dressed in a silk robe. He sat on the sofa and whispered into the ears of a woman sitting not far from Limmie and me.

Sitting there it was different than the first time, because I had someone to talk to, a witness for all of this. There were radio personalities, music promoters, people from everywhere in that suite. Some just came to get an autograph or to shake Freddy's hand. Others came to gawk, have a kiss, get their picture taken with him. He obliged and seemed used to spending lots of time this way. Freddy talked a lot about himself, his family, about his popularity and how different he felt being able to do what he wanted, do whatever his money would allow, as opposed to the days of not having money and living "in the ghetto."

After realizing that I could sit there for the rest of the night and nothing would change, I decided to leave. I nudged Limmie in the side and suggested we go. She smiled and agreed. We got up and walked to the door. He followed and stood in front of me. He looked into my eyes and thanked me for the poem "and everything." Then he grabbed my breasts through my coat, kissed me on the mouth and told me I was beautiful. I told him he was beautiful, too, and to take care of himself. I could have screamed. It was too cold to scream, but not too cold to cry.

*****

Three years later I saw him for the last time in Atlanta, and hardly recognized him. He seemed beat up, in some kind of stupor, and was no longer surrounded by women. Instead, there were men in his quarters, waiting on him hand and foot. Even Manny was staggering. The palpable sadness permeated the space. Sitting there in the quiet, dark of his dressing room, he had very little to say. I asked him about the poetry. He wasn't interested, except to ask if I was "still printing things with (his) name on it?" "No," I assured him.

Thankfully, I had grown out of that. I left and never saw him again.

Within a few weeks, news came about a near-fatal accident in which he had sustained serious injury. He was reported to have been driving under the influence. The story broke with sketchy details and, for a long time, little to no news about Freddy's real condition was available.

Deeply disappointed, as if lost in a desert, I felt as if I had seen a mirage, an illusion. As if someone or something had not only played a bad joke on me and thousands, if not millions of women, but had gotten away with it. Easily. How in the world could a man like that be left permanently broken?

As Limmie said, "you tried to tell him!" I thought, *if only I had been able to get through to him*. Regardless, he couldn't hear my whispering voice amidst the high- volume life he was leading, amidst such noise and distraction. And so, when this happened, I stayed home from work to pray. To pray for our Samson, stripped now of his power, the Samson we had believed in and loved.

Once.

Worthy Work

Grown folks said they were "goin' to work," proclaiming that they were serious, prepared, unstoppable. Everybody who wanted work could get a job. Most black men worked in uniforms or work clothes and the Post Office was always hiring. Monday morning found everybody talking about the blues, yet, they were glad for the work they had, glad to exceed what their parents had been allowed to do.

Day work, child care, taking in sewing and laundry. We had moved beyond the work of fields and houses. In America, we gave life to the idea that every generation would exceed the one prior. Our understanding of this idea was firm. We wanted progress that would prove our ability beyond any doubt, prove our worth by what we could do. In America, we would rise to be more and have more than our parents had had and been. We were determined and had still more to prove. We also lived with a religious mandate to be good people. Being good meant following the Bible. Having more and being more meant status, power, and money, all of which had to be earned, and we were up to the task. We forgot that America had become America through war, had developed an appetite for whatever she wanted at the expense of others so that, no matter what, **she** could have more and be more. We were Americans.

* * * *

Work. Responsibility. Hard work was admirable. The harder you worked, the more odds you defied, the more you were respected. Hard work won pride in the community and pride boosted self-respect. Work meant you were an adult. It was the way you proved your power. Earned your keep. Moved up in the world. It was how you could "be somebody."

Working, smoking cigarettes, drinking alcohol, hanging out in the neighborhood taverns, eating whatever you wanted when you wanted it, spending your money however you wanted to, paying your bills, driving a car, going to bed for the night whenever you got good and ready, and, having sex, these were the privileges that came with being grown. But working topped the list because working gave you money and money kept you free.

* * * * *

Work had interesting twists in my family. My mother worked for seven years as a secretary after having been a telephone operator when I was a baby. My birth certificate lists my father's job as "mechanic" at a place called Diversey Garage. My father couldn't work for the telephone company in the 1950s. It was acceptable for my mother to work inside, dressing in her best clothes and doing mental work and for my father to wear a uniform, face the elements and get his hands dirty. Grandmother worked for a while in a laundry doing ironing. With great pride she ironed, and when I was old enough, she showed me how to iron with a professional touch. She had gone to college to be a teacher but never finished her degree because she "had to get married." Doing laundry had been her one experience working "outside the home." At least it had until she learned to speak as an "Elocutionist" and perform her sacred poetry on a love offering basis.

* * * * *

And what of value? To say that a woman who does not work "outside the home" is looking to be taken care of trivializes and demeans everything she does to run her household and keep her family going. To say that a woman who does not work "outside the home" is not earning her keep devalues the demanding work of mothering and homemaking. All my life, I have heard talk of "women of leisure," but have never met any. For the years that I did not hold down an outside "9-to-5" I worked as hard if not harder than when I did, worked for the first time ever, to *uphold our efforts* — develop and manage a budding career, support my husband's pursuits, make a home and run a very busy household, taking care of all its inhabitants — and in so doing stirred the resentment of tiny eyes peering from outside, eyes who misjudged and mistook my position at the time for something it wasn't. The key word describing what I did at that time is "manage." A skill I had learned by then.

* * * * *

There were songs about work in our community. Sam Cooke's "Chain Gang" saluted the men working for no pay. "Hard Work" by Eddie Harris and "I Got Work to Do" by the Isleys portrayed the ethic, the pride, the volume, the swagger and value of hard work. The harder the work, the bigger the importance, the greater the respect. No work, no value. No money, no respect. Work is how we learned to value our lives. And this value system runs deep and stubborn.

Later, the songs changed. "Skippin' Work Today" was an Eddie Kendricks song, sweetly raising the question of work and the value of one's own time and life off the clock. In the movie, "Claudine," Rupert, a garbage man, articulated the sad truth about his position as a working man when it came time to get serious with Claudine, a mother of five children receiving welfare support, also working as a maid. "It takes a lot of money to be a daddy, and I just ain't got it . . ." What an unforgettable line.

We tried to dignify our jobs. Florence, the maid in the television sitcom, "The Jeffersons," preferred the title "Household Technician." Florence would have reminded us that Rupert's preferred job title was "Sanitation Engineer." For a while, I was a secretary playing the role of "Administrative Assistant," but received the pay of a clerk. Workers wanted to balance the key roles we played with the responsibilities we held. We wanted to forget that these demanding jobs were generally heavy on work and light on power.

* * * * *

My first job was arranged by my uncle through a non-profit community organization. I took a typing test and was told to see Ms. Streater in the Legal Services Division of the Great Lakes Region U.S. Office of Economic Opportunity. I'd be the Clerk Typist in the Office of the Chief. I would earn $2.22 per hour, and work full-time, 9:00 A.M. to 5:00 P.M. in the Summer Intern Program, set aside for college students.

I reported for work, assigned a desk, told I would be doing light typing, filing, answering phones, running errands, and lots of Xerox copying. Xerox was the latest thing and I spent entire afternoons at the machine, watching the lamp go on and off, sliding under the green window, as the whole top part of the machine moved slowly, back and forth, as I stood there, opening and closing the floppy rubber cover, turning every page, and pressing the "x" again and again. We used color coded carbon sets religiously for all communication, and typed on those wonderful IBM Selectric typewriters.

Work was a mad mixture of stretched coffee breaks, clock-watching, eating pastries, running downtown for extended lunch hours in between assignments, and perfecting the art of looking busy. It was experiences like this that helped me to totally relate and laugh uproariously watching the movie, "Office Space," which touched on the ridiculousness and psychological slavery typical of many work scenarios.

* * * * *

Getting there every day, moving my brain in the direction of the el station in the mornings, was hard. But it was expected. So, I did it, paying the many costs of work. Work was already so hard that for balance, I insisted on rewards and comforts.

I bought two things. A window water cooler to help me make it through that summer, and a personal black and white television, both from Walgreens. First the cooler, then the television. The cooler made it easier to sleep nights. The television was a privilege. I could now watch what I wanted in the privacy of my room. Before this, we all sat together and talked, sharing stories of the day, watching selected television shows. With my cooler and my television, I could stay by myself and not necessarily be with everybody else. They could visit me. In my cool room.

* * * * *

I remember rushing with the morning herd of commuters off the train, down the green steel stairs at South State Street, and east onto Balboa. One morning, a white guy just ahead of me was swapping impressive shoptalk with another white guy. Just as we crossed the alley, a pigeon flying in a small flock overhead deposited his morning dump on the back of the guy's suit coat. I busted a roar while he kept walking and talking.

During my time in this job, I got to know Alfred, one of the attorneys in the office, who'd ride the train with me sometimes. He said he made $6.00 per hour, an amount I couldn't imagine. I also got to know the bookkeeper, Bobbie, another black woman, and another intern, Mary, a law student, who attended the same school as Joey.

My job was over at the end of the summer. I returned to school, without much success, and soon decided to reenter the job market. I finally landed a job at Michael Reese Hospital making $3.75 an hour. I was hired by a wonderful woman named Mrs. Gist, impressed by the fact that I had a brother in school on scholarship. I would start right away.

I worked in the "surgical suite" as the OR secretary. Besides typing surgical procedures and generating the daily surgical schedule, I would relieve the clerks at the front and back desks for their lunch and coffee breaks. Their work was very exacting, demanding, and had to be flawless. There was heavy traffic in the operating room. There were doctors coming to perform surgery, technicians and nurses who assisted them, and, of course, the orderlies who transported patients to and from their rooms, and the scrub orderlies who sanitized the rooms between procedures. The all-important surgical schedule for each day had to be followed, and, sometimes there were last minute changes to be made and emergencies to fit in. The desks were traffic centers, and the clerks directed the flow of traffic with amazing precision. There were doctors to page, special instruments to be ordered, patients to be "prepped" for surgery and then sent for, patients in the holding area to be sent to surgery, from there, to recovery, then back to their rooms. Mistakes could be very costly and even harmful.

Learning the early morning routine, getting there by 7:30, changing from my street clothes into scrubs, slipping into the paper shoe covers and covering my head with a paper bonnet was fun. A Marvin Gaye song reminds me of those cold, early mornings.

"Don't go and talk about my Father, God is my friend..."

In the OR lounge, an urn of fresh, hot coffee was on hand for all who needed it. In my laundered green attire, I quickly learned to drink and love coffee. It also did not take long before I realized that the caffeine brought more zing to my mornings than I could stand. So, I switched from coffee to hot chocolate.

* * * * *

During this time, a physician in South Africa, had made headlines as a pioneer in the field of heart transplants. Soon, we had a young doctor from that part of the world come to work at our hospital. One afternoon in May of 1971, an rare emergency surgery was arranged. I happened to be filing in at the front desk that day as the clerk was on vacation.

A twenty year-old black man had fallen from the third floor of a building and was bleeding heavily. His parents sat in the waiting room expecting word about their son. After a while, the nurse in charge came to the desk and told me to order the kidney tray. There weren't any kidney procedures on schedule. I asked to make sure I heard her correctly. She told me to "just get the kidney tray!"

Then, in what seemed more like one smooth step-by-step dance, she called for the doctor from South Africa, told the young man's parents that there was no hope for their son to survive because they were not able to stop the bleeding, and convinced them to sign over consent to use their son's organs. Immediately, a patient awaiting a kidney transplant was brought to surgery. Tissue typing and cross-matching was done, and, without delay, the young black man was pronounced dead and the transplant followed.

When I realized what had happened, realized the thing I had not only witnessed, but taken part in, I left the desk without notice, walked in horror to 31st and South Park, stood at the corner and heard a piece of new music that fit the occasion exactly. "What's Goin' On?" was blasting from the speakers of the corner record shop. I walked in, bought the album and clung to it, clung for dear life as I listened over and over to the words that said what I couldn't.

I was never a smoker, but I smoked an Eve menthol cigarette that night. I smoked it as an aid to my thinking and then as a fashion statement. Surely the Eve menthol would add adult depth to the experience of listening to this music, so I sat there mesmerized, covered in smoke, letting my tears flow. Though I knew I couldn't stay, I didn't have to quit that job. I was fired by the charge nurse several days later, for insubordination, after working in the OR for about 6 months.

* * * * *

By the time I stopped working in the OR, I had a serious case of morning sickness, the cause of which I did not have to be told, and was planning to be married. The following year, when I decided to return to work, I went to the hospital to reapply. My record indicated I should not be rehired. I called Mrs. Gist at home and told her my dilemma. She suggested I come to her new office at Northwestern University Medical School. I did and soon was hired as a secretary in the physiology department of NUMC.

Mostly I typed research findings that the scientists drafted in longhand. There were several research projects operating in that department, most of which were funded by the National Institutes of Health. The research had to do with reproductive biology, or, more specifically, cyclic nucleotides. The faculty seemed amazed at the speed and accuracy of my typing.

I enjoyed working in that casual, quiet setting, frequented by students my age who I found extremely interesting. There was another secretary in the department my age, named Shirley. We wore jeans and sandals to work and hung out talking every chance we got. We had lots in common, except that she didn't have children and her husband was a dentist. She had been raised in Indiana. Shirley had her words and had thought deeply about things. I admired that about her.

The campus had lots of tunnels and out of the way places. The VA hospital was part of the campus, and we could shop at the commissary. The campus was located a stone's throw from Lake Michigan in the heart of the gold coast. I learned to walk to Sachs' and Bonwit's at lunchtime, hunting for bargains. During those mid-day escapades, I saw famous people coming out of the stores. Johnny Mathis, Count Basie, Melba Moore and Ben Vereen.

The job had little to no pressure. It was fun, mostly. I mastered the work asked of me. I wanted more of a challenge. Mrs. Gist retired. I asked for the administrative assistant position when it came open and was denied. A woman with a degree was hired from outside. I knew there was nothing about that job I could not do and do well. She stayed for about a year. I asked again and was denied again. This time, an older woman was hired. I left the department after two years. I went to work for the legal clinic at the law school down the block. I stayed there six months. I made a bunch of new friends, and enjoyed the work. The pay was $600 per month, and we were paid monthly.

* * * *

By this time, I had learned something important. I could work at any hospital or university almost blindfolded. Public service was a more comfortable and rewarding environment.

Promotions for this black girl with skills were available only if I took them. Doing that meant working somewhere long enough to learn new skills, terminologies, procedures, and then moving into another environment that called for them. I adopted this strategy. It worked. At one time, I left a job after one week, with two other offers waiting. I was never out of work. My mother reminded me that there were people looking for work and couldn't find it, and that I had jobs backed up in queue. She told me now and then that she admired me for my hard work. This was one of the few compliments I got from her. This was the way I expected my life to be until I could figure out another way.

* * * * *

My mother taught me the importance of volunteering in our community. In her nutritional research, she had learned enough that she compiled her own encyclopedia, something she shared with me. She shared it all with me, to include an opportunity to serve. She developed and taught a basic nutrition class, introducing people in our community to natural nutrition, food principles, food combining, food preparation, herbal remedies, the works. Her class was offered at the Institute of Positive Education, free to anyone who signed up. By 1974, she asked me if I wanted to teach a class, too. I did, so I developed and taught the advanced nutrition class, focused on real prevention, natural hygiene, and healing self-care, alongside her, until I left Chicago. Not only was I able to share this knowledge with my children, but I was able to take care of myself with it, help others with it, and much more.

* * * * *

By that time, I knew power in the work world was a strange animal. Women with it could be good to work with or not.

Men with it could play a few games. I had learned how to work around them more than with them. I felt as if I lived in a different sphere than men. We spoke different languages, cared about different things. I steered clear of them as much as possible because I did not trust them, generally speaking. I knew that they wanted my skills, since it seemed as if they could do nothing for themselves. But, I knew that they would take whatever they wanted. In my work experience, the exceptional man was worthy of trust and respect. I still remember those rare, safe men.

I also realized that I could help folks I knew who might be looking for jobs to get them. When I saw openings that I could share with friends, I did, and helped them get work whenever I could.

In 1977 I got a job at Provident Hospital in the purchasing department. After being there for a few months, I was offered a surprise promotion. I had cleared up a purchasing requisitions backlog and enjoyed the relaxed atmosphere of the place. I transferred to a higher position in the Medical Director's office. In that job, I was asked by the Executive Assistant, to hire emergency room physicians. This was the hot potato part of her job that she wanted to toss my way. Not comfortable hiring physicians, checking out their credentials in a hurry, and quickly getting them on board to be sure our ER would have no gap in service, but I did. That job was so crucial that folks would call me at home to let me know we had no ER doctor, and I was supposed to get one in there. I don't remember how I got out of there, but it was hardly worth the stress that came with it. Shortly, I was asked to work in the executive director's office, both of these positions were offered to me without applying. If I took it, my pay would immediately increase by $3,000.

I said I'd think about it. I immediately drove to my mother's office to tell her what was happening. I parked my car and got out. Three thousand dollars. I walked past her office and almost to the next corner before I realized that just the thought of all that money had put me deep in a daze. When I went to work at NUMC, my gross salary was $400 per month. Now, four years later, I stood to gross $1,000 per month.

I took the job. There was one problem. The director had one executive secretary who took the news of my hiring the way an old wife being replaced by a newer model would. His idea was that he would divide up duties and use both of us. He was having a little fun. There was work in that office to be done, but not THAT much. The old secretary took to correcting and belittling me. I stayed there until the following year, when I found something comparable at another hospital.

I worked for a small black engineering firm. The company had government contracts and the head of the company was a brilliant man. I was proud working there and happy to be close to home again. It was about a 15-minute commute. All this time, as I figured these things out, a national movement of women office workers was brewing. In this movement, women began to talk about their working conditions, their pay and benefits. There were conferences. A movie "9 to 5" was made, starring Jane Fonda, Lily Tomlin and Dolly Parton who also wrote the theme song. I didn't pay much attention to the work these women were doing, making things better for us, but I did realize that I benefitted from it and was grateful. I didn't think I'd be doing office work forever, but doing it long enough to learn the ins and outs meant that this movement was helping me. I was not alone out there.

Finally, I found my dream job, administrative assistant to the President of a university consortium. This organization was housed at Chicago State University, also close to home, and I had my own office. This was a special project formed by presidents of local colleges and universities who decided to start a college television station that would be mostly funded by the State of Illinois. My boss traveled a lot. He and I, a staff of two, administered the project in its planning stages. He did lots of writing and communicating with folks in public television. We attended board meetings. I'd take notes while the men pontificated about how things would be, where the transmitter would be located, how many students could be served by our courses on television. How the changing electronic media was about to revolutionize things, as things called videocassette recorders and cable television made their way into the mainstream. I made $13,600 in that job and loved every minute of it. It was the only job I had where I was treated with equality and respect, and where the work was challenging. I kept all the books, paid the taxes, everything. Had it not been for the move to Georgia, I never would have left.

Always I worked for leaders in their fields, folks with no more intelligence than mine. Once I moved to Georgia, everything changed. Salaries were a lot less. My first job paid $11,900, and I was an office manager with supervisory responsibility. The loss of that two thousand dollars was a hefty tax on my family.

By 1983, computers were all the rage, and my boss demanded that I learn to use the computer (via the self-instruction method), both the word and data processing programs. The computer was an HP. It was expensive, clunky, and overly technical. Instead of alleviating my workload, it made my work more stressful. I left my job over a dispute about a manuscript for publication that I had typed into the computer for several days that suddenly disappeared, probably because I had pressed the wrong save button at the wrong time. Using manual methods over the life of the project, I had administered our grant of three million dollars with only a

$69 discrepancy, and had taken care of all other administrative functions for the program, with the help of student assistants. The computer stress was very frustrating and hurtful, all things considered.

I went to work for an historically black college as an office manager in the student dean's office. I loved the environment, and the convenience of being able to bring my baby to the day care center. After one year of being snared in the political crossfire of both minor and major management issues, I left that job to work in a law firm. I figured if I had to deal with that much stress, I might as well get paid for it.

The term "sweatshop" became familiar once I assumed the role of a legal secretary. I worked for the second and third largest firms in Atlanta. At the time, we were still using IBM Selectrics, and I could probably type 90 words per minute and use the Dictaphone, which I had learned along the way. Most documents were typewritten. Court pleadings were put on word processing, at the time all done by operators using scanners and WANG dedicated word processors. Although I had to dress for the occasion of working in these posh surroundings — another work-related expense — the pay was not enough to compensate for both the added stress and expense. Something had to give. Melvin left the family for good during this time. This single Mom was growing tired.

I saw one well-dressed black woman appearing very content and relaxed, coming in and out of the offices. One day I had an opportunity to have lunch with her. I assumed she worked for an agency and was curious about how that worked. I asked her if the agency kept her busy. "What agency?" she corrected me. I was intrigued. "Don't you work for an agency?" I continued, not trying to pry, but really wanting to know. "I work for myself. I am a freelancer." A warm glow rushed through my body. She continued, "I get calls to come in when they need me, and I bill them $12 an hour." More warm glows. No wonder she seemed so content.

I buckled down and figured out ways to get started. Eventually, I found good contacts, followed this woman's example, and worked for several years as my own boss, making anywhere from $14 to $18 an hour for straight time work. My clients included architects, lawyers, and physicians. Technology was new, and the best most offices had was dedicated word processing. I learned about 13 different software programs. I slung an almost empty briefcase, filled with software templates. I worked when I wanted to, built some good relationships with my clients and for the first time in my adult life felt like a free human being. The flexibility gave me more time at home with my children, and cut down on my stress which left more energy for living. In my best year, I worked 10 minimal-stress months, and doubled my salary, slinging that briefcase with a smile.

* * * * *

Once I realized that I did not want to sling an empty briefcase for the rest of my life, I followed my aunt's persistent advice, and returned to school another time.

I enrolled full-time in the Atlanta School of Massage in March of 1988. Studying there was like a daily trip to heaven. My entire being was so ready for the culture and experience of massage, being touched, being present, mattering, dreaming of a new life and way of working. That year, my daughter was a senior in high school and preparing for college, and, I had sufficient contacts in word processing that I took assignments on my days off and paid my own tuition and hers too, when the time came.

The program taught me much, not just about massage, but about myself. It showed me that I had been a right-brain dominant learner. I was able to apply much of what I had learned back in Naprapathic College to my training where we were taught the importance and health benefits of reducing stress in the soft tissues of the body through touch. I have to add something here. If I don't include this, it will go forgotten. While in Naprapathic College, I aced four classes. Naprapathic Theory, Nutrition, Botanical Studies, and Genetics. These subjects laid the foundation for the work awaiting me. In massage we also reduced stress through manipulation of the body's soft tissues. We studied in circles and sat in the floor. We were learning what it meant to be comfortable in our bodies. The whole environment was one of comfort, nurturing and healing.

In business class, we were told to imagine our work in its ideal state and then to write a statement of purpose about it. I wrote "to make an important contribution in the field of wellness." I never intended to open just a massage therapy practice. At the time massage therapists had to prove themselves as professionals and earn professional respect. I wanted to apply massage to overall healing, and use it for its many benefits. I was serious. I wanted to be a healer.

My first practice was home-based. At the time, my mother was a chiropractor, and she referred patients to me who had been in automobile accidents. I worked on them, and on anyone who complained of anything. For the first year or so, I worked on people experiencing physical pain. Somehow, using my hands and intuition, I was able to touch them, as one woman said, "at the core" of their pain, begin to untie the knots and alleviate the pain. My youthful hands were strong, full of heat, and I was happy to put smiles on people's faces. People who had been in pain for years came to see me. One woman, a legal secretary, had suffered from headaches for ten years and was accustomed to taking pain killers daily, came to me by referral, and after two sessions, she was pain-free.

I graduated in August of 1988 and began building this practice. I took my licensing exam and passed. I joined our professional association and realized I wanted more certifications to build my base of knowledge. I was asked to work at the school as a student clinic supervisor. I loved the work. I kept my new practice going for almost two years. During that time, I received my second certification in the modality of colon therapy known as the Wood Gravity method. My husband was transferred in '89.

In the summer of 1990, I joined him there. Soon, I found connection with practitioners in the area. I joined a group of therapists at a place called The Relaxation Center, located in a beautiful part of town.

I had come there knowing nobody. It couldn't have been more perfect. After one year of working with these women, I decided to branch out on my own. By this time, I had ideas for expansion. I wanted to find and focus on the keys to health, things like wellness education and lifestyle development. My partners "just wanted to do massage." I completed training in support group facilitation using the model developed by the Center for Attitudinal Healing, and received my third certification. My partners and I parted ways. I opened my own center, The Mind/Body Connection.

* * * * *

Chiropractors and physicians referred patients to me, and I to them. I formulated a schedule of free community wellness classes and billed my approach to soft tissue work as "corrective myotherapy." My suite of offices had about 750 square feet. I had a team of colleagues, a nutritionist, hypnotherapist, psychotherapist, chiropractor, physician. Every month, I met the overhead. I never made enough to pay myself much of a salary. This was self-employment of a whole different sort. In the first round, I billed clients for my time and that time assured a certain amount of productivity. My overhead amounted to the cost of printing business cards, getting to work, dressing for success, and the time required to market my services, learn new programs. Now, I had brick and mortar overhead that remained constant no matter how much or how little business I had. I covered my overhead gladly.

I was excited about the work. The work was extensive, drawing upon and stretching every bit of my experience and knowledge to date. One of my colleagues at The Relaxation Center had said that I was "really angry." I scoffed at her words, but never forgot them. Whatever could I be really angry about?

Soon, a reporter from a community newspaper, *Inside Recovery*, came to interview me. He asked me what the Center was about. This conversation pointed out the need to be succinct. His question pushed me to think along those lines, to reduce the excitement into few enough words to help others catch it, to engage them with a few simple ideas to illustrate what we were doing.

Another challenge pushed me to frame the work systematically. I tried formulating personal wellness plans. I thought it would be a simple matter. It was not. A dentist coming for treatment had requested a plan. I tried and couldn't do it. Not yet. Then, something else happened that would tie all the challenges together.

Women began coming to me with a need. They wanted to talk about their abuse. Their sexual abuse. Initially, I was stunned by this, but willing to hear their words because I thought my experience had prepared me to. Yet, I must have believed that my abuse was ancient history. Slowly, I began to see the connection between my clients' emotional pain and their physical pain. I took notes as I heard their words and treated their bodies. I began spending as much time listening to them as I spent touching them. My education as a healer was opening up an exciting new realm of work.

* * * * *

One client brought a tape series to the office. It was called "The Higher Self," by Deepak Chopra, M.D. I had never heard of him. She complained that she couldn't really understand what he was saying, but that his words reminded her of me. Touched, I took the tapes, popped them in and listened as I drove back and forth between home and the office. I was never the same after I began listening to Chopra. His words reached in, located the strands of my true calling and introduced me to a deeper, more holistic way of thinking. These special teachings were the map for my journey forward.

Soon after this, I mentioned these things to one of my colleagues. I told him about how the stories of sexual abuse were increasing in number. I told him about the Chopra tapes. He suggested that these things were happening because it was time for me to heal my abuse. I hadn't told him anything about that. How could my work now be taking me back to that story? It could and it was.

* * * * *

I found a women's support group for survivors of sexual abuse at Washington University's Psychology Department. I joined the group after being screened and invited. It was a rich and harrowing learning experience. For the first time I was in a place being asked to explore and speak about my pain, to take time to think about myself, my life, as it had been affected by that pain. I felt old emotion and said new words that broke through the façade of the life I had. I listened to other women speak. I was both excited and afraid. The facilitators were graduate students. One was a survivor, the other was not. Someone asked how long the healing takes. How long is the journey to recovery from sexual abuse once you begin? They suggested an average of five years. To a woman just turning forty, a woman as much in a hurry as always, five years seemed like a long time.

During the six months of the group sessions, I read as much as I could about the effects of sexual abuse. I would wake up crying, sobbing, emotions overflowing. At that time, John Bradshaw's popular PBS specials on the "inner child," would come on and I would spend entire weekends watching these specials, crying, being with that child who was not safe and could not speak. I had no idea I had carried around so much pain for so very long.

* * * * *

At the end of the group, I knew that the one thing missing from the experience we'd had was information about the mind/body connection, and ways to take care of and be responsible for our own healing. I looked for a program that included this. I didn't find it. I decided to develop one. Things were beginning to look very promising for my St. Louis practice. I had established a base, a solid and growing network, a following of clients, and was learning so much. My team was beginning to gel and to receive inquiries for corporate wellness programs. The seeds we had planted, the things we were learning, the vision we were creating, all of it was beginning to take hold and take off.

It was 1993. I had spent twenty-three years seeking ways to be authentic through my work, to do something I could love, and had finally found it. Little did I know, the excitement, the learning and the healing were just beginning.

Mister Magic

Within the years I'd known Rev. Golightly, I would *make* myself go see her, to help myself, to learn something, anything I could do to change things. Going to see her did change things. She told me just enough to help me stay strong and hopeful, but not enough to scare me.

Mostly, though, she told me about the men in my life. She told me to keep hope. That what I was going through would soooooon be over! Hallelujah. In one of my sessions, she said she saw some chickens, and chickens was "a good sign!" She advised me — that was what Rev. called herself, a "Spiritual Advisor" — to get as far away from Melvin as possible, and to stay there. No explanations.

She said that I would be married again, and be happy, that I'd have two more children. She also told me to be patient and not to worry. Meanwhile, she suggested I get myself a John the Conqueror Root, for protection. I was to wrap it in cotton and keep it somewhere on my body. If ever there was an important thing I had lived without, protection was it. Obedience to her wisdom was easy. A woman could use all the protection she could get. So, I'd go one step further and wear the root close to my heart.

Then she said the words I didn't want. She told me, in nineteen seventy-nine, that the older I got, the more like her I would become. The moment her words entered my ears, I strained hard to see myself having the gift of spiritual sight. Her words fell abrupt, forceful, like a bag of ice up side my head. What would I do with spiritual sight? Could I refuse this, please, ma'am? Not me, I said to myself, determined to shake it off. What else could she be talking about? I didn't know anything more about her. Then she "woke up" from her prayer, stopped talking and just rocked for another minute or so.

We walked back upstairs and, as usual, she said good-bye and quietly disappeared behind a curtain. The clerk carefully painted my root with blessed oil, wrapped, and put it in a tiny brown paper bag. And as I watched her work, I felt a surge of excitement. Something really good was happening. I really was changing things.

* * * * *

After two miscarriages I thought from time to time about mothering after thirty. My mother had adopted a baby boy. Loving him, helping raise him, seeing him grow reminded me of this, as if his presence activated an ancient code my body carried. Mother. So far, mothering had been my purpose.

Mothering summoned my creativity, kept me kicking, stretching and growing. More than an occupation, mother was a name, an identity. To be somebody's mother was to live in consciousness with and to reflect a set of holy commandments, assumptions, expectations. A sacred agreement between my body and God, mothering was a teacher, a guide, a blessing. It wasn't about me and my husband, for I had learned. I could not trust my husband with my dreams, and mothering was my dream, mine and mine alone. And for reasons he never explained and that I never asked, like clockwork, he would disappear whenever I became pregnant. Gradually, inevitably, bit by bit, leaving . . .

Mothering brought me voice . . . It brought me, through toil and sacrifice, precious children to take care of and protect.

Domesticity, my dream of family, alive in my heart of hearts, a hidden desire and gift is where I had started. Buy a house, make a home, run a household. Start with a structure and create an experience. Watch people grow and develop. That was what I was doing and I loved the fine art of it. But what model did I have for mothering, or even for pregnancy? Now that my children were growing up, I needed this language more than ever. I had always needed it but only now knew that. I needed it since I felt no other reason beyond mothering to be.

Being pregnant meant being on my own at my most vulnerable, living with silence, distance, intense longing, when I dreamed about feeling loved, loved when I needed love most, pregnant and most determined. Oblivious that everything I felt my baby felt, once again I stuffed the emotions, the sadness, rejection and uncertainty, as far down as I could to get through that ninth month. I took all the vitamins I needed and lived to get to the end of the heaviness in one piece, and through it all, to bring a healthy baby into the world.

A supreme commitment, mothering welcomes life through a door swinging between two worlds. I knew mothering only in ways that kept it remote from fathering, severed, as it had surely been on the plantation.

* * * * *

Toward the end of my time in Chicago, I found myself in a position that could have propelled me forward. I had received an unexpected promotion at work and was blindsided by the extra money, money that meant I was making the same amount as Melvin. Sudden money I didn't know what to do with. I saw an ad in the paper for a condo in a secure building in South Shore, just off Lake Michigan. I went to see it. Three bedrooms, two baths, fireplace, elevator, indoor parking. Fifteen thousand, nine hundred dollars. One hundred more for the assessment. I could easily have purchased this, rented it out, managed and held onto it. I asked Melvin about it, thinking I couldn't do such a big thing on my own. He said only, "no, don't do it." So, I didn't. I try not to spend time regretting things in hindsight. But this is one thing I have regretted. Wait a minute! I see that unbeknownst to me, this particular property is located in a red-lined zone and as such, would not enjoy the same rate of investment and appreciation as properties in white areas of the city. So, no need for regret.

* * * * *

Angie and Richie were becoming more and more independent. After much pondering, I vowed that any more children needed to come before thirty. I also prayed that my purpose beyond mother would reveal itself.

My mother-in-law had had thirteen children, Melvin being her middle child. Grandmother had been the youngest of thirteen. I had two children, and my dream was to have four. Children of the same man and woman. A new trend. We would create and cultivate something beautiful. Yet, like every other major decision, this one was also one-sided, taking shape in my mind only and coming with pain.

For I could not trust my husband with my dreams.

I would inform him once things were set and on course. I knew no other way. In my family, I had little experience of men as trustworthy, vulnerable and feeling people. I knew men who were beautiful on the outside, with hollow space beneath. These men did not make decisions. They mostly stayed out of sight.

In those rare times, those emergencies, when Melvin rose up and reminded me of his feelings, it was as if someone had grabbed and shaken me very hard. For he, loyal to his gender training, had worked nonstop to hide his feelings. And hide them he did, all of them, except his anger, and, by this time, he was pretty mad.

The years had been rocky, even replete with domestic violence (not the bodily harm kind, but the intimidation and power-over kind, as in immobilizing my car when I was at an event — removing the distributor cap, — stalking me, threatening to mar my face with a screwdriver, nabbing my baby in front of the church as we got out of the car, locking me in the bedroom while he took my children, as in fighting me for custody of them and hanging me up in court, taking away everything he knew that I loved as in Grandmother's silver, my favorite albums of music, destroying my wedding gown, and more). It was violence, a language of force to keep me in my place, reminding me that I was not in control of my life. Reminding me that I would not rule the nest. He would, and that's the way it would be until he gave up the fight.

The everyday things we needed to say to one another were said in the actions we took. It was true mainly because we knew very little about ourselves, apart or together. Mainly knowing we collided a lot, and we both believed it could be better. When even with all of this, as I began seriously considering my life without him, I got weak in the knees. After all, he had me convinced hands down that nobody else would ever be able to make me happy. Could he be wrong?

When I reached that certain point of recognition, of knowing, the point of no return, of needing to make a decision to free myself, I made myself consider my life in terms of freedom from violence and harm, and only then did light begin to shine. That is when I decided to move to Georgia and began taking steps to make the move.

* * * * *

I sought the counsel of my elders.

Grandmother asked me two questions. "Does he bring his money home?" "Does he love you and his children?" When I answered "yes" to both, she advised me to take stock of the good in what I had. My co-worker, Brother Beni, shed a different light on the subject, "Men begin to mature when they're about 35 or so . . ." he said. That was another ten years down the road.

This counsel needed interpreting. Here, I received wisdom about the bitter, dark side of marriage I was unprepared for, the side of marriage nobody came right out and talked about. Encoded wisdom I did not feel inclined to accept. So, I stepped around it, as if to avoid the hard work that came with those bitter, dark places. Stepping around it assured I'd revisit it in hindsight, when those ringing words began to make sense.

Life in this relationship was a struggle. I knew that I could not simply go to Melvin and announce my need to move forward, "Hey, Mel, d'ya wanna really get divorced now?" for fear of his reaction. For it was with panic that this mostly nonverbal man received change to his very steady routine. And panic for him sent ripples of the same, along with chaos, throughout my life. So, I created a kind of tentative, underlying plan to be free, a plan even I hadn't figured out, something sweet to look forward to, I kept stepping toward it, preparing for it, dreaming about it. Melvin and I had stopped living together the year before. With chaos, some years earlier, we had divorced legally but not emotionally. And although we had no idea what emotional divorce meant, my plan to be free was, simply put, motivated by something I later learned to call "emotional starvation."

In this paradox, I was entangled and would have to find my way out of these twisted places little by little as I gained strength, grew up, learned to respect myself more and more, and in a way that did not threaten him, I took the reins of my life.

He had taken a small basement apartment nearby, and we continued to see one another regularly. In this arrangement, he suddenly became very involved in the children's lives with things they did together, and, when things were peaceful, this would spill over onto my life as in him inviting me to participate. Although I did not participate and pretend that we were still a family, it was all I could do to keep the lines drawn. But I reminded myself that my children were safe with him, that I never had to worry about him abusing them. The default virtues. Here was yet another one that he would frequently remind me of. "We never argue." With his way of solving conflict, who would dare arguing with him? Then, of course, he added that he hoped I would "have the decency" to keep things the way they were. At other times, he would make light of the way things were. "Hey, I'll dance at your next wedding!" he'd smile and mock, . . . out of habit.

Initially Melvin blocked the move. Later, when I found and spoke the clear words I needed, words about feeling jailed and controlled by his maneuvers, those words got his attention. My open words shocked him into laughter. And after he heard me, he yielded. Open, clear language and dialogue were firsts, real language that created shockwaves, new understanding, and change.

* * * * *

My Aunt Dolores, by then living in Atlanta, had helped me make plans by listening, giving me job leads, introducing me to her friend who sold real estate. Her realtor sent me books with pictures of listings. I took a weekend subscription to the Atlanta Journal Constitution. I found and bought a house without Melvin, a bold move for me. And so, the weekend of Mother's Day 1980, the children and I moved into our new home in College Park, Georgia.

In the move, Melvin helped me get the children to Georgia. I wanted it all: my independence, change, more of life. With more space, more beauty, a warmer climate, better schools for the children, a better life.

* * * * *

Settling into the home environment was challenging. As though they were all non-existent, Nature encroached all boundaries of home. It was so quiet at night all you could hear were the crickets. In the mornings, all you heard were birdsongs. The gnats were so tiny, they flew in right through the little holes in the window screens. Bugs bigger than I had ever seen, shiny lines of slime across the carpet left by slugs, some without shells, appeared out of nowhere. There were baby frogs, turtles, lizards, you name it, none to be denied entry. One of the dogs next door ate our kitten alive right on our front lawn. The air was moist, thick, hard to breathe, like water vapor. Southern Nature would not behave.

Our house was a split foyer frame on a quarter-acre lot. There were no sidewalks on our streets. After dark, it was best not to drive the narrow, curvy roads, because streetlights were placed only at main intersections with few between. The time and distance from home to work was twice what I was used to. It didn't take long before this became a big deal, because I wanted to be home and present for the children, by now in 4th and 2nd grades. And, when we arrived, I was horrified to learn about the cases of Atlanta's Missing and Murdered Children. This created an urgent need to get home as fast as possible.

Grandmother had been gone for two years now, and, since I hadn't attended her funeral, I still stepped to the telephone, reached for the receiver . . . to call and tell her all about the new house and our new life . . .

* * * * *

I met Caroline, my new neighbor across the street who had a daughter about the same age as Angie and they became friends. I missed my friends back home so much that I called them frequently. So frequently Southern Bell called me one day to ask if there was a problem. The representative said that I was making so many long-distance calls that they wondered if everything was all right! Months later, when I couldn't pay my bill in full, they turned my phone off, that time without the call. Then, my Aunt Dolores asked me with that chuckle of hers, every chance she got, "When're ya gonna get that *phone* turned back on?" "When're ya gonna go back to schoooooool?"

* * * * *

Until that time, Melvin and I talked regularly. He visited too, when he could. I must have forgotten my spiritual advice, forgotten all that he put me through. I must have gotten scared in the course of moving. We shared whatever we had, and he continually provided for the children and me.

The holidays were approaching. Thanksgiving was my favorite. Joey, now in school in Atlanta and my friend, Kim, from Chicago, would both be with us for dinner. I began my celebration early. Melvin asked me to fly to Chicago and come to him. I took the children to Aunt Dolores, who dropped me off at the airport. Our plan was to have a couple of days alone. Then, we would head South for the holiday by car.

To my surprise, Melvin met me with flowers and a wrapped gift box. These things were rare, and meant a lot. Seeing him there dressed to the nines, smiling and waiting for me was too much! He took me to lunch at R.J. Grunt's, and we talked mostly about the children, about our jobs. I worked as an office manager at Emory, and loved that environment. We knew that

Louise was right. We had time ahead of us. We knew about the years that had gone, that we stood at the crossroads of what had been and what was coming.

The lush, red roses were fragrant. I opened my gift. A black lace negligee. Out of character, nicely so, for Melvin. He was telling me something I was happy to hear. He had reserved a room for us. For the very first time, he had painted a picture for the two of us, with the flowers, the food, the room, the gown. In the time we shared, we felt harmony, closeness, as though there were new parts of each other yet to explore.

With few words and steady ways, Melvin kept things going. With him around, I never worried about upkeep for the house or car. On the Saturday mornings that he didn't have to work, he'd be up and on the ladder painting, or cutting the grass, trimming the hedges, or taking the car in, before I knew anything. We did not discuss these things. He simply took care of them, and his work was always good. This offered me security, freed me up to deal with other things. The children, running the household. This was how he took care of us. By freeing me up. This is one of the ways I learned to understand masculinity. A man who was handy, took initiative, kept things in good working order and freed me up.

* * * * *

Once in Atlanta, he built a fire in the fireplace, went to hang out with my uncle, and left me to cook. I baked an apple pie with a whole grain crust. Joey politely took a knife to cut his piece of pie and, when the crust wouldn't yield to hard sawing, he asked with a smile, "what *is* this?"

Frankie Beverly and Mays. "*Joy and Pain. Like sunshine and rain.*" Energy was winding, giving, taking, rising all around us. Before the end of the holiday weekend, new life was stirring, and on the way.

* * * * *

Christmas would be different. Mel called to say that he would have only enough money to get to us for the holiday and to make sure this would be all right. We wanted him there more than we wanted gifts. By Christmas I had begun to feel pregnant, but did not talk about this. Too many unanswered questions. More stress than I could deal with. But by January, I was sure.

Melvin promised to seek a transfer to Atlanta, but by the time he decided to take action, A&P had all but folded. This sent him into depression. He became quieter than usual. Meanwhile I landed a new job within our department, but located downtown, about 15 minutes or 10 miles closer to home. Good change. Things rearranging for the better.

By April I was angry. And sad. How could this happen again? I wrote to my mother about it, and it wasn't until I read my words to her that I saw the connection between what had happened to me in 1969 and again now, in 1981! I couldn't believe it! My father asked why I was "still having babies for this man," for the one who couldn't quite come through. "What is wrong with you?" he demanded to know, stopping himself mid-sentence, almost saying something about my "inability." What right did he have to criticize me? Especially now?

* * * * *

The people I worked with were supportive and kind. Our research project was funded to study the effects of severe emotional disturbance of mothers upon their young children. The staff worked together like family. I learned a lot listening to the case studies and watching the women, hearing their words, seeing them interact with their children. Was any of this familiar?

My boss hosted my baby shower and everyone from the office came. I received gifts of all kinds, maternity clothes, everything I needed. Melvin was more distant than ever. Yet, with my lovely home, my healthy children, the baby on his way, a rewarding job, and good friends, I felt fortunate, even without his support. Melvin was consistent. I had to remind myself of this and keep going.

I worked full-time through the eighth month of the pregnancy, and planned to rest the whole ninth month. This pregnancy was very different because I was not as physically active as before. I gained about 35 pounds. Yet, I had no problems with water retention or high blood pressure. After about the fourth month, I felt just fine. Meanwhile, I had my favorite foods for comfort. Cottage cheese. Jalapeno brick cheese. Sardines. And, all summer long with an unquenchable thirst, I chewed crushed ice by the tumbler full.

As the time drew close, I knew it was important to pray for the baby. I prayed for a healthy baby with a sweet spirit. As planned, my mother drove to Atlanta with my baby brother in tow, to spend the week I was due to deliver. The doctors said I was progressing according to schedule, and that the baby was fine. We expected a normal delivery. That Sunday night, we had just retired for the evening and whooosh, my water broke! A surprise! With my first two deliveries, the water had been broken for me. I got up and told my mother who called the hospital right away. They said to time my contractions. We tried, but, they only came and went.

We called again with an update. The concern was for infection or dry birth. My mother drove us to the hospital on the dark Atlanta roads. They admitted me, gave me an enema, and told me there would be no food until after the birth. My doctor came the following day and examined me. He ordered oxytocin drops to get the labor underway. Once the drops were started, all hell broke loose.

* * * * *

Despite his parents' uncertainty, Alex was born in his own sweet time, healthy, peacefully, the following Wednesday afternoon, weighing 8 pounds, 4 ounces, measuring twenty inches in length. When I laid eyes on him and touched him, I was careful to say, "Welcome to the world, Alex Haley Jackson! I'm so glad to see you!"

Then, I made a big decision. I had my tubes tied immediately. I had vowed to have children by just one man, and in that moment, I closed that chapter forever.

It was a step.

* * * * *

Alex looked like his sister and brother, his complexion more like mine. Beaming with peace, he was born with just a patch of hair on top. Thanks to friends and family, we needed nothing. And, with enough milk to start a butter factory, I began nursing him immediately, successfully.

* * * * *

I remembered a ritual from the miniseries, "Roots," and, at the first full moon, I took Alex to the front porch, lifted him toward the heavens and declared, "Behold! The Only Thing Greater Than Yourself!" Richie and Angie couldn't believe it.

I had arranged things simply for my baby, nurturing him as he grew, shielding him from violent images, loud noises, and whatever outside forms of chaos that I could while I could. I sang to Alex, and had a special little song just for him.

There's somebody in the world that I love so much,
you're sweet as you can be.
There's somebody in the world that I love so much,
  you're precious in the world to me.

At his first Christmas, Alex portrayed the Baby Jesus and I was the mother Mary in the church Christmas play. In pantomime, we played our roles doing what we do naturally. At the end of the play, the people sang, *"Jesus, What a Wonderful Child,"* and Alex stood, smiled, and danced to the beat while I held him up by his fingers.

I nursed him for the first fourteen months of his life. I blended fresh fruit and vegetables every morning for him, and he always ate whatever I served him very well. By the time he began using his walker, it was as if he was learning how to fly. He would start at one end of the long hallway and go at top speed until he reached the other end. Sometimes I'd close the door at the other end and he'd stand and beat on the door saying, "open the door, open the door!!!" Alex changed our lives, slowed us down, brought a bright light into our days, and his brother and sister who had both witnessed his birth, helped me care for him, and watched him grow.

* * * * *

Melvin came to be with us and while there, took care of the baby. By now he was depressed because of the combination of a lingering back injury and being out of work. So, he stayed at home while I worked. We talked about things, how out of character for him the situation was, but he couldn't help it. He had worked himself into a rut. He couldn't climb out and he felt as if I "couldn't cope" with his "illness." It was an illness he hadn't named or described. Otherwise, he was correct. I couldn't cope. I could see it and feel it from my side of things, but I didn't know what I was looking at. He was still very hesitant to try expressing exactly what was going on. But he seemed happy to be there with the children. So, not knowing what else to do, I waited for a while thinking it would give him time to wake up, time to get unstuck, and when he didn't, I gave him a choice. I asked him to decide to either stay and work on himself, to be the man he could be and that we would start over. Or, to leave, but that if he left this time, it would have to be for good.

This was the most honest I had been about him and with him. And in my heart of hearts, I knew what his decision would be. But it had to be his, it had to come from him, so that we could begin the next new chapters of life in a way that was best for all of us.

As we talked and listened to each other that night, like another kind of birth, the truth emerged. He admitted that he had "known all along" what I had wanted from him, and added that he just couldn't bring himself to give it. He was talking about intimacy. It had been too frightening for him. I was surprised to hear him say this. I was afraid, too. If he had given me what I wanted "all along," what would that have been like? I was so accustomed to his game that, truly, I couldn't imagine our lives any other way! Too much honesty for one sitting!

What I could imagine was humiliation, being played with, but thankfully, this hurt was fleeting. More important, more urgent for me were questions, questions about being a single mom for real, for good. Could I take care of everything on my own, be independent? I was willing to try now if I really couldn't count on him. What we said to each other then was more honest pain. Knowing we had come to the end of a very long and challenging struggle, that we had completely run out of words, options, mileage is when we cried together.

Before he left, he said something else. "You will always be number one."

* * * * *

And when Melvin Jackson left, Richie, now age 10, cried his primordial cry once more. Then, automatically and without question, he took on the "man of the house" role, protecting his baby brother, asking me questions about where I was going and who with, repairing whatever was broken around the house, or trying to. Doing the yard work. I even bought a small riding mower for him, since by then, our new custom built Decatur brick ranch, had almost an acre of grass. I thought this was just the way males worked. I was proud of my son, not knowing that this was a role he didn't need, that he needed to be allowed to just be a growing boy until he was a growing boy no more. And the most relevant song I remember from that time was "I Keep Forgettin'" by Michael Macdonald.

That was the end of August, just after Alex's first birthday.

I was fortunate enough to find good, affordable home-based day care nearby that I had to change a time or two. He was a healthy, happy baby, easy to take care of.

* * * * *

Alex the toddler was mostly content. He knew he was loved and cared for. This was my objective as his mother. But, as he grew, I got the feeling that he thought he needed to catch up with his sister and brother, an impossible feat. And I kept him close to me, hoping to calm the hurry and settle him back into his own time.

Alex grew to preschool age and I enrolled him in a day school nearby where he transitioned easily to classroom settings and being with his peers. He loved music and would sing from his heart. He loved a song called *"Suddenly"* by Billy Ocean . . .

"life has new meaning to me. . . . wake up and suddenly, you're in love."

Singing with his mouth and eyes wide open, his round face sincere and centered, Alex sang like the lone performer on his planet, singing a song for one. When he was little, he really loved family movies like "The Never Ending Story," "The Blues Brothers," and "The Gods Must be Crazy."

* * * * *

Given my experience with Melvin, I made it a point to get my children talking. I would ask them what they thought whenever we went to see a movie. I encouraged them to express within the family circle. Just before Alex was born, we went to see the movie, E.T. It was very touching for all of us. In the parking lot, looking for the car, Richie told me urgently, "Mommie, I'm sorry for all the bad things I've ever done!" and I silently prayed for more movies like E.T.

Not very long after this, we were driving home one Saturday and ran directly into what looked like the aftermath of a Ku Klux Klan rally. White men riding on the backs of pickup trucks, wearing white sheets and hollering, "NIGGER!" All just about a mile from our home. Having never seen anything like this in person before, the three of us were horrified, and I told my children over and over, as calmly as I could, "it's all right; don't be afraid." Alex was just a baby then, and did not know what was happening. When we got home, we sat and tried to talk about what we had seen and felt.

* * * * *

PART III

WOMANING

1990s & 2000s

Prime Time, Part One

Looking back to that promising decade of the 1980s, the skies were clearer as new doors opened to us and we walked in, the very first generation to do so. In that time, love was fresh and redefined for our emergence, our music now lavish, orchestrated, our songs longer, liquid-like. Our maestros set this love to a melody and tempo to usher us through those open doors and into the shiny new world of our middle-class dreams.

This 30-year-old, hard-working, home owning mother of three had climbed from a Midwestern, fast-paced, urban life into a slower, Southern suburban one. As a woman whose existence orbited my children's lives, there was no way to miss what was happening now. They were approaching the portal to the dreaded teenage stage, I was holding my breath as we entered the Unknown Zone, their mysterious growing up time, watching it, letting it unfold. There were times when I wanted to stop the clock. But how? On my own I performed my duties pretty well, but the music had reached me, too. I'd been listening, remembering the other part of my dream, feeling lonely for companionship, for a loving bond that would survive this mothering season.

With so much to do, I gave myself credit for the line in the sand I'd recently drawn. After fourteen years, I had put my foot down, closed and locked the swinging door between Melvin and me. This time he had no key. Gulp. Moving on, considering my future, and in this quiet prayer, I asked myself what felt like a bold question. What kind of man did I want? Could I list his attributes?

Yes, I'd been to The Circus. Now I was woman enough to carefully spell out what I wanted in That Man. And drafted a strong list from my deepest imagining. Then, I wondered. What if I overlooked something essential? That wouldn't do.

So, I prayed.

Lord, it's time. You know what I need much more than I do. Won't You send me the one You have set aside, just for me? Thank You. And so it is.

After my prayer, I knew it was now time for me to DO something. Unless I started going out, I wouldn't meet anyone. But where to go? I asked Marjorie, a graduate student from work to meet me for Happy Hour at a new place I'd heard about. She agreed. Seven-thirty. We would hang out for a couple of hours and unwind after the long week.

It was Friday, December 10, 1982. I told the children my plan to go out to a place close by. Then, by the time I'd fed them and sat down, I quickly dozed off. When I opened my eyes and looked at the clock, I began to waver. I'd gotten comfortable. I could call Marjorie and cancel. There'd be other Fridays, of course. I told Angel.

"No Mom. You need to get out of the house. We'll be all right. Go on!"

She convinced me. I splashed a handful of cool water on my face, got ready and went. This was my first Mom's Night Out. As I drove, I let myself feel the excitement *and* the fear! For the first few minutes of driving, I teetered between "This is it!" and "What am I doing?" That is, until I parked my little car and had walked through the front doors of this new place called Babe's.

On the ground floor of a small hotel set back from the main road, the club occupied the rest of the open space beyond the registration desk. The atmosphere was relaxed and intimate, the space accented by layered, limestone walls and a two-sided fireplace. The far corner of the room opposite the desk had pool tables where some guys were playing. As if I knew where I was going, I went quickly to the back area where I found the bar, the DJ's booth, the dance floor and a few small tables. I scanned the place for Marjorie and didn't see her. No one was in the back except for the bartender. I picked a place to wait, sat and took my coat off, bent over to adjust my boot, and now saw two feet standing next to mine.

I sat up slowly and let my eyes follow the legs, body and face of a man dressed in a plain black suit.

"Do you mind if I join you?" Said the big smile.

"Help yourself!" Straight face.

"My name is Ramon." He extended his hand.

I smiled back, answered, and met his handshake.

In the ice breaking and fact finding he told me that he was married, the father of four children, but that his marriage was "on the rocks." Yet he wore a ring. They were separated; he had left the marriage in his move to Georgia. I appreciated his honesty. Four children? That's a lot. Born in the Carolinas.

Turns out we had arrived in Atlanta at about the same time. When I said where I was from, and that I was a vegetarian, he looked shocked. He'd never met anyone who didn't eat meat. Then he asked my birthday. When I told him, more shock. This felt weird until he took out his wallet to prove that his birthday was that same day, only a few years earlier! That's when we exchanged phone numbers. With my first drink, my defenses and my short-term memory began to soften. I kept asking his name, and patiently he kept repeating it. Ramon. By my second drink, I was too tipsy to be embarrassed. And so, knowing I had to drive home, I stopped drinking.

Incredibly handsome, very well-spoken and with a proud, radio quality voice, an educated man with an arresting presence. A departure from the males I had known.

"Are you ready for the '80s?" Another big smile.

"What do you mean by that?" I could assume, but I wanted him to tell me...

As we talked, Marjorie showed up, checked on me with her eyes, smiled, and sat at my other side. I introduced her to Ramon, filled her in on what she'd missed, and the DJ fired up the evening's music.

Ramon wanted to know what I like.

"Do you dance?"

"Ha! Don't worry about me on the dance floor. Do you think you can keep up, my brother?"

He took my hand and we laughed like old friends walking to the small parquet floor. He extended his other hand and we began our slow dance. I was curious about Marvin Gaye's *"Sexual Healing,"* just what was it, beside the first song we danced to?

This man's perfect height and warm skin invited me in, and I rested my head just a little on his broad shoulder. Contoured precisely for my head, that space between his neck and shoulder welcomed me. Our first dance was tender and magical. I felt at home with him, sort of, and could not stop smiling and relaxing, in brief, alternating waves.

At evening's end, I was grateful for such a short drive home and for the cool breeze in my face as I drove with the window slightly cracked. I pulled into my driveway dazed and happy to find my children, the house, and Frederick the dog, standing safe and sound. Mom's Night Out had worked just fine.

* * * * *

Right away, Ramon started calling, and I felt hurried and unsure about the whole thing.

"Hello?"

"Well, hello there! I've been trying to reach you, but haven't had much luck."

"I'm sorry."

"How about we meet tonight?"

"I can't."

"Oh . . . ?"

"I've got a lot going on here at home, you know, with the kids and all."

"Look, this is nothing serious. We just met. I want to see you. That's all."

"Let me think about it."

"Just come on out. A friend of mine has this after-work thing on Candler Road. Meet me there. If you don't like it, we don't have to stay. What do you say?"

I went. It was a professional get-together with fancy finger food. The more we talked, the more I liked him. It turned out he attended church with his mother right across the street from where I worked. He wanted to get to know me. We went to lunch a few times. He was generally upbeat and cheerful, easy to be with, to talk with, and these conversations added thrill to my routine. I was helpless. The man was thrilling.

We began to date. He didn't know how to dress. Not at all, but I decided to overlook that for the time being. His body. Muscular, not like a jock or anything, just really sculpted and solid. His smile was like sunshine, his touch made water in dry places, and the sound of his voice was my personal music. I liked him more and more, and just as the year came to an end, I invited him to come and meet the children.

Naturally, they were standoffish. By then, Angie was 12, Richie was 10, and Alex was not quite 18 months.

* * * * *

Soon, we fell in love. The next two years with him turned my life inside out. Pause. Rewind. The falling in love was not immediate nor was it simple. In answer to my prayers, I recognized and received a strong, influential sign of coincidence. Synchronicity. If by then I was in any way unsure that we were supposed to be together, little messages kept me convinced and encouraged. Numerous times on the expressway, someone with his three initials on their license plate would cut in front of me and hang out there. Rather than get upset, I just smiled.

The love songs of that time were so fine. Quincy Jones' *"Just Once," "Baby Come to Me," "One Hundred Ways," "How do You Keep the Music Playing?"* and Michael Jackson's *"Lady in my Life,"* were ours alone, as Ramon drove me crazy, slowly rocking his pelvis from side to side while we slow danced. We sang the world's best music into each other's ears and candy coated our moments over and over with sweet, sweet love.

* * * * *

During our first year of dating, he finalized his separation. When he told me it was happening I stepped away from him and remained silent until it was complete. He'd leave messages on my answering machine saying that it was "painful," but I would not comment or engage the conversation. This was their business, and I wanted no part of it. I thought that if he could finish this on his own volition, then, just maybe we would be all right.

* * * * *

But my struggle started with the love. Love. My driving force, true, but the closer I came to it, the less I comprehended it. My life was a sacred space, a busy place, filled with action and responsibility, but who wanted me? Major decisions would impact my family. The relationship soon became intense, presenting me with a double, magical, complicated pressure. With the intensity, I sold our little home and moved us to a larger one. Then, once I knew that the relationship pressure was mine alone, I found an affordable condominium and moved us again. It was a nice enough place tucked away in Clarkston, where the schools were really good. Then, not long after we settled in, I lost my job! Mom said that it was "the best thing that could have happened." That may have been true for the long run, but what would I do for income now?

Sure, I was worn down and bored to tears by office work. I needed new direction. But, this was not even embryonic thinking. How does a black woman with a family to support take action on anything pre-embryonic? I ventured no place. Without viable options, I felt stuck where I was. I signed up for unemployment insurance benefits and registered with an agency that sent me out on long-term assignments, some even close to home. With this, I earned enough for everything but the mortgage. I qualified for assistance, but never applied. I refused to raise my children with that stigma. Stigmas for the women in my family were frowned upon. As I write this, I am reminded that these women were not the ones raising my children.

And so, when the heat in the kitchen of my complicated life reached a boiling point, I would find a cost-free escape where I even lost time. That's right, I would drive around the corner to the Wallpaper Store. Wallpaper — something to totally rework and re-create a room — was a craze in the 1980s. And this special store sold only wallpaper. I'd go in and disappear. The store even had a closet with stacks and rows of sample catalogues. After I'd browsed the store and absorbed the latest trends in color combinations and fabrics, I'd ask to see the catalogues, knowing I'd be escorted into a private space where I could sit and look and touch and imagine having that kind of pattern, texture, ambiance, that kind of beauty in my home. Imagining yet more beauty in my life, imagining how much better and sweeter, more appropriate, and classy everything would be with more beauty on the walls. Before I knew it, I had spent over an hour of luxury in total solitude at the Wallpaper Store. And I came back to myself, realized that my children were in the parked car outside, waiting for me. I went to them, and there they were, with my Angel, crying. She said she thought something had happened to me.

* * * * *

Meanwhile, on the other side of so much life change, Melvin began to stir. He was curious about my newfound independence. That year the kids and I flew to Chicago for Christmas where their father and I spent time finishing our conversation. We stayed at Joey's place where the TV was always on. Cable, where they showed the same movie over and over, was all the rage then. As we came and went, I kept seeing snippets of "Arthur," with Dudley Moore, and hearing the movie's theme about getting "caught between the moon and New York City . . ." And to this day, every time I hear that song, I think about Christmas 1982 in Chicago.

After our visit, Richie said that his father had asked him if I had a boyfriend, and that he had happily replied, "yes, Ramon!" In no time flat Melvin announced through his son that, since I now had a boyfriend, I should "get (my) money from him." Until that time, he had been semi-faithful with child support. We had been to court so many times I don't remember what amount of child support we had agreed to. He had fought me tooth and nail every step and stitch of the way out of the marriage. Now, accepting my new life pushed him as far away as he could get: to the west coast where he disappeared. I pursued child support. After the turtle hurtles and legal red tape, I finally began receiving regular checks in the amount of sixty dollars a month. It was low because Melvin was now, consistent with what he was trying to tell me when he left, "disabled." This last development boosted my average monthly income to just shy of $800.

To supplement this, I brought home my typewriter from work and started a weekend typing service. I posted flyers in the Emory student center to publicize my service and got calls now and then from graduate students and lawyers. I charged $2.00 a page for typing all kinds of things — term papers, short stories — and for us this little bit of extra money was like gold. I even considered ways to grow that business, but, it was all I could do to manage everything I had going already.

* * * * *

I gathered my wits and forged ahead. As best he could, Ramon kept me inspired and supported. He even expressed resentment for my pursuit of child support. "Forget him; I'm here now," he told me. But with Ramon, money was a pretty tricky subject, registering anywhere on an emotional scale from *neutral* for amounts of less than fifty dollars, *delicate* for amounts between sixty and ninety, to *raw* for anything beyond one hundred. I made these delineations by the volume and length of his hems and haws when the subject and amounts of money came up. While I saw money as something to work for and handle carefully (although at the time money used me much more than I used it), I soon learned that for this man, money was one of life's weapons, and, for the duration, with or without it, money was his Achilles heel. This fact would take me some time to learn to navigate.

* * * * *

Once we reached our first dating anniversary, I got the exciting idea to break the silence and propose marriage! In my mind — where all my communicating was happening — one year was a real landmark, long enough for water testing and to see if the boat would float. Besides this, as a mother in my thirties, raised in the church, I had no time to waste. This anniversary would have been hard enough if I was merely a single woman, but as a Single Mom, come on, now! Despite the deliciousness of this arrangement, I had no idea how to stay cool and "just have a boyfriend,"—as he referred to himself — have an intimate relationship with a scrumptious man with a truckload of potential, and no plan whatsoever for marriage.

To prepare for our special evening, I practiced the two sweet songs my parents had swooned by, *"Our Love is Here to Stay,"* and *"The Nearness of You."* These old songs said exactly what I felt and wanted to say to this man. To celebrate the occasion, I bought a bottle of wine and a special cup with a sky blue "Aquarius" sign, a cup large enough for two, and wrote a poem.

Once I had everything set, I asked Ramon to come over. Surprising him was never easy because he always asked so many questions. Sometimes I knew the answers, like now. At other times my idea could still be percolating. And at those times I wished he would just shut up and trust me but, there was something else.

He hated surprises! But I loved him, never tired of doing things for him, things I didn't want to convince him were worthwhile. I loved making him smile, which he always would, once the surprise wore off. This part of him was tough for me since surprises were my specialty. I had given everybody

I loved the most a surprise birthday party. Grandmother, Mom, Melvin, my children. Hands down, he was next in line.

* * * * *

As a young woman, my verbal communication was slow going. I left at least half of what was going on in my head right there. Saying everything was taxing work. Saying everything was risky. Saying everything was something I had never seen or heard of. No woman in my family or my home community that I knew of had been transparent, spontaneous, or totally open with her words. What's more, from what I had learned so far, womaning involved strategies and plans to be thought through, built up, and implemented slowly. This was a process, like conceiving, gestating and delivering. Although my thinking had to take shape, warm up and incubate in my own head before I could mention or try to describe it, whatever "it" was, the truth about it is this. My thinking was always light-years ahead of any man I knew, and so, keeping him informed of my thoughts was a risk, a chore, a thing I was not at all sure I could do safely or with proficiency. There was nothing simple about it. I'm trying to describe what all went into the way I talked as a young black woman living intimately with men at early stages in my young life, and without full awareness of or any language for my experience of oppression. So, I safeguarded my dreams, ideas, and plans from men who would most assuredly try stamping them out if only with their words.

This caused problems for Ramon. I couldn't just give him "a straight answer" when he asked me something and of course, he assumed I was being coy! In fact, over time, he even began accusing me of keeping a "separate agenda," questioning my motives and loyalty, although I was never unfaithful to him. His distrust was much, much older than our relationship. From the start, it made me uncomfortable, like something that disagreed with my stomach. But I figured I could deal with this, too! Enough time would prove me. He'd see. I thought this part of it *was that simple.*

Nada. Ramon's suspicion falsely accused me. I fit the profile of the suspect, I was arrested in the vicinity of a crime I did not commit. It was my job to prove my innocence. Crazy making premises. Turns out Ramon's hurtful suspicion was related to things I'd learn more about later.

The same was true with his anger, (or, shall I call it rage?) his other ultimate weapon, and money's bookend. Early on, he'd warned me about it, even described it as some remote part of himself that I "never wanted to see." During those years, his own version of Mt. St. Helen's, erupted twice. Both times when nobody else was around, this twisted wind and fire blew from his mouth in a storm of words directed, of course, to me. For a moment or so, he became Dragon Man, capable of great destruction. Dragon Man's steamroller legs flattened and left me in the middle of the road, toasted, ground into the pavement. And then both times, after he came back to himself, he picked me up, dusted me off, and apologized profusely.

* * * * *

Nevertheless, I loved me some Ramon. Nevertheless, I could not hold this or any list of "challenges" as the sum of what was true about him. What was true about him as I saw it was that he had a good heart, he was kind, articulate, sensitive. He listened to me in a way that no man ever had, he understood me — we understood each other — and this is what I knew. He loved me. He gave me a love that I had waited all my life to know. He was gentle and helpful with my children. This is what I would hold onto and build upon. This is the compartment that I hoped would save itself, that I would wait for, that I wanted to come back to, that I counted on to be there, waiting after the storms passed, once he was ready to retire, when everything and everyone else was gone, when the way for our time as a couple had come, the road to it was finally clear and the traffic light forward was green.

I especially loved the sound of his voice. He couldn't carry a tune, but he didn't have to. His voice reverberated so well that he could speak his way through a song better than many could sing it. I loved listening to him speak. He had a litany of sayings that he would keep handy for use as needed.

Now, that's a tall order.
I'm just trying to get somewhere.
I have no illusions left.
It's clear as a bell to me.
Wrong answer, Buddy!
I keep the high ground.
I won't fall on my sword.
I won't shoot myself in the foot.
We don't do no knee-jerk reactions.
Let me see how I can make that happen.
Patience!
I don't want nobody who don't want me.
I feel a movement in the Force.
... Now, not to be outdone ... ,

There were more like this, little things he would say at just the right time to help alleviate confusion, provide levity, and even restore the peace. His voice came with gifts of peace where his words and presence would calm us.

And even though he couldn't sing, he did have a few songs at the drop of a hat ... mostly singing to himself.

" ... Or, will you walk ... out the door like you did ... once before ..."

"Someone's sneakin' 'round the corner ... could that someone be Mack the Knife?"

"Go Stagger Lee! Go Stagger Lee!"
"I'm a hog for you baby, can't get enough of your love!"
"With these last two dollars, I'm not gonna lose!"
Yes, I was smitten with just the sound of his voice.

* * * * *

But for now, did it matter that I kept quiet about my deepest thoughts, hopes and desires? Did I notice that this was the way it was? With him deferring to me for the little things like what to eat, where to eat, yet expressing what he really wanted in painful, sometimes passive ways on high volume, while I did the opposite? And what about those times when he would talk aloud to himself right in front of me, questioning and answering himself, as if he really was alone, as if to show me the place inside himself that he hid from the world, where he stashed and kept his secrets? What about how alone I felt in those moments? Did it matter that I was busily managing all things mundane and freeing him to concentrate on the major things that required his attention, so that having an honest relationship would take a whole other kind of effort, starting from scratch, without instructions or examples? Who knew what that was?

Now and then, though, it did feel as if we naturally complemented each other in our roles. That was a good feeling, a cool, quickly evaporating sensation, like rubbing alcohol. And, I learned about abuse in that marriage. The what's and why's of it. How to recognize, name, call it out and change it. I wrote my first book in that marriage, a book about abuse. These are the things I can't say I was willing to overlook in the beginning, because, again, I couldn't fully see them. My eyes could not see them, not for quite a few years. Nevertheless, I wanted this to work so much that I expected to be able to work blind miracles, push past the hurtles and make all of it go.

* * * * *

Back to December 10, 1983. When he arrived at the house, I was ecstatic. I drove us to a small, secluded area tucked away at the back end of my neighborhood. The evening was cool and clear. Once we found the little wooden footbridge over a stream, we both stood there and enjoyed the full moon's glow. As I sang to him, he blushed, took my hands, joined in, and we sang together. Then I read him my piece and popped the question. Caught off guard, he was dumbfounded.

That's when Ramon's barreling voice fell silent. Now in this awkward moment, I waited patiently, sure that he would rebound and respond with love and when he didn't, my heart sank. Out of my element with this move, with no plan beyond asking, I was unprepared for the silence. In my rehearsing, I hadn't considered the possibility of rejection. Was his silence rejection? Whether it was or not I'd have to wait and see, but while I waited, it sure felt like it. Wordless, we slowly drove back to the house.

Finally, we argued.

I told him what I knew. I said what Grandmother had told me about the cow, the cream, and the man not needing to buy. That infuriated him. He left. There it was again. How and why was it that the "M" word continued to be his open sore, smarting whenever I touched it?

* * * * *

He was rebuilding his military career according to plan. He would take another year of exercises in Florida and apply for a six-month training in Missouri to begin after that. He completed these exercises, and then got the approval for the training. Even with sketchy details, we each had plans and dreams. His revolved around a career, mine revolved around a marriage. Soon, the New Year rolled in.

In what would amount to two more years of dating, like it or not, I had a boyfriend. And I learned how to have a boyfriend, a man whose role in my life beyond loving me was undefined. A man I loved. A man worth waiting for. A man I loved to watch doing manly things, like shave. I had never been around a shaving man. A ritual of "ablutions," he used a razor and lather first thing every day. And the process of dating, growing closer over time, was exciting. We enjoyed good food, good movies, clubs, live performances, and house parties, in that order. We danced and laughed together a lot.

It was 1984 and we moved through another year. He spent the night with me at least once each week, and I cherished every second we spent together. We spent regular family time, too, with dinners and holidays. That Fall, my Aunt Dolores died suddenly of respiratory arrest. Her boyfriend called that night from the hospital with the news, and I said I didn't believe him. Ramon was there with me, so I didn't have to feel the shock alone. It was really true. She was gone. Just like that. Beyond belief. Gone, and her sudden loss was a heavy weight, more than I could bear much less begin to grieve... So, I put it away.

* * * * *

We got along. That is, until the subject of marriage cropped up. When it did, he would try to ease his way out of the conversation. I resented that the decision was solely his, and that while I waited for him to move, the question/the waiting solely mine.

Even though these were things I did not discuss with my children, my daughter once said to me. "Mom, it looks like he has all the benefits of being married without the responsibility of it." As usual, she spoke beyond her years.

I reasoned with myself. Marriage was the next logical step. We talked at length about almost everything else. Our children got along well. We truly felt like family when we put the bunch together. He had introduced me to his mother, and the two of us developed a friendship. When his brother came to town, it was tons more of the same. Together, those two were like a fireworks show, ready to explode any time of the year! As I got to know his brother, thinking now of the extra energy that it took to be in the same room with him, with the pair of them, the song, *"True"* by Spandau Ballet takes me back to those hilarious moments.

Of Ramon's four children, he had custody of his two eldest while the youngest two lived with their mother. He would visit them but only rarely discuss them. His eldest son, Ramon, Jr. was headed to college the following summer. I would help him raise Rudy, his younger son. Rudy and Richie were one year apart in age. Rudy would stay with us whenever his father was working an exercise. By then, the boys naturally referred to each other as "brothers."

I realized Richie had artistic talent when, smiling as if he had surprised himself, he showed me his beautiful pencil sketch of a horse. I soon enrolled him in a weekend art class at the mall. Of sports, he loved Michael Jordan most. With Rudy, he watched the football games, and collected miniature helmets. They read Teenage Mutant Ninja Turtles comic books, and played PacMan and Super Mario in the local arcade, the dark place where kids gathered, bought tokens, and lost themselves for an hour or two at a time to those big, noisy machines.

* * * * *

Clearly, and perhaps even understandably, the subject of marriage frightened Ramon. He wanted to buy time and keep things the way they were for as long as he could. Rather than explain this, he just did it. With his sense of independence, he worked things out in his mind first. Very similar to what I did, but I didn't notice this parallel so easily at the time.

Still, I silently yearned for things to progress. During the hardest times when neither of us had very much, we shared resources, and the sharing seemed to make everything go farther, as in yeast, water, flour, and dough. Assured that breadmaking was not only the next logical step, I knew it was the next practical step, too. In my mind and heart, this was not a question of "if," but of "when."

* * * * *

By the end of 1984, enough time had passed without my taboo subject coming up too much. Now it was Christmas Eve, and we spent that whole night wrapping presents. He had helped me buy gifts for the children. As we wrapped them, he fell silent, took my hand, looked into my eyes, and sincerely, said the words,

"Will you marry me?"

Unbelievable, I thought.

"Yes; when?" I asked.

"Let's not worry about a date yet. Let's just agree that we're gonna make it happen," he said with that bright smile, then he took me in his arms, kissed me, and I was lost.

And found!

At long last, Ramon had spoken these clear, direct words to me. Knowing and feeling the deep assurance that I was now a woman engaged to be married, knowing the truce to keep us from fighting about the "M" word, knowing my wait for that question was all over, was comfort and relief! Knowing the time we spent getting to know and learning to love one another was well spent, knowing that the man of my dreams had finally asked me to marry him in his time was my best Christmas gift ever. At last, I could live like a normal woman, an Honest Woman — not fully understanding *that* concept — but in that moment, I began to fully breathe.

When I broke the news to my mother, reflexively, she asked to see my ring. I told her I didn't have one. She said an engagement is not official until the man gives a ring. Why? Why had she not told me this before? But wait. It's that way in the movies, and that makes it true! Somewhere I read that the engagement ring is a symbol of a man's appreciation.

Why was there always some other thing, one more twist that I didn't know about? Why did the man's every move hold the power to completely change a woman's life? Like water off of a duck's back, I let Mom's words roll. She didn't know. How could she know how much work and patience in two years it had taken just to get engaged, and I would not try explaining any more than I had already. Now, I knew things finally felt right and in place. For now, the agreement to be "engaged" — even without diamonds — was real enough for me.

* * * * *

Meanwhile the kids and I still lived more or less from day to day. But this new future on the horizon put an extra twinkle in my eyes. Now this young mother in the prime of life was also a woman happily engaged to a beautiful man with so much of life to look forward to. I had always known I wanted more from life than what I had in Chicago and with Melvin. But if anyone had asked me to be specific about my dream, I couldn't have gone beyond the larger family, the husband, the house with a fireplace, because beyond the sense of bliss, I had few details. I just knew I wanted more, that I was determined to have more. Now, here it was. Suddenly, besides doing a good job as a mother, homemaker and being a good secretary, besides high-level functioning in all of these areas, I now felt for the first time truly beautiful and totally sensual. No man had ever loved me with compliments and affection. Ramon's attention encouraged me and drew new happiness and joy out of me, as if they had been there all along, just waiting to be called.

That year, Barbra Streisand released, *"The Way He Makes Me Feel,"* a song I loved to sing, one that expressed exactly what this new time felt like . . .

"I feeeeeel as if I'm floating every time I close my eyes . . ."

Every breath I inhaled was an elixir. I sang, smiled and laughed constantly. I was high, and my whole life exploded with promise. I felt wanted and loved, and this love, albeit imperfect, was my invisible blanket. I felt good in my bones, so good I wanted to tell everyone, but most people were far away. So, I kept it for just us two. Just as his lotiony love smoothed my body, his nourishing words kept me well fed. Like the soulful groove of my favorite song, the sight, sounds and feel of him and his love settled and moistened my mind. I was a ripe pomegranate attracting hummingbirds that hovered overhead and then chased me for my juice. It was the summer of my life and I was aglow with awe over absolutely everything.

* * * * *

"Every time you go away, you take a piece of me . . ."

Just before he left, I went ahead and gave him a surprise Going Away party to celebrate the occasion. As he prepared to leave, this new song came out as if once again, some songwriter was eavesdropping on us. What in the world would I do for six whole months without Ramon? The night he left, I cried like a baby.

We phoned each other often, wrote letters and sent cards. I visited him. He bought the new car he needed. We went to

Helzberg Diamonds, and I selected a channel diamond wedding set. As we signed the papers, he assumed silent, slow motion, moving as if dreading the transaction. I assured him it was all right, rubbing his leg and arm and back, trying to bring him back to us, to pull him back from whatever memory mire had trapped him. Again.

* * * * *

Richie, 12 by then, had taken up with a new neighbor boy who had already been in the county juvenile detention center. When the officer came and explained about some trouble they'd gotten into, I whipped and corrected my son for his misdeeds, fainting in the process! Some part of me — that thing that keeps my legs standing up straight — suddenly fled when I raised my voice with all my might. Without that thing, I fell to the floor like an emptied potato sack.

My son was seriously misbehaving, I didn't understand why, and I was trying to solve the problem alone. My son had enormous potential and this is the way he was using it. I was blinded by my anger, and I tripped over my own body. I did not feel myself fall, but heard myself thump against the wall and into the hallway floor. I was probably "out" for only a minute or two, but awoke to the sound of Richie's cries as he stood over me, "Maaaaaaaa maaaaaaa!" The sight of me in the floor may have gotten to him much more than my scolding. Too great a price for either of us, that was the last time I used all my might to correct him.

My first inclination was to imagine the year ahead in terms of Richie's development. He was at a very crucial age. I had an idea. What if I applied for a Big Brother for him, someone to mentor and listen to him as he matured? I called and made an appointment where they interviewed us both. But when I told Ramon the story and mentioned this idea, he took offense and asked me a probing question.

"Just what am I, chopped liver?"

That stumped me. It's the very question I'd been asking him in different ways and so carefully, for more than two years now. "Who are you in my life?" "Where are we?" "What will this relationship mean to my family?" "Is there a future in this?" But, so long as I was the one asking, we didn't get very far.

* * * * *

Not knowing how else to juggle Ramon's ego with my son's immediate needs, I canned the Big Brother idea. As for Richie, I stayed in his face, tightened his circle of activity and paid closer attention. I knew that once I was married, I wouldn't have to face this challenge and uncertain time in the life of a precocious teenage boy as a single mother taking my next steps ever so cautiously. The marriage will end my struggle and prove to be good for all of us.

Daddy. It was a hole in the family that we all saw and sought to fill.

* * * * *

"Who's Melvin?" Alex, now three, just came out and asked me one day.

"What? Where did you hear that name?"

"Richie said it."

I did not elaborate. I was surprised. He had a right to know the story, but I hadn't planned on talking with him about his father until he could understand more. But he brought it up himself. Now in pre-school, one evening as we drove home, he said even more.

"Mommy, the kids at my school have a Mommy AND a Daddy." I thought about what he was saying and smiled at him.

"That's what I want, too," he said and smiled back, so proud of himself. Apparently, this was already important to him, something he had been thinking about and had kept on his mind because, at Thanksgiving dinner, he turned to Ramon and spoke in an audible whisper.

"Ramon,"

"Yes?"

"Will *you* be my Daddy?"

Ramon took a breath. "Yes, I will."

As Alex smiled and relaxed with satisfaction, there was not a dry eye at the table.

* * * * *

Daddy. Angel stopped me one afternoon and asked to talk. I sat down with her on the side of her bed.

"What is it? Is everything okay?"

"Sure, but I've been wondering about things, Mama."

"Yes, about what, Honey? Tell me."

"Well. I just . . . It's different for me, Mama. When I think about the new marriage, here's how I see it." She paused and took a breath or two.

"Richie's getting a brother. Alex is getting a father. You're getting a husband. What about me? What am I getting?"

"Oh, my! Well, for starters, you're getting a father and a brother, just the same as your brothers. Don't you know that? Everyone in the family will be blessed by this marriage. Don't you know that?" I didn't know how to convince her more, but that is what I wanted, to convince my daughter that she would share in the blessing of the marriage.

What a probing mind, I thought . . . Pause. Rewind. She was 15 then. Angel fell silent and tried to smile in response to her mother's defensiveness. And I left it at that, hoping she would get on board our Love Train. But she didn't really, and her feelings grew, bubbling into more complicated manifestations, asking, demanding over and over again and again for my attention.

The spirit of this exchange felt vaguely familiar. And it should have, because I had had those same feelings about my mother's marriages. Recurring, predictable feelings I could never tell her about. At least my daughter could tell me what she felt. And I was always proud of that. But, what I didn't hear my daughter say, but now in hindsight, what I know she meant, is this,

"We've always been close, Mom. He's already taken up lots of your time. Will he *come between us?* Will this new marriage mean more than the closeness *we've always had?*" I know now that this is what she meant to and needed to ask me, but didn't quite know how. And, sadly, I answered her based upon *my dream* and did not provide the answer and reassurance she needed from me.

* * * * *

Ramon's career plans were taking shape. When word came about his new assignment, he called to share his good news, his relief and happiness. Things were changing for him. He felt his feet on firm ground. He now knew what the financials were, and that's when we set our date. We would be married when he completed his training, and then "get whatever kind of house we want."

He had shared the abridged stories of his two marriages that hooked my empathy. Understandably, this left him both gun shy *and* nearly blind to what was in front of him. Then, there were times when we talked and fantasized about how things might have turned out had we met each other first. But we didn't linger in the fantasy. Meanwhile, he couldn't see me. Not from the way I cooked and fed my family that

I would keep him healthy with nutritious food. He couldn't look around my home and see that I would make for him the best home he had ever had. He couldn't tell that I would be faithful to him, be careful with money by not wasting it, be an asset to his career, and love him better than he'd ever been loved. His past left him both drawn to me and my attributes yet somewhat blind to them. His past mocked and dared me to exaggerate my attributes to see if I could shake him awake with them, shake him into seeing me for me rather than through the thick, stubborn shadows of his past.

His blindness and statistics were scars, irrefutable parts of The Package, real and not to be minimized. They caused him to move oh so slowly and with great caution even when he was safe. I've learned that this is common among people who've been traumatized. They continue to live as if the trauma is yet to happen, expecting the same horrible thing to happen again, and fully prepare themselves, brace themselves as if it surely will. And although this slow pace was not easy, it turned out in the long run to be best. For, together, my bliss and his reality created our bumpy course extending all the way to the altar.

* * * * *

When Aunt Elaine saw Ramon for the first time, she gasped aloud and peered at me with one highly lifted eyebrow. I immediately rejected her spot-on nonverbal prophecy. What did she know? This brother's potential far exceeded his rough edges, and I loved him enough already to handle all that she perceived.

Mom's cloaked caution and Aunt Elaine's intuitive warning were but two among a list of signs I could not mistake, signs our slow pace magnified, signs I ignored. Now after two years of monogamous dating on my part, our engagement was set. There had been another, much earlier caveat that I hadn't recognized when I received it. My first mother-in-law, Louise, had said to me one day as we sat talking on her front porch, "You know what you've got, but you don't know what you're gonna get." I had no idea what to do with her words until this writing. But, at the time it was simple. *Nothing and nobody* would deprive me of my dream.

And so it was.

Until then I had starved for love. He fit the bill. This marriage, the grand prize at the end of a one-way road, was mandatory, and there was no Plan B, no other basket for my eggs, nothing else in the cards. In my heart, we were already married. I had given myself to him, and, I don't play around with my love. I had proven myself consistently, so the marriage to come was about his commitment, and that was worth the wait. This is what I believed. Our trajectory was set, we were loaded up, and the cannon fuse was lit.

* * * * *

Since my poetry was still all about love, it was almost effortless to write poems for Ramon, and during those years I wrote plenty. Whenever I read and gave him a poem, he became like the happiest kid on Christmas morning!

"Have you read this?" he would smile and ask me repeatedly, with such emotion.

I didn't have practice reading my poetry yet, but, I began reading for him, since, he would read them aloud, trying to give intended phrasing, but not being able to. It was good. Good for us both. I felt really, deeply heard, and it seemed Ramon felt deeply known and truly loved in those moments.

* * * * *

I used the whole six months he was away for planning. We would be married in a simple ceremony at the church he attended. Still, I had no idea there was so much work involved. Once I got started, the dream became real and the work snowballed. The day I put the wedding invitations and supplies order into the mailbox, I stood there and asked myself one final time.

"Really? Are you really doing this?" "Yes," was my answer, and, after seriously pausing for another moment, checking one last time as I opened the door to the chute, I let the envelope drop from my grasp and fall inside. Yes. It was done.

* * * * *

The excitement peaked as I rented a house for us in Stone Mountain, we moved in, he returned from Missouri, we celebrated Christmas, then close friends and family came and shared the weekend with us. On our wedding day, Saturday, December 28, 1985 after everyone was gathered, dressed, and in place, after I was dressed, I felt equally ecstatic and nervous. And in that dissonance, Ramon's best friend, Irvin, whispered something in my ear.

"Can I ask you a question?"

"What's that, Irvin?"

"Do you *really* know what you're getting into?" He looked into my eyes.

"Of course, I do." I smiled and held his gaze, as he smiled back.

"I'm just making sure." And with that, he went and took his place with the groomsmen. Irvin's words felt sweet and thoughtful. I wanted him reassured. I had paid my dues here, and could handle whatever was in store. I was up to the challenge. My love for Ramon was that strong. That little exchange helped to lessen my nervousness. And then, as I stood in the back of the church, I saw our guests, and everyone in place, so beautiful, smiling, waiting for me, including all the children. Richie and Rudy in their suits as ushers, Angie dressed as my Maid of Honor, Ramon, Jr. as a groomsman, and Alex as Ring Bearer. Our mothers in place. Suddenly someone started singing Billy Preston's *"You are so Beautiful to me,"* our wedding song, and, Joey and Papa, one on each side of me, whisked me up by my elbows and practically carried me down that narrow aisle! I felt so loved. Good thing none of us was overweight.

Once I reached Ramon at the front of the old sanctuary and stood by his side, I felt composed, centered, and spoke my words clearly and from my heart. Aware of my body — my legs, feet and back — tall and solid, my whole body stood with me, every part of my life, my energy, in that moment, hummed and tingled, saying "yes," supporting, affirming this act completely. It was my day, and as I stood there, I felt in synch with it all, the activity, my wedding, myself. The tear stain on Ramon's left cheek reflected his feelings. Our combined emotion was palpable.

One friend whispered in my ear at the reception, "You had to be devoid of feeling not *to feel the love in that ceremony.*" With tears in my eyes, I nodded and agreed.

After the ceremony, picture taking, cake cutting, bouquet tossing, champagne toast to the couple, and so much hugging, I felt very tired. One last time before we left, I stopped to make sure the children were all set. It was really done! We had survived the courtship, the engagement, the training hiatus, the planning, the wedding, the reception, and now, the married couple left the church and headed to the hotel for a very timely meal and wedding night. As we walked into the door and through the hotel lobby, people stopped, stared, and smiled at the happy, gorgeous couple.

In a booth at one corner of the dining room, we enjoyed a delicious dinner from the elegant ice sculpture buffet before checking in. We talked a little bit, as I tried not to fade. Able to exhale and feel restored as we ate, relieved for the Big Day to come to a close, I wondered how I would hold onto my bridal aura, as evidence of the day.

As if I was on a carousel, the continuing movement of the Big Day persisted in circular fashion, and I now felt slightly dizzy. Out of the elevator and into our room, I carefully removed my veil, dress, shoes, stockings and garter belt, shedding the outer layer of my wedding skin . . . and beginning to feel a little bit regular again. By then I had learned that whenever Ramon felt most vulnerable, his habit was to talk, quickly revert to humor, or withdraw completely to regroup and save face. With everything finished now, as he half-joked about the importance of consummation, I knew that he was trying to settle down too. What a full day! In the last bit of excitement, I kept my earrings, the tiniest proof of our celebration, some part of my special day *on my body* . . . kept them on even while we slept, proof I hadn't dreamed the whole thing up.

* * * * *

A sweet, new Luther song marked our short, quiet honeymoon.

"Let me hold you tight, if only for one night . . ."

Nestled by a running stream, our rented cabin smelled like fresh cut wood, my favorite nature smell. The weather was brisk. Winter in Helen was crisp, clean, accented by naked trees and clear, cold water rushing everywhere. Ramon brought along some books to be sure and not overdo certain things. We built a fire and stayed warm, ate lots of good food, and ventured out to explore some of the Bavarian Village. Among other things, we found an old-fashioned shop where they made homemade fudge while you watched, and, we indulged just a bit with samples, and one slice of maple nut fudge.

* * * *

Since my dress was intricately beaded, I had selected my wedding earrings carefully. They were clover-shaped, three small pearls clustered in a tiny gold setting. And I wore them through our honeymoon and for the entire week after.

Once I finally took them off, something happened. Intending to hide them along with my other wedding keepsakes, I got distracted. I knew what I did with everything else, but when I looked for my earrings, I could not find them. As time passed, I missed them. I wanted to wear them on several special occasions, but no matter where and how hard I looked, I could find them nowhere. Helpless about it, eventually I stopped looking . . .

* * * * *

There was so much about married life to discover. We talked, and even had talking rituals. He'd come home from work. We'd sit over tea while I finished cooking dinner, and we'd talk about the day, catch up with each other. I finally had a true friend and confidant. He got me saying out loud what I was thinking, and before long, I trusted this part of us. Some Saturday mornings we would wake up and talk, share stories, laugh, ask each other questions and listen closely. We would talk this way for hours, and the deeper the dialogue, the more it encroached. Although he did share, it was usually me doing the opening up. Our bed had four massive posts, a ceiling, and lots of space. It became our cove, and from it, there was nowhere to run. And I wanted to run sometimes, even though I figured this was good for me. This sharing, the quiet, easy talking was something I needed. If this was what it felt like to have a husband, it was good. It was making me happy.

When we were alone together, playful, totally away from everything except the couple, this was our love, warmth, skin, freedom, bliss, and for me, fleeting, not enough. Under siege. For those few moments, those golden, rare times, I can still feel them, feel the luxury and the thrill of them. Remembering the preciousness of those sweet, selfish moments, I don't know if he still has that, but I do.

One Saturday night, we came to bed, started talking and wound up singing random rock-and-roll songs from our teenage years. One of us would start and the other chimed in. And we sang together that way all night long. Sang and laughed that way until sunrise. These were the times of my life and I enjoyed them so much, never ever taking them for granted . . .

* * * * *

And at that time, something special, some quality of warmth I hadn't known before took up residence in our home. Whatever it was made other couples comfortable enough to open up, and made our parties momentous. As often as we could, we gave parties that turned into tender, heartfelt discussions about the serious parts of life we were all discovering and trying to navigate if not understand.

For us, despite the love, with the love came insurmountable issues and unfinished business from both sides. I spent those first few years learning a hat trick, trying to re-imagine myself in my busy new roles as wife and stepmother while keeping the hungry part of the marriage from swallowing me whole. This was something else, a struggle I couldn't articulate, but felt the deep complexity of, and I somehow expected Ramon to help with. How could the dream I prayed for, focused on and sacrificed for so long to have also bring me such inner struggle? I couldn't find the right words for the pain. He didn't know what to do. True to form, he reverted to humor and started calling me "Thunder Thighs," from time to time, his "mermaid," or his "diamond in the rough," but then sometimes, offhandedly saying, "you're not well," as if there was something I was supposed to do with that one, as if he had a right to dismiss me with judgment. I hadn't experienced such upheaval as this the first time around.

Or, had I?

Nobody said that once the honeymoon is over and the dust settles that the big issues come round, begging attention. Luckily, I was discovering these questions along with the rest of my generation, and people everywhere, not just our friends, were talking about them. A woman named Oprah now had an afternoon talk show that gave women permission to speak openly about what they felt. Her show helped me a lot. Authors wrote books about these hot topics, and I bought some of those books and read them. I also watched PBS specials on marriage and the family. During that time, I learned one of the most important lessons of my life. I was not alone.

* * * * *

Yes, it's true. He owed far too much to far too many off the bat. Ramon's professional receiving line was pretty long, but I had a chance to meet and get to know most of those folks. Although his personal receiving line was much shorter, I would never know some of the folks there, as if his past was in some ways off limits. Sometimes I resented this. I resented them, too. Folks lined up for small pieces of him and his love. I didn't believe at the time that there was enough of him to cover such need. I didn't like the fact that the short line never seemed to go away. I didn't see that there may indeed be enough love IF we both understood it to be coming from a place higher than Ramon, the man. But he seemed to enjoy being the center of the tension, and so tried to generously, sincerely whether he had it or not to give, give something of himself in each case, as if this part of his life was still alive and calling. And for him, it clearly was.

I wanted him all to myself. Wanted the room and togetherness that any couple needs to establish their home life, and so I learned to find and seize these moments when they presented themselves. That's what they were, quiet moments of closeness and contentment. Years later, I remember relishing an evening at home together after a storm, with no electrical power. We lit candles, told stories without distraction. A whole evening together, maybe two. The weather was mild so we didn't have to worry about heat. We snuggled, listened to each other, sang songs. We felt connected. Something in me knew to pay attention to this time because I felt it dwindling, as if I was finding and seizing something of my own, something also fragile and temporary.

Prime Time, Part Two

One of my most tender memories of those first few years was when I had a short hospital stay. When I awoke in my room, Ramon was there with me, asleep in a chair. The sight of him there was healing. I called to him, he awoke and then kept me company for a little while. This was a first. I had asked my doctor for an extra day to rest and got that too. Another first. I felt fortunate to soak in the healing love, the time and the rest.

*****

One self-help book I read at the time entitled *"You Can Have It All"* by Arnold Patent, stands at the top of the prosperity ideas emerging at the same time that the cost of living took off. Little did Patent know, having it all went hand-in-hand with doing it all, which went hand-in-hand with living life at an unforgiving, bruising pace. But we were young, and this is America, so, we tried it . . .

During this time, I recall a newspaper article in the *Atlanta Journal Constitution*, reporting an important story. It said that by the end of the 20th century, the average American middle-class family would need an annual income of $100,000.00 to maintain its present way of life. This after only ten years since Jimmy Carter said it should take an American family of four $10,000.00 per year to live. I remember the jolt brought by this new information, and how we talked about what was going on. We did not know what it was, but something irreversible had already begun to change the trajectory and quality of all our lives.

Yes, my years with Ramon caused me to reinvent myself, something I did for him, for us, and to the extent that it stretched and helped me, I found it exciting. I spent more time than ever attending to my appearance. I learned to cleanse, tone *and* moisturize. I watched Oprah to learn more about hair care and used all I learned to look the part of the role I was now playing. I paid more attention to the social graces. I read about what is expected of a military wife and thought about how far down that road I was willing to go, giving myself that choice. As I got to know some of the other wives, they totally defined themselves by their husbands' careers. That was too far out of bounds for me.

* * * * *

Those years challenged every part of me. They woke me, helped me catch a glimpse of the woman hiding inside, obscured behind all of this new and fast action. This woman — a stranger — was dying for a life of her own, for a chance to live and find her way. For starters, I began having recurring dreams. Three of them.

* * * * *

The first dream was about my childhood home in Wheaton. Repeatedly I would find myself hurled back there by some unknown force, hurled again to the place I never wanted to leave. I discovered another family living there, and I'd hide out undetected, under the crawl space, in a tree, quietly, anywhere on the property, just to be back there again, just to know that the house was really mine, by right. After all, Daddy Maurice had built it for us with his very short and pain filled life. Home place.

The second dream was triggered by major purchases. Whenever we bought a home or a car, I dreamed of a phone call in which we would be told, "there had been a mistake." That they were "sorry, but . . . ," we'd have to bring the car back or get out of the house. We hadn't qualified after all. Worthiness.

The third dream took me back to Chicago, to the block on Seeley where we had lived. I was running hard, like Trinity in a Matrix chase scene, and a S.W.A.T. team was after me. I'd be out of breath, jumping from rooftop to rooftop over the houses on our street. No matter how hard the chase, I would always escape. My crime? I hadn't made my mortgage payment. I would awaken from this dream exhausted by the black tax on my life. Sufficiency.

The questions at the heart of my dreams were essential. To have a home, to be worthy and to have enough. Wasn't this all part of the American Dream? Were my dreams saying something about how available this Dream was to me?

* * * * *

Back on the home front, it seemed as if I couldn't please Ramon for very long. Early on, he would chide me for "not reading," and then by habit, discount however much money I made. Even in my banner year of self-employment, he complained that there wasn't enough to run the household when there always was. In fact, that year I saved ten thousand dollars from my earnings for the down payment on our first home in Stone Mountain. This way we began our homeowning journey from a "position of strength," to use Ramon's phrase. It was my dream home, perfect for us.

Speaking of money, over the years, the first of the month became dreadful for me. I came to think of it as his Bill Drill. He wrote out each check sighing, as if the ink from the pen was his own blood. For us, collective money, together money, marital money was a war zone I traversed for the first time. We approached that volatile place from opposing purposes. For Ramon, it seemed that money was something propping up his image, something he needed to handle like gold, his ticket to admittance, to social acceptance. For me, it was a utility, something to take me beyond survival habits of counting, figuring, silently praying for enough, sleeping and waking automatically, practically dreading if not avoiding or somehow negotiating everything that involved cost, and even after doubling my salary, something was still wrong. Though I never wasted it, I dreamed instead, that I didn't have what I needed, not according to the world's all-seeing eye.

When we went grocery shopping together (we learned to stop doing this), he'd stand at the register and ask me to guess "how much damage" we'd done. I always knew within the dollar because I silently counted item by item. This was something I had learned as a small child, watching my mother, the "smart shopper." Anyway, he'd seem surprised when I was correct, because he wasn't so much at the mercy of money as I had always been. And until I learned better, I was a little bothered that he considered the price of feeding his family in terms of damage.

He would criticize me for not being satisfied just being his wife. Of course, I was happy as his wife, the role presenting me with social status, the role turning into something of a full-time job, the role probably thankless in the end. I was blind to some things, but I could see that much. I wanted my own career, one that would survive whatever change was in store, one he couldn't touch or complain about. In hindsight, I am grateful that I insisted upon keeping and actively developing a work of my own, an option my marriage afforded me.

During the first two years of the marriage, I began taking steps in that direction as I learned about and transitioned to self-employment. This made absolutely everything better and more manageable. Until the next year when Ramon was transferred to St. Louis.

* * * * *

Alex attended Woodridge Elementary School from kindergarten through the third grade. I remember his first day, watching him walk away on his own, catching and boarding the school bus at the corner, never looking back. He had what I had wanted for all the children. He had what he needed, more of me, more of my time and attention.

He had his own bedroom at last. His first pet was a box turtle he'd found in the yard. We tried feeding him food from the pet store, keeping him in a tank with rocks, but he didn't live long. Alex was such a tender child, an old soul in a new, little body. I never had to tell him to go to bed. Whenever he was tired, like a little old man, he would just disappear and take himself to bed. The only problem that I knew he had as a little boy was eating too much. He loved his food and, on Thanksgiving, he would eat and eat and sometimes eat himself sick.

* * * * *

We had lived in our new home for three years and were very comfortable there. I had begun my new career in natural health and had a small and fulfilling practice. Angie had graduated from high school the year before, and was at art school in Virginia. Richie was in the twelfth grade. That summer many things happened. Rudy went to St. Louis with Ramon. Angie "wouldn't be going back to school." As hard as I tried to convince her to continue, she was set against it.

My heart was broken. I was willing to bear the expense and get her through, but no. Regardless of all my efforts to force the issue, Richie refused to work up to potential in school and had to be redirected so that he would finish on time. Frustrated, and not knowing what else to do, I put him in a G.E.D. program. After he finished, he wanted to join the Coast Guard. But the Coast Guard would not accept folks with a G.E.D. More heartbreak. Both of them refused to move to Missouri where I could have done more for them. I was responsible for all these people and now felt pulled in every direction between stay and go.

I took my time getting everyone and everything settled so that I could eventually join my husband in Missouri with a clear head. Meanwhile, he and I met regularly in Nashville, the established midway point, to spend weekends together every three weeks or so. We kept this routine until I sold the house without an agent, and got the children situated. Situated meant suited with full-time jobs and housing. With the help of a friend who owned a clinic, I managed to get Angie employed, and it didn't take her long to find an apartment that she liked not far from work. As for Richie, he got a job at UPS, we got him a car, and for starters, he lived with Mom.

* * * * *

Now, Ramon's transfer to St. Louis felt abrupt. What I did not yet understand is that these specialty positions he needed to reach his goal had to be applied for. The selection process was not random. This meant he had applied and was already expecting to go without letting me in on this part of his plan. This was a slap in the face. What happened? I had forgotten what he had already told me about resurrecting his career. Every bit of this was a step-by-step plan he had already thought through, but did not talk anymore about.

We discussed the timeframe of the move. It was the middle of the fall semester! He would need to report for duty by the first of the year. Our lovely home in Stone Mountain was very hard to leave and I never considered not going. Picking up stakes involved a lot of work, of course, but I handled it. I hung back with the children, marketed and sold the house. He went ahead, got temporary housing and got acclimated to his new job.

We lived that way for about seven months, yet another form of adjustment. I made it with musical assistance from Dianne Reeves singing about her Grandma, and her special invitation to *"Come In,"* not to mention Anita Baker's fairy-tales and happy endings. But, let me not forget Quincy Jones' *"In the Garden,"* with Barry White promising to take good care of me because *"that's what a man is supposed to do!"* Something about that line comforted me every time I heard it. Yes, I made it. As far as I knew the commute was working.

By phone, I got acquainted with Ethel, Ramon's new secretary. Then one day when I called, Ethel said something strange.

"He *really needs* your home cooking," she said gently.

"What?"

"I said that he *really* needs your home cooking," Ethel repeated herself, adding extra emphasis . . .

"Okay, Ethel. Thank you." What else could I say? (Black folks in St. Louis talked to me right off the bat like they'd known me forever.)

Soon, I had a disturbing dream.

I was in a room somewhere with three women, and they were laughing, mocking me. Laughter between women strangers can mean but one thing. And they said it cruelly.

"WE have had your husband."

I awoke in a panic... it was the middle of the night. I called Ramon at sunup and told him about the dream.

"Oh, Baby! That's just your imagination, running away with you." With no breath or second thought, he turned the spotlight back on me. I was worrying needlessly again. I needed to stop, he said simply.

When I got to St. Louis, no sooner than we finished the move did I receive communication — one handwritten letter and two phone calls — from three jilted, insulted women, all looking for Ramon. One of them went so far as to report being told that I had "abandoned" him.

Confronting him was like capturing a greased piglet. He refused any responsibility for his cheating, or to even discuss it with me. Why had I opened the letter addressed to him? How many times were we going to have this conversation? Why couldn't I just let it go? No, he wasn't getting counseling. Nobody was going to tell him how to live *his* life! It was like talking to air, talking to air about *my* world turning upside down, about losing faith in *my* marriage, about the pain of the whole situation. *My* pain.

But worse than the piglet, the air, the betrayal, I felt violated. As if he had taken what belonged to me, my most cherished gift, straight to the street and left it there. Disgusted, I got myself a bottle of Takara plum wine and headed to bed, as I had when Grandmother died.

Had something died? The trust had. Now, the part of me with my head in the clouds had, too. After a day or so of this, I knew I had to do something. Something for myself. Slowly, again, I turned to my elders. Surely, they would know what to do!

Starting with Mom.

"I'm so sorry you're having to go through that. Oh. How do you feel?"

"I'm not sure, just hurt. So hurt."

"I know. Are you sleeping all right?"
"Pretty much."
"Eating enough?"
"Yes."
"Talked to any of your friends?"
"No. Not yet."
"You probably need them now, don't you think?"
"You're right. I will call, but this hurts to talk about."
"That's because it's still raw. You do know that I went through this with your father?"
"I know Mom."
"... Any headaches or other pain?"

I had to think before answering. "No other pain, except that my stomach feels weak, like, sometimes when I would normally eat, I'm not hungry in the usual way. I don't want much food."

"That's the stress. I'm going to send you something to help you calm down."

"What is it?"

"Magnesium. Just take it according to what the label says, okay?"

"I will. Thanks, Mom."

"You're welcome." Then she asked very delicately...

"Sweetheart, have you told the children?"

"Oh, God, no. I can't imagine telling them this. I have no idea how they'd take it."

"Well, there's no rush. I just wondered."

"You're right. There is no rush, and please don't ask again. Just the thought of it makes me shiver . . . I know I have to tell them. And I will, when the time is right, okay?"

"That's not a problem." My mother sighed before she spoke again. "But, remember this, Dear . . ."

"Yes?"

"This, too, shall pass. I love you."

"I love you, too. Thanks a lot, Mom"

I waited before calling friends, and stayed with the elders for the time being . . .

* * * * *

After she paused, Aunt Lucille replied with her one important question. "Well, is he *violent?*"

"No, Ma'am."

"Then, I want you to really think about this, now. When a couple celebrates their golden wedding anniversary in the church, everybody knows that that wife has had to put up with something! Either it would be drinking, he messes up his money gambling, or, there have been other women! But if she wants to celebrate her 50th anniversary, she puts up with it. Remember your vow? Until death us do part."

"Really?" I loved this woman. She was one of the strongest women I knew growing up, and this was NOT the answer I expected from her!

"What are you thinking now?" She asked.

"Well, Auntie. I'm thinking that it hurts. I need to do something other than just take it."

"Do what?"

"I don't know. But I feel as if things between us have changed too much. I won't accept that I have to live with being cheated on."

Silence.

"I won't. And, if that's what it takes, then I won't be celebrating my 50th anywhere, because I need more than just this ring. This is not what I signed up for. I need the real thing." I was adamant.

More silence.

Later that week I called and talked with Daddy. He listened. He had much more to say. I'll never forget our conversation that day. We talked for over an hour. He heard me, and offered his counsel.

"I don't know, Baby. But, this is just something that men do. I'm not making an excuse, but it's true. Here's what I mean. Right now, if I walked into a room of 100 men and asked who hadn't cheated, I'd bet not more than five could stand and answer no. I tell you; it's just something that men do. So, the question is, how do you want to handle it." He paused before asking his question.

"Are you going to go after him?"

"What do you mean, *go after him?*"

Daddy didn't answer. What could I do? I was crushed, not vengeful. In full view of the offense, I'd felt blindsided, unprepared. I might have been in full view of it. But, did I know what I was seeing? Could I really see what I was looking at? Having good insight (as in my dream) and actually seeing (as in the betrayal) are two very different kinds of sight, and now, like it or not, I was learning that difference, learning to believe myself, to trust my own perceptions.

I had believed in my husband. Until then he had been my stallion *and* my knight. Corny, but true. Had he earned my trust? The pedestal? No way, in each case. But I desperately needed him up there. That was news! This devastation was an important thread. Once he fell off his horse, I had to learn about this Other Reality, this foreign enemy now staring back at me. Who in the hell was this person? As my wound healed, my work now was to find out.

And Daddy, the one man who respected my intelligence, still didn't answer my question! My learning curve felt steep, but I was determined to discover the truth.

* * * * *

My elders had answered based upon what they knew. They had offered support but . . . really? Was *this* what I had to look forward to? Knowing they had heard me helped me feel a little better, but it wasn't nearly enough. I needed a solution they didn't have and was very surprised by this. Even with their experience and wisdom, they couldn't help me see my way out of this mess. Looking back now I realize that for them, there was no way out, only a way through.

Times really had changed. Besides, it wasn't their marriage! It was mine. I was angry now because I couldn't work this out with Ramon. But even if he had been willing to talk openly, I didn't have all the words I needed to say how much he had hurt me and us! For me this cut deeper than words could go. And I had many questions bubbling up. Is this kind of betrayal so common now that folks just accept it? What had I missed? Would I ever get over this?

When I did talk with my friends, one conversation in particular stood out.

"When *my* husband had an affair, I had to ask myself what *I* was doing . . ."

"What?"

"Yes, I had played some part in it, and I had to face up to that . . ."

I look back on this episode as my personal awakening because, from that point on in the marriage, my eyes and ears never completely closed again. I couldn't afford the luxury of a normal on-and-off kind of awareness. No, I wouldn't buy into the notion of having been an accomplice in Ramon's cheating. I had given him one of my nighties to take along to St. Louis. I told him to hang it up in his closet and think of me. I wanted the nightie to be a symbol, a reminder, not a scarecrow.

For now, I was on notice to "let no more grass grow" under my feet. And so, I kept watch. I watched his schedule, his checkbook, his habits, his pockets, his sports bag, and the trunk of his car. I was in his face, finally naming what was going on, because, despite his promises to the contrary, it continued. Then, a couple of years later I finally understood what my father was asking me to think about.

* * * * *

We lived in St. Louis for the next three years, in the Village of Bel-Nor, a step back in time. To walk through the village gates was to walk onto a movie set from the 1940s. All the homes were brick and stone, most with stained and beveled glass, each unique, ornate, some built as early as the late 1920s. I power-walked the neighborhood every day I could, planning my day, taking in the beauty, the character, imagining the untold stories hiding all over that village.

We transformed our new house and made it our own. A Cape Cod brick built in 1934 with a beautiful yard. Ramon and I sanded and varnished the wood floor in the living room and had the kitchen and basement refinished. I made curtains, painted and created a sitting room for myself, put in a swing for the screened porch, put in new light fixtures. We made a home.

I loved that old city, reminiscent of Chicago, only smaller. There was something lovable about the people there. We made a few good friends among the salt-of-the-earth folk. We attended a Baptist church eerily similar to the one where I grew up. It was in this place, as Alex was baptized, that the pastor prayed over him prior to immersing him, lifting him up to the heavens with both arms, consecrating his life in a way similar to his newborn dedication.

After the first year, Angel became ill and needed help back in Atlanta. We brought her to St. Louis to live with us. Having her there, I knew I could help her, that she could rest and get well. While there, she bonded with Ramon and began calling him "Dad." And, as we listened to the radio one day, *"What Does it Take?"* by Junior Walker and the Allstars began to play. Angel said, "Mommie, that song gives me a funny feeling, like I know it from somewhere." I told her that it had been our song, mine and Melvin's. She smiled and told Richie.

* * * * *

Alex was about 10 years old by this time. He very much loved and admired Ramon, the Dad he knew. They found things to do together, like taking a father and son road trip to Fort Leavenworth for the dedication of the Buffalo Soldier monument. For fourth through seventh grades, he attended Lutheran School, was a good student, played cornet, played basketball for the school team, played little league baseball, played soccer, and was still a little shy until you talked to him. One Sunday at church service, he brought along his cornet and played "When the Saints go Marching in."

Around the corner from my office was a great community recreation center, with a pool. I'd pick him up from school, return to the office and Alex would walk to the center and swim while I wrapped things up at work. Little did I know, he was up to something. This particular day I, too, had my swim suit, walked around to the center and decided to get into the water. But before I did, I noticed my son climb the ladder to the short diving board, walk to the end of it and dive in. Then he swam! He hadn't had lessons. I couldn't believe my eyes. He stayed in the water while I took in what I had just seen. I asked him about it, and he told me this. "I just knew I could swim, Mama. That's all. So, I did."

* * * * *

One afternoon, he and I were walking through the neighborhood, talking about racial prejudice. We had watched a TV news special on *Race in America* the night before. Some of the program had been filmed in St. Louis, a city divided by racial lines, with whites living in South City, and blacks in North City. The reporters, one black and one white, had taken turns going to a car dealership, pretending to be potential customers. The black reporter went and had one experience. The white reporter went and had a totally different experience. They repeated this exercise in applying for apartments and for jobs. Same result. All filmed. Alex and I talked about what we had seen and how we felt about it.

* * * * *

Though this was years later, the habit of sharing came in handy. Alex had not yet encountered this problem in his young life, at least not to his knowledge. Racism . . . After he thought more, finally innocently, he said, "Mommie, I wish people in the world would just be fair. Why can't people *just be fair?*"

In that moment, I gave him a reassuring smile, held his hand tightly as I really heard his words, the words of a child learning about meanness in the world, meanness I wished I could keep from him. Thinking back to the months when I carried him, remembering my repeated prayers for a baby not only healthy, but with a sweet spirit. It was clear as we walked those old cobble stone sidewalks that my prayers had lovingly been answered. Born and growing in the midst of change and uncertainty, this child had brought peace to us. It was clear that Alex was both our peace and our blessing.

* * * * *

In St. Louis, we were away from everything familiar. For our time there, it felt as if we were freeing ourselves. Yet, I learned that the old demands of the past, part of The Package, were going nowhere.

There was the alcohol. It took me a while to notice Ramon's alcohol problem. This was hard to see so long as I was drinking with him socially. His drinking was never out of control. But slowly, it grew into something more. He drank away the tension of a tough day, drank to celebrate everything, drank rather than talk, just an habitual, mandatory, unlimited drinking that became as much a part of The Package as the money, the suspicion, and the rage.

And with the women, the infections and the lying, the underbelly of The Package, I opted to work as hard and as for long as I could to keep it from flipping, being exposed to the light of day. This was the full picture of what I had to work with, push against, revealing itself more clearly with time, creating and shaping our relationship, and I only saw the picture in pieces, gradually, as I was able.

I did see the good job he did as a father, providing, teaching, and helping me to raise my children. They each took important lessons from his strong example.

* * * * *

From courtship and through marriage, I supported his career and helped him reach his professional goals. I resented the fact that, in his eyes, my focus had to be either/or. The two careers would not equally coalesce any more than the two people could. I could not fully be, express, and explore myself *and* receive his love. I would grow, and growth was my mandate. But Ramon would not respect me for supporting his career while also developing and attending to one of my own. And, no, Ramon would not support my career in the way I had supported his.

From start to finish, this marriage was an education, as in Graduate School. Among its deepest lessons, I did learn something about sexual healing. I learned what being on the receiving end of infidelity felt like. I learned that while dreams do come true, they're hardly free. With sacrifice both to himself and to the marriage, Ramon's career success had been expensive. As for me, I found my dream of a marriage wrapped not only inside the home I was able to make, the happy times we shared, and the glamour and fun of entering a room coupled with a charismatic man who made me feel beautiful. I learned the hard way what Aunt Elaine knew at first glance. This much beauty came with numerous, painful challenges.

* * * * *

Yet we settled into that decade of bright sunshine, the '90s, with some really enjoyable rituals.

As a family we shared dinner together daily. During dinner there would be more talking back and forth about the day, what was going on and lots of teenage laughter. I would do my best cooking, with the food many times putting smiles on their faces, and sometimes not. Like the time I served one whole baked white fish on each person's plate. And we laughed. We had company that night, which made for even more laughter. No matter what I had served, Ramon had an encouraging and thoughtful habit of saying, "Dinner was good, Baby," just before he left the table. That was something I became accustomed to. It was my new normal. This was our dinner ritual.

After dinner there was evening family TV. Weekend TV included sports. Usually when they watched sports, I'd do housework, or go shopping. I never liked watching sports on television. Sunday TV became important. Once home from church, I'd prepare Sunday dinner, usually something special which meant adding gravy and dessert. After dinner, we'd watch "Roc," a great African American (we took our name back in the early '90s) weekly series starring Charles S. Dutton. Roc was written in a setting with such a St. Louis feel, making it even more relatable! After Roc, we'd watch "In Living Color," and laugh hysterically. Later in the evening, Ramon and I would watch 60 Minutes, and finally the BET news show with Ed Gordon and other black journalists discussing weekly news events of special interest to our community. Ramon and I would discuss these issues after the show. This was our Sunday ritual.

As a family we would play UNO, work puzzles, go to the movies, have picnics, go to church, take road trips, and attend family reunions, his in Carolina, mine in Illinois and Tennessee. We'd have birthday parties for the children and invite their friends over. Of course, as the children grew, they wanted to do more and more on their own. We would take them to group activities with their friends like sleepovers, the skating rink, to the mall, to school games and programs. Then one by one they started driving, and dating, and leaving for school . . .

Every Christmas we would wait until the children went to bed, to begin unloading the closets and trunks of our cars of the gifts we'd been hiding. I'd make tea and put music on. We'd sit up talking, laughing and wrapping presents, building the evidence of our hard work that year with the display of gifts under the tree, growing as we wrapped more and more. We'd literally wrap presents all night, and save the ones we bought for each other until last. That's when we had to split up, one of us in the kitchen, the other in the dining room.

Wrapping. When it was finished, we took a picture of the beautiful Christmas tree. And then we'd go to bed and sleep until the children woke up. When they did, we would gather in the living room and read the Christmas story from the Bible first. After gift opening, we'd take the paper and burn it in the fireplace. Then I'd prepare breakfast and return to bed. This was our Christmas ritual.

Every year on our birthday, we would wake up and sing "Happy Birthday" to each other and then, later, exchange gifts, and celebrate the day together. This was our birthday ritual.

We would take long walks, ride our bikes, and play badminton together. These were our outdoor rituals.

We created a long-term marriage support group with two other couples. We would meet with them once a month for dinner and conversation. Sometimes we would take trips together. Within the group, we could talk about almost anything, knowing that our friends could relate. This group formed itself. As couples we were similar in age and had been married for different lengths of time. We all lived in the same area of town. We grew to care about each other's marriages, as if we had a stake in them. And we did. There was nowhere else that we knew of where this kind of support was available. We grew to love each other. We looked forward to our times together and felt better when we had spent that time. This was our marriage support ritual.

We frequented a few special Asian restaurants. One was on Wesley Chapel Road, where they had the best Chinese Vegetable Soup with what had to be the world's best broth! We'd go there to eat in good times and bad and always felt better after having the soup! Then, if we had something special to celebrate, there was a bigger place with spectacular fish tanks on Memorial Drive, going back toward town. This was part of our food ritual. When he was home and not traveling for work, we indulged and rewarded ourselves with good food at the end of each week, because we both worked so hard. Good food helped us to relax, communicate, move through misunderstandings, build and maintain the bridge.

Even with time spent talking together and with friends, family time, Christmas, our birthdays, outdoor activities, support, and good food for every occasion, the walk across that same bridge ultimately felt longer and longer. Finally, I stopped and asked myself this question. What was it? What was the conundrum, the cognitive dissonance in this marriage? The lesson revealed itself as I was ready to learn.

* * * * *

Our lives were busy, but eventually I did get back to the nagging question Daddy had asked me. The question I still did not quite understand. Bill Clinton was being impeached at about the same time as we returned to Atlanta. There was also a high-profile military scandal in the news, and as I watched these reports unfold, reports filed with such polite, circumspect language, I couldn't help noticing a common, telltale thread running between them. I couldn't help wondering why men in high places behaved this way . . . why infidelity was so damned predictable. But Daddy's simple words rang true still. *"This is just something that men do . . ."*

There were no easy answers but the more I considered the cultural aspect of this issue the angrier I felt. My dream had by that time begun to feel more like a fairytale, one I had naturally outgrown. This meant that one of us — the dream or I — would soon have to compromise to hold things together, just the way they were.

* * * * *

With all of this occupying my headspace, I still had a child at home needing some of my attention. One day he reminded me of this by coming in and hopping up on the kitchen counter top to talk to me. I had heard the end of a report on the news that afternoon that sounded like they mentioned Alex's school, but I had missed it. By then he was in the eighth grade, in our neighborhood middle school, and said that something had happened at school.

"What?" I asked Alex.

"We were changing classes, and I saw a boy pull something out of his bookbag. It was a gun! And he just shot another boy in the leg, right in front of me, just a few feet away from where I was standing."

I took him in my arms right away. And until he was calm, we talked about how he felt after that shocking moment. I went into action, visiting the school, talking with the assistant principal. He knew me since I had been volunteering a couple of days each week to learn as much as I could about the school. I asked about his plans to be sure incidents like this would not happen again.

He told me he was doing all he could to prevent future incidents of gun violence but that he could not guarantee me that it would not happen again. This was his answer. I could not leave my child in an environment like that.

For me, this was a crisis. I would have to find a private school for my son where weapons were not permitted. I looked and found a black Seventh Day Adventist school, got the paperwork and learned how much I would need to enroll Alex in the eighth grade. I asked my family for financial help, got it, and made the transfer. Ramon said I should not do this, that I should let Alex remain in the public school and ride this crisis out. "Public school was good enough for me," he said, knowing that was not the point.

It was times like this in the marriage that I did not try to work things out with my husband, to persuade him to see it my way. I knew that he never would, so I didn't bother. I simply put my child in a safe place and that was that. I made enough in my practice to cover his tuition. Alex did just fine in the SDA school and, except for a bump in his senior year, did well there until high school graduation.

* * * * *

My husband was up for promotion again. By that time, I had pinned him in three official ceremonies. Career officers were expected to be loyal to their country, their mission, their unit, and, to their families. That was the expectation, the standard they had sworn to live up to. And when they strayed, getting caught was their worst offense. I became friends with one of the wives in his command who kindly helped me see that I wasn't alone in this either. I could have blown the whistle and stopped the presses. But no. When the day of the fourth ceremony finally came, we stood as I pinned the star on his left shoulder, stepped two paces back and saluted him, knowing that this was my last official act as his wife.

* * * * *

The foundation had been breached beyond repair. After more than a decade of throwing out buckets of seeping water, making sure the basement didn't grow mold, I finally realized what I had been doing and how angry I was. "I never had a woman to cuss me like you do!" He said in the end. "That's because you never had a woman from the South Side of Chicago!" We were from opposite ends of the same world. I realized after so much fighting, internal and external fighting, that I was burning up my precious time just as sure as if I had lit a match to it. I realized at long last that I had a decision to make.

My second marriage introduced me to my dreams. Intuitive and recurring. They're not just messengers. They're healers. During especially challenging times, they come bringing at least one important truth. Now, to emancipate and help me transition, my Dream tenderly presented a bill. My freedom would cost me something. When I was ready, I would surrender all trappings (lifestyle, friends of the marriage, most of the benefits). I would do this as the anger dissipated.

Who knew about the tremendous anger looming as the marriage dies? Anger looming, waiting for me to fill the ravenous void. I'm talking about the anger that was probably always there but that I had learned to function in spite of, or to distract myself from with so much work and responsibility. Anger over all the waiting, waiting to see and get to know the real man living outside that uniform, the musician, the humanitarian, the artist, the man who could actually relate to the things that I cared about, the things having nothing to do with war. But, let's face it, that man wasn't coming home to me.

When I was back to myself, when I eased and settled into this new way of life on my own — for the first time ever — it would be done. And only I would know "done." In our divorce Ramon was calm, declaring us "no enemies." Funny, I heard Gary Zukav say once that there was "no difference between divorce and war." I'd been through it before. Gary's words felt accurate. I was braced for another war, and this man could have fought one to be sure. But he knew when to back down and retreat. He knew when not to fight. He knew when to prevent any further loss of life.

* * * * *

By then, the music had completely changed. Love had all but disappeared from the songs. We had sacrificed it for something else yet unnamed, for some other feel and sound while smooth jazz emerged as a hot and worthy substitute for grown folks now too busy to realize what had happened.

I wanted to know and love my life too, without the dream, the betrayal, and the frustration of not knowing my potential. Who was I beyond a marriage that made no place for me? I wanted a chance to live free of so much tension. And as long as I was questioning and wondering, I asked myself the Big Question. "If I had enough money to live on, right now, would I still be here, going through all of this?" That answer was easy. I would not. The "D" word. To tear us apart. And then one day, unaware of the silent process I was undergoing, Ramon asked me for his freedom. Without hesitation, I agreed it was time. Yet, for me, that word packed what I imagined to be the same wallop as the "M" word had for him all those years ago.

A fitting end, our split was a slow, organic undertaking, as gradual as our courtship had been, only now, on my terms. I assured him that he would no doubt show me the respect in divorce that he had denied me in marriage. My resolve was fraught with emotional upheaval. I needed to sort through the remnants of the life I'd had, my life with the man now leaving. The man who, despite every evidence to the contrary, I thought would be mine for life.

No, I wouldn't make the long walk across that bridge again. I could give up the fight at last. And as I thought about the fight, I checked in with myself one last time, just as I had that day when I mailed the wedding invitations. Is this what I really wanted?

To be sure, I sat with that question. It wasn't a question of love. I was just so very tired of fighting, tired of looking at him through angry eyes. Tired of fighting something secret, something of my own that may have been older than the marriage. Whoa, what did I mean by that? Sure, I could have fought for the marriage and held it in place if I had wanted it that badly and suddenly I didn't anymore. I could have held onto him and all that we had made together. Everyone said I should. But for what? I was *really* tired. Tired of settling for less than I deserved in the love department, of knowing him better than I knew myself, being able to complete his sentences, anticipate his needs. Tired of putting all my waking energy into taking care of everything but me. Tired of keeping my longings and desires on the back burner, longings and desires that suddenly felt urgent.

* * * * *

And while I was trying to deal with this, my Aunt Sandra died. She was 54 years of age. She weighed over 300 pounds, had numerous health problems, and one day just stopped taking her medications. It was the Fall of 1998. I took my mother to Texas for that funeral. When we got there, we learned that she had left her daughter a letter. Aunt Elaine showed me the letter and asked me not to speak about its contents. By then I had begun to connect the dots to some of the secrets, but didn't understand why the women were still hell bent on keeping them.

* * * * *

The following Spring, we separated for good. Nineteen ninety-nine was the year of great change, and I went to work embracing it. Quickly, as if my life depended on it. Alex was completing his senior year of high school and had a plan to go to college. I returned to school, became a grandmother, experienced empty nest syndrome, entered menopause, wrote my first book. I co-wrote and produced a play, joined an African-centered writers' workshop and found a home for my work there. Just as the life I had was now turned upside down, I lived on full blast now, expressing what was inside me.

Agonizing, I knew that I needed this divorce, and although my heart still disagreed, it would take much more time for her to catch up. In this emotional process, I entered a divorce support group at a United Methodist Church where the veteran facilitator warned a room full of members that divorce typically causes "breakdown," and that we might even "lose teeth" making this transition! What she did not tell us is that sometimes breakdown is necessary before new construction can occur.

When he left for good, when he pulled out of our driveway for the last time and waved good-bye from his car window, I stood watching, feeling a part of my life being torn off, I waved back, glad to be willing to say good-bye in relative peace. The slow dance was over now. And in his leaving, the fresh squeezed tangerine juice of a life we had turned to dark red vinegar for me, and right away, my recurring dreams simply stopped.

Clearly, divorce was a form of death that made a widow of the part of me that had loved him. The shadow of his departure slowly turned our marital home into the marital mausoleum, leaving the place fit only For Sale.

* * * * *

And, it as if by script, my earrings would reappear only then, in the year 2000. Those ensuing years taught me what it took to be married to someone with such a self-described "checkered" past, a past that would only partly reveal itself. But the irony was, that although I had secretly compared my marriages as two separate chapters, I had actually experienced them as contiguous, just the briefest pause between, with no true punctuation. They were one thing, a run-on sentence, written to legitimize my youth, to legitimize me. So, there in the midst of much chaos, the first marriage came tumbling back into focus to be dealt with now that the second was over. Melvin arrived in town the same day as Ramon drove away. With time on my hands, I did what came naturally, rolled up my sleeves and started writing. But before I immersed myself too deeply into that, Alex came and let me know that he needed help.

* * * * *

We had a long, honest talk about the fathers. One had just left, and now the other was on his way back. Alex had chipped in with Richie and sent for Melvin at that time struggling on the west coast. Admitting to me that he was angry at them both, Ramon and Melvin, for short-changing him. For Alex, Melvin was little more than a mystery. But Melvin was at least imminent, a conversation about to happen, discoveries yet to be made. I encouraged him as clearly as I could.

"Do your best with this. We can keep talking about it, if that would help. I understand whatever you feel. You have a right to feel it, but be sure and don't get stuck in any part of it."

At the same time, Ramon, the Dad he knew, was gone, and had not looked back. What a major, painful thing for an 18-year young man to process. Could one father replace the other? No, and I didn't want him feeling torn between the two, as in loving one meant being disloyal to the other. I told him that he had a right to a good relationship with them both. This seemed part of the lesson for our family. I reassured Alex of one thing.

"You're loved. You're fortunate to have a family where you belong."

"Thank you, Mama. I'm going to try my best."

And he did. Still in a hurry, he just wanted all of the pieces in place, the way you would feel in your new home as you worked to unpack all of the boxes quickly. It was still new, and the settling in would not happen overnight. Our divorce had indeed rippled throughout the family, and Alex, growing up and trying to show his determination and strength, was the only one of my children willing to point this out and to ask for help with the pain and the work of it.

* * * * *

And now, back to me. It was not until after the marital post mortem, as I cleared the house with help from the women who loved me, that I found those tiny earrings. Not until my sense of self started peering wide-eyed, up and back at me through the rubble of my earlier years, would I see or hold them again.

There they were. So carefully wrapped in a single, folded tissue and pushed far into the toe of my wedding slippers is how I had missed seeing them. Once off and tucked away, my magic earrings sat forgotten for fifteen years while I awoke from this, the world's oldest tale of love. Ah, at last I saw it. This dream hadn't really been mine. It had been the world's, served up early on by dream merchants, served up in such a cunning way that, without such a journey with these two men, waking up may have been impossible. Finally coming back to myself, I dropped to the foot of my bed, my keepsake in my hand, exhaled deeply as I opened the tissue, held the earrings to my face, and wept.

Sexual Stix, Stonz & Broken Bones

It's Tikkun Olam time. Time to put the broken bones of my sexual body back together, and to let them mend. Slowly, as if no amount of time is too great for this work of repair. As if the work is a gift in itself. As if the time and way of this world will not stand in the way.

"*Sticks and stones may break my bones, but words will never hurt me.*"

From the pile of ruin, my elder heart knows that, as do all things, "breaking" in this world begins with words. Memories, stories, all the pieces, need to be reassembled. And in the slow process, I pray the bones will speak anew. I begin by welcoming the timeless woman spirit into this space. I give thanks for my ancestors, those mothers and daughters who also knew this silent, crushing breaking so long ago. I give thanks for their tenacity, for their dream of healing, of which my life is proof.

* * * * *

Girling: The secret blood came with power that I never recognized. In the church, everything to do with the female body was generally treated with shame, and what's more, we didn't even honor Mother Mary. At school, it wasn't much better, but at least there, we could use book language. As 8th graders we girls had an agreement, since it was happening to all of us. As we crossed this threshold into womanhood together, we agreed with our teacher and my shero, Mrs. Frances Wilson, to chip in twenty-five cents each. With the money she purchased a large box of sanitary pads. She then put each pad into a single envelope, and when we needed one, we could ask and receive a clean pad. Together, Mrs. Wilson shepherded us across the threshold to womanhood, turning this milestone into something good. Not the "curse" as some called it. Thus, Mrs. Wilson broke the silence. Maturing *together* step-by-step was something to be happy about, just as when we all got training bras as 6th graders.

The church missed an opportunity here. Rites of passage for young women at this time could have been conducted to mark and celebrate an important part of girls' lives, something sacred and mysterious.

* * * * *

Nobody, I do mean nobody, except Aunt Dolores ever talked to me about my abuse, my father's absence, about how any of it made me feel, as if it mattered. Except for her, there was only silence.

In the silence of my pregnancy, at 17, I made clothes. For myself, for my baby, and I waited, I ate, I went to the clinic, I sat and watched movies. And eventually, when I couldn't keep my feelings quiet any longer, I stepped inside them long enough and wrote the poem describing The Longest Walk.

Being left alone and pregnant. A girl like me should not be pregnant and unmarried. A girl like me. My mother was disappointed, but in time, I would make her proud. My cousin said that all I needed to do was to "have that baby," and, she added, that once I did, "everything would be all right." Thank God for my cousin.

Ms. Gwendolyn Brooks said my poem was good enough to publish. But, how could I publish something I couldn't even speak about? Sure, I could write it on paper, but not say it out loud. I had no voice at 17. And at 17, I didn't know she was trying to help me get one.

* * * * *

Mothering: Men hurt and left me. With me, where I was most needed.

Before I ever knew his hug, loving touch, or teachings, Daddy was gone, never to return. Over the 25 years we had, our contact either by letters, by phone, or by my visits with him in New York. As if helpless and not knowing what else to do, teaching me what to expect, Melvin left. Repeatedly. Ironically, for living with Melvin's part of this, Daddy ridiculed me.

* * * * *

The summer after Angie was born, I took up with Willie, a boy from high school. He'd call and sing to me over the phone, playing his guitar. He wanted to get into the music business, performing with his brothers. Anyway, part of the mass exodus of our classmates "downstate," Willie went to SIU. He was home for the summer and had a job driving a truck for the Quick Biscuit Company. He had had to marry a girl from school, and they had had a baby. But they were separated now. During the summer break, back home with his parents, he wanted to take me out. I let him.

We'd go to Old Town, have handmade pizza and beer in "The Alley" there. Willie loved to do different things. He was exciting. We talked about everything imaginable. Back in high school, when he called and right away asked me for sex, I refused so he stopped calling. Now that we were out of high school and I was a woman, things were different. He showed interest in me. Melvin was gone. I was a mother; I was also 18. I went with him to Carbondale one weekend on the train.

I wound up pregnant and infected. I went to the clinic and got medicine for the infection.

Later I told my mother that I was not having my periods. She found a doctor on 63rd street. Mama and Papa knew about this doctor. You had to say the right thing then because what he was going to do was against the law. We did not have the money. Together, we raised it.

* * * * *

It was horrible. The doctor gave me nothing whatsoever for pain. He only gave me ether which made me feel high, and then vacuumed my womb for what seemed like an eternity. Hell's punishment. His machine made loud, continuous, grinding sounds, while his nurse held my gripping hand and dried my tears. He packed my vagina with iodine-soaked gauze, told me to leave it there for a couple of days, to go home and go to bed. My mother said that I was not to see Willie again. "He's too expensive," she said. By then, Willie had started saying that I "needed to be with the baby's father." Hit the road, Willie. By then, just the sight of him made me nauseous, and to this day, the scent of iodine reminds me of him. And so does *"Still Water Runs Deep"* by the Four Tops, *"I Love you More Today than Yesterday"* by Charles Earland, *"Does Anybody Really Know what Time it is?"* by Chicago, and *"I Wanna Make it With You"* by Bread.

* * * * *

Soon Melvin came back. And I didn't know what we were doing, but at least being with him made me respectable. A few days after Christmas, his sister called out of the blue and asked if I wanted to go out for New Year's Eve. I was so happy. I said, "oh yes!" and he came to pick me up in a cab, looking so cool, and took me to a tavern at the corner of 79th and May where he knew the bartender. We wore funny silver New Year's Eve top hats. We sat at the bar for what seemed like forever, not talking. Melvin ordered Harvey's Bristol Creme Sherry and a bottle of champagne. I loved the Bristol Creme. The chubby bartender sang along loudly with the music while he worked. They played one special song that night, *"I Just Don't Want to be Lonely,"* by Ronnie Dyson. Ever since I saw him on Johnny Carson belting out the first line of Aquarius, "When the moon is in the seventh house . . ." and gave me chills, I've loved Ronnie Dyson. They played *"Stir it Up"* by Johnnie Nash, and the bartender — a little tipsy himself by then — kept singing along. I sat there sipping my sherry, wrapped in smiles of contentment and joy, able now to chuckle as I watched him serve the drinks. I was with Melvin Jackson, the man worth waiting for, and Melvin Jackson was with me, ringing in the New Year, 1971, when just a week before I was still alone and blue, celebrating Christmas Day with Baby Angie.

We left the club headed to the Clover Grill on 74th and Halsted for breakfast. Melvin had sausage, grits, and soft scrambled eggs. "Over light," he'd say, and the people there knew exactly how he liked his eggs. I had buttered wheat toast, juice and eggs, scrambled regular. He said something about making me feel special, not knowing that in a small way, I did. Then in the cab going back home, he said, "Hey! Do ya wanna get married?" Now, I wasn't sure what I expected from Melvin at that time. My mother had asked me, as if she had wondered. I didn't know what to tell her, so I said that, and she dropped the subject. I was glad because I hadn't thought ahead when it came to him. Thinking ahead with him didn't pay off. So, I'd been in a holding pattern. But I surely didn't expect him to blurt the question out just like that — a one-liner, no lead-in, no warm up, no hand holding, no music — nothing. Oh well. But it was Melvin. "Sure," I said, and that was it. It had been so rough. The struggle, The Longest Walk, the lonely times I never told him about. Willie. But now it would be different, better. At least I hoped it would be.

We were engaged, and, like anything else with Melvin, the details would shake out later, almost by themselves, as if they'd been written down somewhere, just waiting for us to catch up to them.

In the meantime, more and more he would call and tell me to "bring that baby" to see him, and I did. The first few times when she saw him, she would bolt, leap away from him, to get back to me, as if he scared her, as if she knew immediately who he was and what he had done, no explanations necessary. It didn't take long for her to warm up to him, though. He loved to sit and just look at Angie and admire her beauty. I'd feel excited when he called and asked to see her. When we got there, he didn't talk to me. He would just sit with me. I would oil his scalp with Sulphur 8, or "lotion" his back with whatever he had handy. Then he would touch me with his familiar, welcome touch. We would have sex. Upstairs. Downstairs.

Finally, Melvin wanted me. Finally, I would have love and a real family of my own. And one Sunday afternoon as the three of us rode in a cab from house to house, a song played on the driver's radio. It was Stevie Wonder's new "*If You Really Love Me,*" a sweet song that made you want to join in and sing with him. And Angie, standing up, holding to the back of the seat, was listening, too. Suddenly she just started singing, on key, and with the lyrics, "*Ahhh, if you really love me, won't you tell me!*" as she moved her head from side to side to the beat, smiling. Melvin and I both looked at her to be sure this was really happening, that all of this, that she was really ours. She surely sang and she was surely ours. Then we looked at each other, and laughed together. We were family.

* * * * *

We had one fancy bed covering. It was big, white and furry. We would spend practically all day Sunday under it. Suddenly everything was different, as if I had been released from purgatory, with no debriefing. Was it really all right to do this now? I mean, before we got married, we had to sneak and find places to be together. And now, as if I had entered a whole other world, I just couldn't get enough.

It was the summer of 1971, our first summer as a married couple, and, gratefully, the music helped me make the transition. Bobby Womack sent two soulful songs that didn't let me down. He gave me permission to be a woman happy in my flesh. The first song, *"I Can Understand it,"* a blanket affirmation, came from somewhere that I received and claimed. Then, *"A Woman's Gotta Have it,"* gave Melvin the guidance he needed. Bobby had helped us both at a time when words were scarce and precious.

* * * * *

Birth control was a topic of major social concern in the early '70s. "Choice" was the important, powerful new idea in women's minds. And in 1973, the pill was available, Roe v. Wade became law, and homosexuality was cleared of its "deviant" designation by the mental health profession. I turned 21 that year, and although I was a mother of two by then, I was not a full-fledged participant in all the change taking place. In college, I would have had a totally different experience. But that isn't where I was.

Sex is the spirit of life. It is undeniable, creative energy. Sex is fire, an element of creation, equal in potential to water, air and earth. And we walk around with it in our bodies all the time.

I acknowledge the broken father spirit in this lineage, absent in body/mind, missing, a perpetual disappearance and silencing, reducing, leaving the dream of his best self where he once stood, leaving also the raging damage where he lived unbridled, unchecked, unable to move among his children for very long in safe, nourishing ways.

Our ancestors ask for, long for, cry for healing restoration through us. Time for Tikkun Olam.

* * * * *

Melvin said something very directly. We "can't keep having babies at this rate." So, we used the withdrawal method. After some weeks of this, he explained that this was not fulfilling, asking me to imagine what withdrawal would be like for me. I felt bad. We didn't use that method anymore.

I did not realize at the time that this breakthrough in communication on his part meant that now, because of my silence, *my body* was in for a recurring beating.

* * * * *

Sex with Melvin was our silent talking. He had a way of sliding his hands beneath my hips and pulling me closer. He pleased me. Movement and silent knowing, traveling by a vibe, a simple wavelength that started beeping long before the lights went out, a wavelength from the sky, making him warm and gentle. He had shown me what this was all about. A dance, a wordless conversation, a silent movie. And, living in sexual fulfillment changed me. It made me smile, made me walk a certain way, showing off the changing shape of my young, agile body.

This is the role I was taught to fill, what the mothers taught me, and I followed their example.

After we settled into our new home, he surprised me one day with a king sized, heated waterbed. The heat was wonderful, providing me a warm bed from then on. Other than the heat, the water felt strange to sleep, or shall I say "float" on. Gone were the days of firmness beneath me and I would come to miss the firmness. Not only that, sometimes we unknowingly poked pinholes in the rubber bubble and the water would leak out. He learned to put patches over the holes. It was the 70s, our decade of bold change, of color, loud noise and sexual freedom, and Melvin wanted to keep me "satisfied." I wanted to enjoy the freedom, too, but was still awkward with it, as if still just a kid, even with my marriage and family.

* * * * *

I wanted my children to have a sense of ease about their bodies. This is the reason I did not raise them in the church in the early days. I did not want them hung up and feeling the kind of body shame that I had known. I thought about how this would look. I also realized that everybody thinking this way was having to figure it out. And so, we agreed to bathroom nudity and family baths. No shame. But Melvin had to be the first one into and the last one out of the tub.

How could I tell my children that what seemed like preoccupation on their mother's part was really confusion? How could I tell them that Mr. Latimore was right? I really had been "fighting something." I couldn't. But then I wondered, if he could sense that much, then why in the world didn't he ever break it down and tell me more?

Clearly, I gave my elders credit for knowing far more than they did. I expected them to come through for me in ways they just couldn't.

* * * * *

As a growing young woman, I slowly learned to let the shame and awkwardness go. Sometimes I'd feel embarrassment and I'd cry, laugh, and feel a flood of emotion. In the sense that I was yielding, being made love to, letting him take charge of the love, take charge giving me what he knew I needed. I'd take my turn giving, but my ability to be purely sexual was still blocked. I could initiate sex, especially after we married. Rarely did he deny me sex, but when he did, it hurt, like he was forcing me to hold my breath. Like I was unwanted and unloved. For me, sex was the ultimate, most basic love, second only to breathing.

Little did I know that sex was a life dance, simulating the marriage itself. It was where the power rested. And I yielded to him completely, maintaining that place in the dynamic, until I needed to change it.

* * * * *

I experienced sex at different levels. Aunt Dee said it this way. "Some men screw. Some men f—-. Some men make love. Which do I prefer? Different things at different times!" And then she'd laugh her loud, crazy laugh, talking this way to me because she knew damned well that nobody else would. I listened to her at those times, knowing she was also talking to me this way because there was no daughter around for her to say these things to.

The solely uninhibited member of my family, the only one to freely broach taboo subjects, taught me a thing or two. But no, I hadn't quite experienced sex as bluntly as the way she described it. Or, had I?

And then, in one of these sessions, she told me a story that her mother told her. Her mother had described being embarrassed in and shaped by this story. It's the story of Grandmother's first husband, father of her children, leaving the family for good.

Then, with her children looking on, Grandmother knelt to the floor, cried, begged him not to go, as their father then slammed the door shut in Grandmother's face.

* * * * *

In my world, breathing, the wavelength, the dance and dynamic, was all reduced to birth control. For me, that powerful notion of control skipped over or topped everything that came next, everything from consent to the act itself. (I did not know about or get my copy of "Our Bodies, Ourselves," until the early '80s.). I did not know that I was working with blank spaces and broken places then.

* * * * *

During our first few years together, Papa's premarital warning proved not just prophetic but volcanic. At work, I "fell in love" with a medical student. I was 22. A disaster that was all Stevie Wonder's fault. *Inner Visions* was our background music, and I was *"Golden Lady."* I can't hear *"For the Love of You"* by the Isleys without remembering him. The following year, after I went back to school to study natural health, I loved a very serious fellow student, and again blamed Stevie. *Talking Book.* *"You and I"* was the swooning song.

I hung out with him on the North Side, near school, discovering a new, youthful and transient world. I remember standing in front of an old apartment building and, for just the slightest moment, imagined myself living there, as a single student. It felt blasphemous. But I dared sneaking a peek at such fantasy, something I never told anyone about.

Then at 24, I went out and had a few laughs with a guy who looked just like Papa. These were all during times Melvin and I had been "separated." These young men were students, learning, expressing, questioning everything about life, trying to attain their place in the world. Each of them listened to me, enjoyed my company, enjoyed communicating, and made talking feel adventurous.

Altogether, in the decade of my twenties, I had eight more pregnancies. One of them was not Melvin's, and, like the one before we married, I never talked about this. Hush. Of the two miscarriages, the second — occurring at almost six months — sent me nose diving into a deep depression. The year before, my first miscarriage occurred at four months. Now, with depression I could not shake, my cousin suggested I "go talk to somebody."

Yes, thank God for my cousin! Although therapy gave me a place to remember and talk, I never got anywhere close to the source of my pain.

* * * * *

I terminated the other pregnancies within the first two months at the very latest. My first diaphragm was a gift from my mother. Smack dab in the intersection of this turbulent decade, unable to take care of myself, my body, I could not manage or coordinate or think about or talk about or get in touch with or remember or do anything about my reproductive health except to track my cycle on the calendar. As if time was what it was all about. And, of course, birth control was solely up to me, making the responsibility feel not just unmanageable and complicated, but extremely burdensome. Melvin and I never discussed condoms, not in 14 years. I was afraid to take "the pill." It is crystal clear now that the risk the pill would have posed was probably minuscule compared to the risk of those abortions. My ability to see things clearly and to make good, sound decisions in this area of my life was non-existent. And so, in this area, my mother was still mothering me.

The sexual self-care narrative I got at home had been a disconnected series of warnings.

Stop!
Look both ways before proceeding.
Enter at your own risk!
Never take a man's money because then
  he'll treat you like he owns you.
I will never sign for you to get married.

At school it was body parts and other sterile book and pamphlet facts.

At church, more code. Bible verses iced the cake of DWM (do what you must), but DGC (don't get caught!).

There was no teaching anywhere for, and no mention of the broken sexual bones.

I had probably felt this way, this inability, this sense of paralysis engulfment, or whatever it was, from age eight forward. But, at age eight, in the pre-verbal stage of sexual development, a girl cannot make such a statement about any sense of cut-off from her own body. Was this inability, this impotence, were these also clues? If I said anything to myself about this pattern, it was only this. I told myself in the silence that the pregnancies were between God and me, because it was only God who was with me while I was pregnant.

Years later I dug up the memory of these pregnancies, and I didn't have to dig too deep. The memory was there, about bargaining with God to keep me going in spite of this pattern, whatever it was, asking Him to forgive my recklessness and to see me through. And then I talked with each of these tiny, unborn souls, living in the realm of the heavenly hosts. I prayed for them, for their peace, let them know that they had not been unloved, but that I, their mother, had struggled for existence, that my gruesome decision had not been about them, but about me. And I asked their forgiveness for the pain I had caused them. When I felt they had given it, one by one, I released them back into God's hands. And I felt their peace afterwards, knowing that only God understood the pain and trouble of those times, then and now.

* * * * *

Lasting sexual freedom came for me in 1981, when I made an important decision for my body. By then a surgical option was the best, most viable one for me. Once I made it, I never had to worry or be concerned about pregnancy again. A tremendous relief.

* * * * *

Womaning: Through this relationship transition, I grew up a bit. In 1982 the man I met that night at Babe's, the very first and only man I met there was almost everything I dreamed of, although, at times, he was vague and distant. He used alcohol and marijuana for pain. Married, with four children, one of whom was "adopted." He told a pitiful marriages story. The first by shotgun. The second by deception, he said. These were the clues I missed. But, I talked to my aunt about it. Introduced him to her and she really liked him. Told me that if I "played (my) cards right," I could do this thing.

He looked like Phillip Michael Thomas, only with more hunk. Consciously, I knew that I could clean up this brother, so full of potential. I would do the work, make him look as good as possible and reap the harvest. Meanwhile, from time to time, he tested the waters.

I don't recall what we were talking about that day, but, early on, he hauled off and called me "bitch," mid-sentence, with a smile, as if it was nothing. At the sound of that word,

I stopped, turned and looked at him. "As long as you live, don't you EVER call me out of my name. Do you hear me?" The smile faded as he said, "yes." The vow I made to myself at age 8 would not be broken.

* * * * *

Before long, sex with my second husband felt easy and natural. A masterful lover, he'd come to bed talking, sounding like Barry White. I'd tell him to shut up so that I wouldn't totally lose it. But that is what he wanted me to do. Laugh, joke, enjoy. Then, the feeling I'd get when we were totally under the covers, including our heads, away from the world and everything else except for the couple, felt like pure love.

The problem was that I was not the only one he was this way with. Seeing it took me years, prophetic dreams, and heartache. Sometimes he'd have a memory slip and do the things, make his new moves to blow a woman's mind the first few times he'd have sex with her. A shivering move. I remembered it. When he'd lapse this way, I knew. Again, he had forgotten he was back in bed with his wife. Wife number three. He'd never say names in bed for fear he'd lose track. And he made a special point to announce the news whenever he had tested at work, "AIDS free!" Hallelujah!

Sometimes when we talked in the early days, I found myself in bed with him, squeezing myself into a corner, needing to be as far away from him as I could get, staying in the bed, feeling so much hurt, but away from him. I noticed this, but didn't see what was happening. Between us there was so much potential, the same potential I saw in him initially. With both of us it was exponential, but I didn't understand that much. I didn't know we had power to heal ourselves together. But I felt that power and it scared me. Then in the end, we hung from the rafters trying to feel something, and managed to share pleasure, working harder as the creative energy between us slowly died.

By then, it got to the point where he'd only come to bed after he knew I was asleep, or just go to sleep first to avoid closeness, even on special occasions. Other times I would turn away and hope he wouldn't touch me. There was so much rejection in the end. Rejection felt like a stranger, a whole new thing that stung so hot it got my attention, like a poisonous bug bite. It was painful, making me imagine my life without him. But by that time, it was "all over but the shouting," as Ramon would have said.

"*After the love is gone . . . used to be right is wrong . . .*"

* * * * *

Besides love, companionship, growth, and a sense of freedom from worry, I did not know what I wanted in the early days. Maybe this was enough. Both my marriages were opportunities for self-discovery, and through them, I took the right path. The Longest Walk to me, the flashing red light my signal, and then, the slowest dance.

What lessons! The importance of my education, getting down to the business of building my career, stepping into relationship with myself, learning who I really am, trusting myself, swimming defiantly rather than drowning. The importance of the truth. What abuse is. What addiction is. Walking with me the to the edge of my journey with men. This is literally what Ramon made me see. Among many other things, he was my teacher.

* * * * *

It's time to heal and unlearn what's left of the sexual trauma. Time to learn to approach sex with clarity and intention. Time to approach it with good information.

Learning. Forgiving. Realizing. I had married into a family that treated opinionated women in ways similar to how violent men had been treated in my own. Unwelcome, expendable, replaceable, when they didn't behave. Life looked like the circle they told me about, like the stuff I did with Melvin had come back around. And, as my second marriage ended, and now that I knew how it felt, I sent Melvin a card saying that I carried no grudges, asking him to forgive the pain I had caused him.

* * * * *

Sexual healing. In the beginning, when it seemed I knew nothing, my brain had shielded me. I had developed a habit of not seeing the hardest things and so not knowing what was happening, keeping distant from the pain in it. I hadn't seen Daddy Maurice's body or Melvin's betrayal or the wedge Mom drove between Angie and me, or Ramon's cheating. So many hard things about love and loss I hadn't seen. Until I could be blind no more. Until my life demanded that I see, speak, and know where I am with love.

There was one more thing.

For three years, I watched as my mother lived by choice without a man, and I almost noticed something. Mom seemed happier during those years. Besides this, living manless in a community of free women, *I felt newly safe, free, and relaxed,* in the best years of my childhood. But of course, nothing about this was put into words until I began reflecting and drawing from my own mental notes. I remembered everything about those years, and, like good money in the bank, drew from that savings in due time.

Connected to sex was beauty, the condition for love. I am reminded how essential it was to be beautiful until the 2020 pandemic. How much time and money did I spend pursuing beauty, achieving That Certain Look, getting and maintaining it, until a trendier look came along? Looking the part, improving my looks and impressing those who paid attention, those more curious than caring. Looking the part just as I had been taught. A woman must be beautiful to seduce and keep her man. This is a job with no time off. And now, after all these years, I stop, stand still and catch my breath. I take a drink of water and ask myself what I want now. I ask myself what is real and meaningful?

* * * * *

I want the truth. When I sit in conversation with folks who tell the truth, that authentic energy washes over me and leaves me feeling well. That cleansing energy blesses me to tell my truth, too. Nothing less will do anymore.

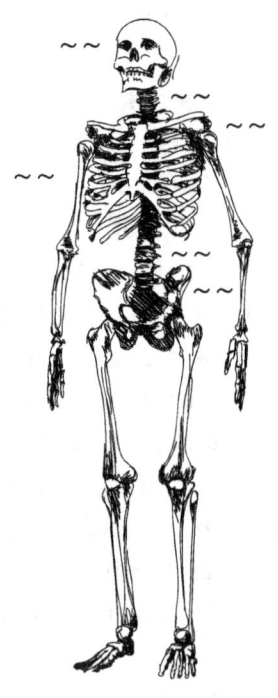

Next, I want consent. The ability to stop long enough and decide what I want in intimacy and then participate at my own pace. Sexual healing for me is about truth, consent, and authority over my own body. Sexual healing for me is about true love and what true love does.

* * * * *

Men I knew. Touched me without asking, sought no invitation and in time, I learned to protect myself in the moment from their advances.

I was molested at age 8, felt up at age 11 and 16, raped at 23, propositioned for money at 25, that same year groped at work, then at 30-something, ignored when I locked my husband out of the bedroom. All as if this was NOT MY body.

It's about consent.

I say "yes" or "no" when it comes to my body. And each time they disrespected me with their presence, their words or their hands, I felt spat on. I figure with untold stories like these, my brain might be struggling with trauma. Sexual trauma.

Looking into this question of what my brain might need, I discovered fava beans. They feed the brain's chemistry, and by that time my brain had taken a beating, too.

But fava beans have a thick shell. You have to sprout or cook them to break and remove the shell and unlock the healing part of the bean. So, I started with sprouting. And when I looked at the sprouted beans in the jar, I swear, they reminded me of the male anatomy. I laughed as I took the shell off, rinsed and then ate them. They were slightly nutty, crunchy, and so, I chewed for quite a long time.

* * * * *

Lurking beneath the sexual self-care narrative lived the teachings, amounting to this.

The church taught me that *sex is sin;* at home I learned that nice girls are *victims of the men they know, not willing participants* in something so shameful and hurtful as sex; at school I learned from watching the goings on that *it's the bad boys who make you feel so good!*

There were no sex positive teachings orbiting anywhere in my world. I was an elder before I felt fully empowered in my body, actively permitting and denying access. I was an elder before I loved myself.

And, with that power, I heal my broken bones with renunciation.

You! Be you ideas, be you Book, words on the page, be you man, be you woman, be you living or be you dead:

Get back! Without an invitation, you may not enter my space.

Be you good guest, be you sane, be you gentler, even understanding, still you must tread mindfully here.

* * * * *

My friends waited for me to get another, new man, after my divorce, and I didn't. Why? Because I didn't want one! And if I did, who? Who could follow the Man of the Hour? Besides, I was seething with anger and did for some time to come. I had no energy left for men. Married practically all my adult life, I needed to know what being single felt like. Taking time for me, finding and healing myself, was absolutely all I could do. This was what I knew for sure.

As for the question patiently awaiting me, I took my time, had traveled a long, hard road getting around to it, *imagining, gifting myself the idea* of partnering with a very special woman. It's a journey I want to take, one I will take when she and I meet at last.

And now, for reclaiming my body.

This is My Body. Mine. Not a thing, a possession, not an object, ornament, not an "it," but my abode, my body. She is. To be honored. She is always in conversation with me. An honest loving, respectful conversation . . . my best, my lifelong friend and supporter. I occupy, embrace, nourish and care for you fully. Thank you for all that you do for me.

* * * * *

In 1992, I embarked upon my healing journey. This decision grew from developments at my Wellness Center where clients were telling me very hard stories, harder than anything I had ever heard. Unexpected, their stories ushered me right back to mine. Not that I had forgotten, but it was buried so deep that I considered myself living separate from it.

I wrote to my parents, asking for their support. My father never responded. After a few months, my mother wrote back. Her unusual letter was a three-page, single spaced, incomplete ("there'll be more") avalanche of abuse secrets, imploring me to "keep them in confidence." Mostly it was projectile news, far more than she could hold back, similar in spirit to my clients' stories!

Her page three ended mid-sentence. Evidence she had at least started page four. But, what did she leave unsaid? She said she'd send it later because it involved people still living . . .

Rather than let this overwhelm me, I put it aside, filed it and instead, focused on my own words, stories and voice. Many years later, after I learned more about stories, what they are, what they can do, I returned to Mom's letter, knowing that the major clues of my journey would be in it, and found even more. Placing my story beside hers, I figured out what she wrote about on page four, the page she never sent.

* * * * *

After thirty years of journeying, I was diagnosed with major depression and PTSD. In 2014, I published my novel for the child in me, giving her the important things she never got. My own medicine worked. From there, beyond my healing journey, was rebirth, where the quest for my real life began.

With story medicine, I can imagine it.

Sex. When I give consent. When I make a choice. When it's what I want.

Being human, showing love. With my body.

Sexual healing.

* * * * *

Grandmother came from Southern Appalachia where they told stories in special ways. She told her womaning stories in a coded medicine, preparing me for the difficult moments she knew would come. She included a simple little spiritual to sing, as needed.

"No harm, no harm, no harm. No harm, no harm, no harm. No harm, no harm, no harm. No, the devil can't do me no harm . . ."

Of Grandmother's many stories, three in particular come to mind. And inside of them I include the one Aunt Dolores shared. Each womaning story included a fracture of some kind. These fractures characterized their lives of one hundred plus years ago, a time in history when women had to be married to be considered adult. They had no rights to speak of, they could not vote, own their own property, and, women of a certain class and race did not work outside the home. A woman's place or value in the world was determined by money. Her husband's money.

His money determined on which side of the line she lived, the sufficient or abundant side, or, the poverty side. Women who were black and had little or no education worked as domestics. With the benefit of schooling, they could be teachers or nurses. In this era, a woman probably cherished her dreams and, if they exceeded society's limits for her, she knew enough to keep them to herself.

I can imagine that women who passed for white or whose racial identity was doubtful had to walk a fine line, protecting the mystery. This woman might use it as a joker card for key moments in the game. With a smile, Grandmother let people guess about who she was.

But for a Southern black woman living in the Jim Crow era, there was violence. From the stories I've heard, violence was a predictable part of life. Both inside and outside the home. Most times the violence was exacted on her mind as she was regularly constrained and reminded of her place. But overt or hands-on violence was exacted on her body at whim. Her body had never been her own. I can imagine that she and her body were strangers. The clothing of her day confirmed it. Everything below the neck and above the ankles was concealed.

If her body showed signs of battering, this kind of clothing worked on behalf of men. If she used the means of detaching from her body, as a victim of trauma might, I can imagine her feeling extreme pain and loneliness, perhaps having no one to talk with. I know that she lacked the full language for or knowledge of what she was enduring, but that enduring was the expectation, the requirement.

And sex was something she was "duty bound" to provide to her husband. A woman's desires, dreams and voice were easily lost in the course of living in such a world.

Sex and all things sexual were men's domain. Sex in a racist, patriarchal, post slavery society was obviously a tricky business, in tricky territory to navigate for a woman oppressed yet interested in preserving her dignity. Bad male behavior was expected, and so the risk was not *if* he would, but rather in just *how* badly. And the big question became whether a woman could endure it. Was his behavior any more dangerous than what she would encounter in the world on her own? Pregnancy became an inevitable "happening" under such conditions. If a woman was unmarried and pregnant, she had to figure a way out. That is, if she ever wanted to be marriageable. Perhaps she used *a four-letter word* to describe just how this "had happened."

Grandmother's clues confirmed this much. The Secret Blood. That Door of Confidence. When a girl child turns twelve . . .

* * * * *

This book's preface tells the story of my mother's birth and raising. This is the story, energy, and the secrecy that she and her children were born into. All my life this story has been the context and container for my feminine experience. I attempted, in another work, to deal with the other, seemingly less complicated story on my father's side. Initially, I wrote this memoir in response to a question raised by my eldest son. Once I hung the stories together, this deeper, living story begged telling in order to finally fill the gaping hole at the center of the book. Stringing the stories together, finding the language, and breaking the silence, was arduous and healing. I compile this memoir to help my son, my children, grandsons, and me, all of us to see how the untold story influences us. The unspoken pain we feel is older than we are and, in this knowledge, there is context and in proper context, there is hope for change.

* * * * *

The first story is of Grandmother's birth. The thirteenth, last child to be born in her family. Oddly, however, she added that her mother never expected her, not for one day. Her mother did not know she was pregnant until she went into labor! Until her body demanded she know. (I wondered if such things were common in her time.) This distance between her and her mother endured long after her mother's death. This other distance, the one between mother and mother's body added to the first and kept Grandmother very tight-lipped on the subject of their relationship. She never said anything else to me about her mother except that she was half Lakota Sioux. She never even discussed her mother's death. The bright side of this story is but a sliver, a presence, of a Sioux elder, Grandmother's grandmother. All Grandmother said about her is that she was a tiny woman who told stories and knew about plant medicines. Her grandmother's memory gave her comfort and put a smile on her face.

Then there was the story of Grandmother's sister, Josephine, or "Jo," as she was called. Nobody told Jo that one day, she would begin to bleed, that this would happen each month. So, when Jo's day came, the blood scared her and, not knowing where to turn, she went running to the cold creek and jumped in, thinking that the cold water would cure whatever ailed her. But instead of that, Jo died.

Because of the silence about all things sexual and bodily in Grandmother's family and time, because of the separation between her and her mother, she admonished and implored me repeatedly as I grew up to keep open "That Door of Confidence" between Mother and Daughter. This is the third story, although I had to reconstruct it using her clues. Noticing the wisdom, the cautionary vigilance hidden in her admonition, as if she herself had experienced this very thing at another time, and so told it to me with an extra urgent knowing. "Never keep a secret from your mother," she said again and again. And she helped make sure I didn't. It was *my responsibility to tell my mother* if "anything happened" to me that should not. It was my job to keep That Door open, a job much more important than my mother's job to protect me from "anything that might happen" in a world not safe for girls.

Finally, when a girl child turns 12. Like clockwork, when I turned 12, she told me the clean bones version of her hard story, and I was so surprised that I told Joey, then 10. Right away, as if by some reflex action, the next time we saw the woman we had until then known as our "Antie," he immediately ran to her with open arms, elated and greeted her in a new way. "Hello, Grandmother!" he exclaimed. And as if by some other reflex, she gritted her teeth and told him under her breath, "Don't you *ever* call me Grandmother!" And that was that. Poor Joey didn't see it. I never needed to call her that. I *had* a Grandmother who filled that role quite well, and had done so as far back as I could remember. I was not confused by biology. This was about love, about the one who had loved us, loved us from the belly of her imagination. She had loved my mother, my brother and me.

* * * * *

This system of silence is all about sexual shame. Shame so vile that girls needed always to be vigilant, to look out for and defend against secret male behavior. Shame over the expectation, the certainty that as long as our bodies are not our own, girls and women would surely be victims.

Sex and the body were secrets. Men were the offenders. The body was a stranger you had no power over, but from it you could always flee when the pain became too great. Something was very wrong. This caution came into awareness through the back door. It entered whispering like a thief or an accomplice.

* * * * *

In this family, womaning came with two things. And like two sides of a coin these things coalesced and depended on one another. The secrets AND the need to persevere. In the face of adversity, Grandfmother's love saved our lives.

There are ancient cultures where the image of nested dolls is used to symbolize paradoxical things in life that coalesce this way. I first saw nested dolls as a very small child. Since then, I have also come to understand something about stories, how they connect, how they connect us. And so, I see the nested dolls as symbolic of the secret stories of women.

To apply the wisdom of the nested dolls, I listen. Listen to their questions. Who are they? And I write what I hear. The outer doll is Grandmother's mother. Each doll nested inside her represents the daughters: Grandmother, her daughter, my mother, me, my daughter, all of us wrapped together in Grandmother's loving, sheltering presence. This bunch of dolls is us.

What is the emotional truth of those women in that time? She whose throbbing black body would not be denied or covered up. She whose tired body swole with new life she refused to feel or notice. She who ran, just running from the blood now running down her legs. She who smiled all the time to make the neighbors think well of them, to think well of herself, until the night time came and with it brought the big hands. She whose father left for good and who grew bitter, loveless, love starved in his absence, desperate with longing and willing now to do anything at all to fill that void. Anything at all, for any man.

By their clothing, they covered up. By day they covered their bodies, their bruises and escarpment. But the shock was timeless and not to be covered. The shock of a body she tried to silence but that would not stop growing! A child and its milk. Undeniable! She who did not mean to sin, who only sought cleansing and healing in the cold creek where she jumped and once she did, the freezing water filled her open pores and sucked the life from her young, throbbing body. She who watched the Family's Power walk out the door while its powerlessness, its need, knelt in the floor and begged it stay. "Please don't go!!!" She cried out, her children watching. A slammed door their answer. The quake of that slam tore through the family and left it divided for all time. The quake dried her tears and left the stains. Then, besides the clothing and shock, like an outer, tougher layer of skin, the secrecy and silence covered everything.

Will *the forbidden language for the old shock heal us?*

Her eyes and ears shocked. Her body. The bodies of these women betrayed them over and over with the throbbing truth of a man's desires. The noise of every man's desires overtook and silenced her own, yet unknown to her. Abandoning her. Leaving her now to her own devices. Shock. Freezing their thoughts. Blurring their bodies, their stories, them, one into the other. Shock. Starvation. Shame. Emotion exploding, aftershock, tremors, one sure thing they found in the wake of the slammed door.

Her proud stepfather dared enter the haunted place. Seeking to fill it with himself. With his powerful, black, learned Christianness, armed with Scripture in four languages, after all! Shock. She was shocked by his beauty, the beauty of his words. Wonderful words of life. Beautiful words . . . Delicious words. And she did eat. Had her fill and loathed the need she could no longer deny or cover with cloth. She was sick of trying, so she fed it well, fed her body with her mother's help, then she fled and hid her body so that some man would have her later. With her mother's help. Disembodied, in the face of great pain. This is the emotional truth of these women whose precious bodies betrayed them, predictably, one by one, in a world absolutely ruled by men.

Now, in the stillness as I listen even more closely, I hear wolves howling in the far distance, howling as if they had always been there howling the daughters'—my three aunts' — sudden deaths. Howling, this sorrowful wail, alive beneath the stories of our ancestors always there, only now am I stopping long enough to hear. Only now do I feel able to hear and try to comprehend. Beneath the stories we know, a nameless pain lived through constant reminders, through shame, through whatever horrors it could cling to, dream, stir up and feed from. It lived as a curse so called in this world, one secret kept from all who didn't know, and judged by all who did. For this pain and curse there would be no help, for she knew of no one she could trust with it. Not even the men who vowed to love and comfort her. Especially not them, for once she told them, they added to it somehow and mocked her trust. Added, as if they had no other way to receive this broken knowing. Inserted into this part of her youth, I remember her sensuality. Her perfumes and dusting powders from Carson, Pirie, Scott & Co. Her treasured Barton's Chocolate Bridge Mix poured into the small, white paper bag, purchased by the pound. "The best," she said. "Make it the best thing they have. I'm worth it." She kept telling herself that, over and over. All night long. Telling and trying to convince herself it was true. True enough to outlast and overtake the pain she felt whenever she looked into their eyes, or, into the mirror.

She turned mostly to food, and then temporarily to alcohol. The best relief she found would be in work, her later relationships, through faith. Relief, when she could give herself totally to something, someone, or to God. And she did it all, pouring all she had into this or that for as long as she could, for as long as the pouring did not come with mirrors, as long as the pouring did not shine a bright light back on her, or advance her status in any way, for that she could not allow. And in this way, she lived out her life until there was nothing else to do, no more striving, attaining, nothing left of consequence. In the end, after raising her children, seeing her grandchildren successfully raised, she methodically as if by plan began to apply brakes to living, tying off the arteries of former interests, one by one releasing the trappings of her life and times. And without exception, she let go of her things, desires, attachments, everything except for her memories, until all that was left were the clothes on her back, and the old hope she managed to hold out. Hope for the one thing she knew of in this world she felt worthy to look forward to. The rapture.

This is the beating pulse, the heart of my mother's pain that she carried all her life, the undeniable, unbearable pain she carried alone until she finally dared lay it down, until it claimed her completely. From the inside out, costing even skin, bone, everything except breath, breath she received from God. Until all she had left in this world to claim was the breath "from God's hand."

* * * * *

We are the stories, and the stories inside of the stories. We are the stories of longsuffering, faith, self-determination, the strength to persevere, the stories of love that, by our very survival, surely triumph in the end.

Together, these stories revealed a few things without doubt — how much love there was for my life, love I hadn't noticed until this writing; how far I've come, how much of my feminine ancestors' wounds, longings and gifts I've inherited — and how far down the road to generational healing I have, gratefully, managed to travel.

So, for now, with the Spirit's strong help, shedding a bright light on these old, living stories, seeing their unattended, interconnected pain, I pray over what is left of that pain in me, and in my children, and their children, asking for its continued transformation into something useful and good. Finally, I pray for my ancestors, those mothers and daughters who knew this brokenness reaching as far back as the stories go. I give lifelong thanks for their tenacity, for their love, for their dream of healing, of which my existence and that of my children is proof. I ask for their healing and for rest from their pain, tears, and hard stories, no longer kept locked away in the silence. I ask for loving peace reaching back to the beginning and extending to future generations. I ask these things in the steadfast, prophetic spirit of my wonderful Grandmother.

Pot Liquor

Sunday is my day to prepare for the coming week with ritual and food. I reminisce about my religious roots, and the hands-on worship black people naturally slip into. The call-and-response, rain showering love and welcome, the harmony, deeper understandings, the chance to hear about what is going on in the world from another black person's lips. These elements feed my soul. I'm touching memories of my place in the old church choir where such food sparked healing and hunger all at once.

Today, as the Scripture is read, my brain automatically imagines something good to eat. Then I crave greens and cornbread, and nothing else will do. By the benediction, I have a plan worked out. This Sunday after church, I will make my way around the corner to The Beautiful.

Chopped turnip greens cooked long enough in onions and peppers to give off an elixir that quiets and restores, is how I describe it. Warm, dark green liquid. Pot liquor stewed from the roots, the skimmed renderings with leaf bits, and oil swimming at the top. Pot liquor. And I came through the line, asked the sisters dressed in orange and white, with little orange hats on their heads, working behind the fragrant steam table, for my vegetables. "I'll have dressing and gravy, limas, pole beans, and some turnip greens, please, with a cup of hot water." I said, since I brought my own tea bag.

This homey little place never closed. Once inside, you walked to the kitchen where the food is served from behind steam tables. Through this surrogate kitchen, into the surrogate dining room I found an empty booth. The rundown booth was all I had for now. I accepted and ignored the ugliness as much as I could, much the way I did back home when my mom bought a sofa at the Salvation Army for twenty-five dollars. More like a seesaw, when you sat at one end, the other end flew upward. At least the dry days at home sometimes made us laugh. At least back then, we had each other.

Here, now, in this surrogate dining room I was one of several anonymous guests dining solo. And sometimes we shared our thoughts about the day's news. Some faces and voices were familiar, but ever distant. I gratefully sat down and said my grace.

Picked up my book and started reading while I ate. Sometimes I do this to help me practice and get used to eating alone. To tell myself that it's okay. Eating and reading quickly fills that alone space, keeps me busy and looking okay, even when I'm not. And so, I read about peace, and how the Christian church has "said" it was teaching "Jesus," while doing just the opposite. Instead, John Stoner explained, the church supported militaristic might, not peace, thus, making the government's agenda easier to achieve. Hmmmm. Mmmmmmm.

By now I had lived South for the better part of two and a half decades. I came South to live, to raise my children, to grow, to grow up, and did, as life had denied me none of the material things, not my dream of family, not the growth I asked and worked for. My father was gone. My three children were grown up — although I felt Alex had left the nest too soon — and each had presented me one grandchild. My children were hard working, home owning adults, values they learned from me. I was divorced from my second husband, sure enough, just as Louise predicted, the one I couldn't trust, but the one who taught me without fail, to find and trust myself. Still, I took the divorce bit by bit, in my own way, turning over every stone and reclaiming myself, my life after marriage.

These years offered me new life, a new mantra. I completed my first round of grad school, came to know and love my blackness more deeply. By soul searching and solitude, I embraced more of my identity, discovered fulfilling new past-times, this new ground still forming under my feet. Imperative self-love pushed me ahead into this new time. I began substitute teaching. I became my own companion. My own elder, too, seeking and keeping my own counsel! No longer could I follow the world's ideas of beauty, decency, respectability, honesty or legitimacy imposed upon *my woman body*. Instead, I drew from my writer's memory and let my stories rise up and guide me . . .

* * * * *

I slowed down enough to taste my food. The creamy limas, the chicken dressing and gravy, the pole beans. Greens and cornbread. Slowly, my mouth celebrated. I don't eat this way often, or even regularly anymore. Yet, my lips did a holy dance keeping the water works contained. My brain and taste buds agreed. Buttery, salty, sweet, over and over, faster and faster. Buttery, salty, sweet, as I chewed, and finally, the explosion of tastes was exciting. Then an intruding thought. Something was missing! The thought courier quickly said it. "Pot liquor!"

Could I? Would I ask?

The sister waiting tables had just come by, asking if I needed anything. When I said I didn't, she disappeared. I considered not asking, but my tastebuds softened and perked up all at once as I imagined the greens, cornbread, and now, pot liquor, all together right here in my mouth, where I could enjoy them.

And I thought about this moment. It is good fortune belonging to a people able to treat sickness with commonsense. A people whose lifegiving, warm, green liquids extracted from fresh leaves, boiled and drained from the bottoms of black pots by black hands, this is our love. A people whose wounds, black strength, and black wisdom were equally deep, a people determined enough to offer healing from their hands to the whole world... my ancestors brought me all the way to this very moment.

Here she comes again...

"Excuse me, Sister, this may sound strange, but I have to ask."

"Of course," she answered.

"May I please have a cup of pot liquor from the turnip greens?"

"Oh, yes you can!" she said, went, and came back smiling with the treasure. And I took the cup of healing liquor. Looked, marveled, prayerfully sipped it after taking a bite of cornbread. Wouldn't be anything *but* a black woman right now. Feeling precious, cornbread in one hand, cup in the other, I parted my lips, sipped and made the ecstasy last. Slowly, I moistened, chewed, swallowed, made sure to get every crumb off my plate. As I took the last drop, noticed my stomach full, and heard him say as always, just as I finished, "Dinner was good, Baby." And I cried a different sort of tears.

The man and his car may be gone, but the soft part of him would remain in my skin for years to come. And as I prepared to leave The Beautiful, I thought about the Latin phrase inserted into the divorce decree, *"a vinculo matrimonii,"* that is to say, "as if the marriage had never happened." The white man has such a strange way of doing business. But this was for the best, and I was willing to journey solo and let enough time pass, time to let him leave me in the soft way, too. Time to let go and be truly free.

In the instant that followed, I noticed. Noticed my full body, alone but not in that booth at The Beautiful, noticed the long miles, dances and many bridges behind me. With hopeful thoughts, the help of the soothing liquor in my full stomach, I noticed that I am new. Original, fully nourished, and new.

Yes, dinner was good.

ACKNOWLEDGEMENTS

This book became a project, labor of love, timeless excursion back, back, back through memory. The Spirit of Perfection offered the needed medicine, making the work feel far more fruitful than expected, and for that I am grateful. Almost all of the people who made this work possible were my elders, now ancestors. For all of them who gave of themselves and took time with me in my youth, the difference they made in my life is inestimable. And to my son who in 2002 asked the pestering question that sparked my need to write these stories, he is a genuine Catalyst. To my first-born child and only daughter for making me a proud mother and grandmother. To my youngest son who believed in himself from Day One. To my mother who gifted me a writing talent, the example and standard of her work ethic, and, permission in 2009 to write the stories I needed "if they would help somebody." To my brother, my best friend growing up, who helped me when I needed it most. To my sweet niece, who asked the probing question that day. And to Grandmother, whose bright light and love saved our lives. To my teachers and advisors who helped me find and hone my work. To the guides who helped me find my path, but most of all, to Dolores Randall, Dr. C.T. Vivian, Lucille Loman, Rev. Clay Evans, and my father, Paul Commerse, Jr. To my Story Medicine Community, for steadfast support, Ellane Chandler, Chris Wells, Mahan Siler, Judy Maris, Jim Stokely, Pat Johnson, Dennis Fotinos, JacKaline Stallings, Evan Richardson, and Matthew Abrams. To Carol Majors for challenging me to bring all the voices forward. To my special friends for their support and love through it all. Darrell Mayfield, Cher Gilmore, Pamela Plummer, Jason Blackwell, and Mama Matanah.

ABOUT THE AUTHOR

Meta Commerse is an artist and social entrepreneur living in Western North Carolina. Meta earned her MFA in Creative Writing at Goddard College.

Learn more about her work at *www.storymedicineworldwide.com*.

www.ingramcontent.com/pod-product-compliance
Lightning Source LLC
Chambersburg PA
CBHW051420290426
44109CB00016B/1369